BALANCING THE TIDES

Balancing the Tides

Marine Practices in American Sāmoa

JoAnna Poblete

UNIVERSITY OF HAWAI'I PRESS

HONOLULU

University of Hawaiʻi Press books are printed on acid-free paper
and meet the guidelines for permanence and durability of the
Council on Library Resources.

Library of Congress Cataloging-in-Publication Data

Names: Poblete, JoAnna, author.
Title: Balancing the tides : marine practices in American Sāmoa /
JoAnna Poblete.
Description: Honolulu : University of Hawaiʻi Press, 2020. |
Includes bibliographical references and index.
Identifiers: LCCN 2019045525 | ISBN 9780824879686 (hardcover) |
ISBN 9780824883515 (paperback) | ISBN 9780824883393 (adobe pdf) |
ISBN 9780824883522 (epub)
Subjects: LCSH: Fishery management—American Samoa. | Fishery
policy—American Samoa. | Tuna canning industry—American Samoa. |
Marine resources—American Samoa—Management.
Classification: LCC SH319.A46 P63 2020 | DDC 338.3/727099613—dc23
LC record available at https://lccn.loc.gov/2019045525

Cover photo of Pago Pago Bay by author.

CONTENTS

As a Filipino-Chinese-Portuguese American PhD student in history at UCLA at the dawn of the twenty-first century, I started graduate school wanting to study Filipino American legal history. After taking an Asian American jurisprudence course at the law school, I realized Filipinos had more legal connections to Puerto Ricans and Chamorros than other Asians who came to the United States due to the War of 1898, the subsequent Treaty of Paris, and the 1901 Insular Cases. From that moment, I knew I wanted to study and write about the experiences of U.S. colonials, whom I define as groups under the direct authority of the United States, across time and space. Overall, my intellectual goal is to make visible and center the histories of unincorporated territories and their peoples within larger U.S. narratives and American perspectives.

While not a manageable dissertation project, my advisor and chair, Henry Yu, encouraged me to think of my desire to study the impact of unincorporated territorial status on colonized groups as a life-long career goal. I have been privileged and fortunate enough to have the ability to follow this advice and engage in research projects about Filipinos and Puerto Ricans in Hawai'i for my dissertation and first book, American Sāmoans for this second book, and U.S. Virgin Islanders for a nascent third book project. In the long term, I hope my research, writing, and teaching can help us think comparatively about historical and contemporary connections among all U.S. colonials for greater understanding and potential future coalition building.

My research for *Balancing the Tides* started in 2008 during my time as a Carolina Postdoctoral Faculty Diversity program fellow in the History Department at UNC-Chapel Hill. The success of my first trip was greatly facilitated by the initial contacts provided by Roderick Labrador, who got me in touch with Jacinta Galea'i, and Stephen Thom, who connected me with the amazing Oreta Togafau (now Oreta Crichton). I am also forever grateful to my mother, Lucille, who accompanied me during the first week of this trip and bravely approached any Filipino she came across. Jacinta and Oreta provided my first taste of the generous Sāmoan spirit, *fa'a Sāmoa,* one loaning me her car during the weekdays and the other inviting me to stay in her home for this trip and every other consecutive visit. The librarians at the Feleti Barstow Public Library, especially Cheryl Morales and Justin Maga, were extremely kind and helpful. Likisone Asotau also gave me an excellent tour of the Chicken of the Sea factory for a firsthand, close-up look at the tuna canning process.

While I was able to publish a preliminary article in 2010 on the closing of the Chicken of the Sea factory, the next several years were full of teaching in my tenure-track position at the University of Wyoming and publishing my first book in 2014. I was finally able to return to my research in American Sāmoa that same year. Support from the Wyoming Institute for Humanities Research, the University of Wyoming International Travel Grant, the University of Wyoming College of Arts and Sciences Basic Research Grant, as well as research monies from my current institution, Claremont Graduate University, funded my trips to American Sāmoa from 2014 to 2016.

I am so blessed that every year I have traveled to American Sāmoa, Oreta and her family have hosted me in their home. I am humbled and proud to be part of their *'āiga,* appreciative of all their professional and personal support through the years. Oreta also helped me set up meetings with several government officials and community members in 2014, who in turn recommended more people to contact and so forth until I interviewed over one hundred people related to my research topics for this project through this snowball approach. I am grateful for the time and support of every single individual who spoke with me, whether their name is mentioned in this work or kept confidential by request. Those who went above and beyond the normal scope of assistance during my research trips or while I was off-island include Clarence Crichton, Saumaniafaese Uikirifi, Nate Ilaoa, Keniseli Lafaele, Hillary Togafau, David Herdrich, Alice Lawrence, Patty Page, Joseph Paulin, Jeremy Raynal, and Fofō Sunia.

In addition to individual interviews, primary source documents, archival materials, scientific reports, and historiographical texts were used to write this story of American Sāmoa. While working in this region has been a personal joy and honor, as a historian this orally based culture has sometimes presented challenges in locating and obtaining consistent written sources and data. Some histories in this work have been reconstructed through the tellings of multiple people and confirmed as best as possible with available documentary evidence. As scholar Fikret Berkes has stated, "The written page will never be an adequate format for the teaching of indigenous knowledge" (2012, 38). This work is not and cannot be an exhaustive look at all historical ocean policies in American Sāmoa. Nevertheless, I have tried diligently to provide as accurate a narrative as possible for the case studies I present. While many issues discussed in this book are connected to several contemporary and current events, out of a need for an end point in research, all statements are based on the policies in existence through August 2018. I apologize in advance for any errors or gaps in information that may have inadvertently resulted from this research process.

I am deeply appreciative for amazing colleagues at the several institutions I have been a part of since 2008. In particular, I would like to thank Maile Arvin, Janet Brodie, Keith Camacho, Faye Caronan Chen, Nicole Choi, Holger Droessler, Lori Anne Ferrell, Joshua Goode, Jennifer Hayashida, Isadora Helfgott, Jennifer Ho, Char Miller, Lin Poyer, Phil Roberts, Carolina San Juan, Kiri Sailiata, Ronald Schultz, Lisa Uperesa, and Kathy Yep for their feedback, support, and assistance through the years. I would also like to thank my research assistants, Kaitlyn Bylard, Jonathan Hanna, Lara Kolinchak, Mike Pesses, and Gary Stein for all their hard work and creativity in finding sources for my work and helping me with manuscript cleanup. In particular, Michael Pesses did an amazing job with the maps and charts. Special thanks also goes out to my cousin, Joanna Sokua, who provided her artistic abilities for some last-minute illustrations on fishing styles. I am grateful to my colleagues at Claremont Graduate University for always being excited about my research on unincorporated territories and encouraging me to teach what I study, bringing along our students for the ride. I truly appreciate all the comments and help from those at UH Press, especially my editor, Masako Ikeda, editorial assistant Debbie Tang, the managing editor and staff at UH and Longleaf, as well as my two manuscript readers. And finally to my pack, Mike and Matli, you are the rocks that I draw strength from FOR EVS.

FREQUENTLY USED SĀMOAN TERMS

'Āiga	family, descent group
Aumaga	untitled men
Fa'amolemole	please
Fa'a Sāmoa	the Sāmoan way
Fono	Sāmoan legislature
Mātai	chief
Palangi	foreigner
Pule	power, political authority
Tapu	taboo
Vā	social relations
Vā fealoa'i	social respect

LIST OF ABBREVIATIONS

ASG	American Sāmoa Government
ASLLE	American Sāmoa Longline Limited Entry program
CFMP	Community-Based Fisheries Management Program
CBMRM	community-based marine resource management
DOC	Department of Commerce
DMP	Draft Management Plan
DEIS	Draft Environmental Impact Statement
DMWR	Department of Marine and Wildlife Resources
EEZ	Exclusive Economic Zone
LVPA	Large Vessel Prohibited Area
ONMS	Office of National Marine Sanctuaries
NOAA	National Oceanic and Atmospheric Administration
NMFS	National Marine Fisheries Service
NMS	National Marine Sanctuary
SFR	U.S. Federal Sport Fish Restoration Program
TEK	traditional ecological knowledge
VMPA	Village Marine Protected Area
WPacFIN	Western Pacific Fisheries Information Network
Wespac	Western Pacific Regional Fishery Management Council
WWII	World War II

Introduction

Where is American Sāmoa? And why does this region have the word "American" in it? This set of five islands and two atolls in the South Pacific is the most southern territory of the United States in the last time zone of the globe. American Sāmoa is 2,566 miles southwest of Hawai'i and 4,719 miles southwest of the continental U.S. West Coast. The total landmass of this region is almost seventy-seven square miles, with a population of 55,519 according to the 2010 census. Through a set of treaties between the U.S. Navy and local chiefs in 1900 and 1904, this area became an unincorporated territory of the United States and has maintained that status through today. Over the years, this location has served as a U.S. Navy port, particularly important during World War II, a major site for tuna canning, and the location of the largest National Marine Sanctuary in the United States.

This book examines the unique experiences of American Sāmoans in contrast to other U.S. colonials, or people under direct U.S. authority, who became part of the U.S. empire at the turn of the twentieth century.[1] The United States engaged in colonialism (or direct government control over another region), as opposed to imperialism (which involves extended efforts to influence another region's governance, but usually does not entail direct control), in places like Hawai'i, the Philippines, Puerto Rico, and Guam.

Despite active protests by the majority of Native Hawaiians, their islands became a U.S. territory in 1900, instantly converting the indigenous population into U.S. citizens against their will.[2] After the U.S.-Philippine War in 1902, the U.S. federal government dictated the Philippines' government and economy until independence was granted in 1946.[3] Puerto Rico was an unincorporated territory under U.S. leadership from 1898 until becoming a Commonwealth in 1950.[4] Chamorros have lived in an unincorporated territory of the United States since 1898 (except for Japanese occupation during World War II).[5] In these U.S. colonies, federal leadership controlled all decision making in the beginning, gradually providing local representation in government positions after a significant period of assimilation to American values, ideals, structures, and processes. While stories of U.S. colonialism in Hawai'i, the Philippines, and Puerto Rico are familiar to many, the history and contemporary effects of U.S. rule in American Sāmoa, as well as Guam, are quite invisible.

The common story of the U.S. government's takeover and control of island colonies was not the case in American Sāmoa. Instead of native customs being erased by missionaries, as in Hawai'i, and intense Americanization initiatives such as those in the Philippines, Puerto Rico, and Guam, American Sāmoa differed from other colonized regions because the U.S. government has historically accommodated indigenous practices in this area. From the beginning of their official relationship with the United States in 1900, American Sāmoans maintained indigenous control over their local governance. While the United States held authority over larger structural affairs, such as international trade, global diplomacy, and the military, the traditional Sāmoan *fa'amātai* (chiefly system of leadership and decision making) managed daily life.

The U.S. federal government consistently used island colonies for monocrop export industries (that profited U.S. corporations) and strategic military sites. In Hawai'i, Puerto Rico, and the Philippines, sugar became those regions' major agricultural export. American Sāmoa became a site for the monocrop of tuna canning, which will be discussed in chapter 2. These island regions, as well as Guam, also became sites for major military bases. However, unlike the experience of other U.S. colonials who have generally come under full federal control, American Sāmoans have always had a degree of independent action. According to a 2012 U.S. Department of Commerce report,

> Although the Department of the Interior has administrative oversight of the Territory of American Samoa, there is only a limited amount of direct Federal involvement there. The Federal government owns no land on American Samoa except for an uninhabited atoll 150 miles from Tutuila.... There are no military installations in the Territory, nor any energy facilities serving an area outside the Territory. The primary Federal agencies with interests in American Samoa are resource protection oriented. With the exception of the U.S. Coast Guard, all relevant Federal authorities concerned with Federal resource protection laws have their offices located over 2000 miles away in Honolulu, or over 4000 miles away in Seattle or San Francisco. Due to this lack of a continual presence, enforcement of Federal resource protection laws is irregular at the Federal level.[6]

The federal government openly acknowledges its minimal economic, bureaucratic, military, and legislative involvement in this unincorporated territory. Consequently, the maintenance of local indigenous rule since 1900 significantly differentiated colonization in American Sāmoa from other island territories of the U.S. empire.

This work examines U.S. federal marine policies and programs in American Sāmoa to highlight historic U.S. colonialism in the region. According to postcolonial ecology scholars Elizabeth DeLoughrey and George Handley, "European Enlightenment knowledge, natural history, conservation policy, and the language of nature—the very systems of logic that we draw from today to speak of conservation and sustainability—are derived from a long history of the colonial exploitation of nature."[7] Imperialism, colonialism, and empire building are at the root of land occupation, as well as resource categorization and use. Subsequently created, as well as supposedly scientific, hierarchies and priorities place indigenous groups like Pacific Islanders at the bottom of social, economic, political, and cultural structures throughout environmental and empire history. Such Western-based ideals about the appropriate use of the environment and proper modern lifestyle patterns have drastically altered the lives of indigenous groups. The following chapters highlight the shifts in marine practices in American Sāmoa away from self-sufficient subsistence living to a cash-based, export economy and the precedence of Western-based scientific and ecology ideals in environmental practices since World War II.

The following case studies also show how U.S. federal ocean-use policies connect contemporary scientific and ecological prerogatives to continued U.S. control and authority over the region and its people. As Sasha Davis discussed, the desire to possess and control Pacific Island regions stems from the U.S. empire's ultimate goals to protect globalization and free market trade in the Asia-Pacific region.[8] The ability of U.S. vessels to move and exchange easily with markets throughout the Pacific Rim remains a key motivation to retain island colonies and continue to regulate ocean use in the region. Mansel Blackford also argued for "the tremendous importance of government policy in shaping the fishery and the fishery's global scope. . . . Regulation and development went hand in hand."[9] The expansion of U.S. federal marine regulations during the twenty-first century results in continued U.S. authority over American Sāmoans, as well as a strong influence on the global fishing industry.

However, like work by sociologists Cluny Macpherson and La'avasa Macpherson, this study views island colonies as "a site where global forces confront local ones, and Sāmoans are assumed to be active agents in the transformation of their society."[10] The following case studies also demonstrate the human priorities of economics, local control, and indigenous rights by American Sāmoans. While Westerners have prioritized wilderness and conservation, indigenous groups are more concerned about "arable land and potable water, public health, the threats of militarism and national debt, and reflect social planning for cultural, economic, and national sovereignty"[11] Often times, native issues are distinct and separate from colonizers' interests.

In fact, ideals, goals, and standards in a colonized territory and for its local population do not always coincide with, support the needs of, or have the same impact or resonance in the continental United States. Stateside environmental efforts and economic regulations, such as national marine sanctuaries and minimum wage standards, seem positive and moral from a lower-48 perspective. However, these same rules have adversely influenced ground-level employment, local industries, and native access to ancient fishing grounds in American Sāmoa. As historian Karl Jacoby has stated about Native Americans, U.S. "conservation was but one piece of a larger process of colonization and state building in which Indian peoples were transformed (in theory, at least) from independent actors to dependent wards bound by governmental controls."[12] Western-based initiatives have also imposed nonnative standards, practices, and ways of knowing on this indigenous group.

Native issues versus federal issues in colonized American Sāmoa are complex and layered, sometimes tense and fraught. Examining the intersections of environment and empire widen understandings of fundamental questions of difference, power, and privilege that postcolonial ecology studies emphasize. This work discusses the complications involved in the unique shared governance in American Sāmoa, the impact of government policies on this indigenous group and the United States, as well as the ways in which native American Sāmoans have expressed their views about government regulations of marine practices and ocean-related management policies in the post–World War II era.

Brief Historical Background

Researchers believe the first Sāmoans, known as the Lapita people, originated from Melanesia. This group migrated from New Caledonia to Fiji, then Tonga and Sāmoa more than 3,500 years ago. Over two thousand years ago, Sāmoan political and social systems "were fully developed and operating" at independent village, clan, and regional levels.[13] These people then started to explore regions in more eastern areas of the Pacific, influencing cultures as far as the Hawaiian

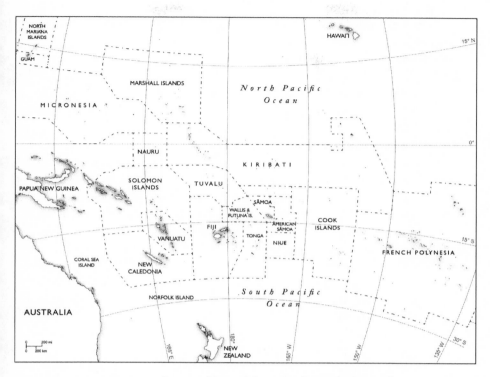

FIGURE I.OI. Oceania. (Created for author by Michael Pesses.)

Islands. According to *A History of American Samoa,* during this period "there was much exchange and intermarriage between Samoa, Fiji, and Tonga."[14]

More than 1,300 years ago, Tonga occupied the Sāmoan islands for over 300 years until Sāmoans from places like Manu'a in the east and Upolu in the west revolted against this empire.[15] After that overthrow, a series of Sāmoan chiefs competed for control over various islands in the archipelago. More than four hundred years ago, struggles over royal titles heightened and divided communities across the islands into the nineteenth century.[16] During this period, strong rivalries among *'āiga* (descent groups) throughout this region resulted in violent clashes among Sāmoans.

In 1722, the first Westerners made contact with the Sāmoan islands, led by Jacob Roggeveen, a Dutch expedition leader for the West India Company. However, Western settlement did not occur until Congregationalist members of the London Missionary Society arrived in 1830. Just ten years prior, some of the first informal missionaries came from Tahiti and Tonga.[17] Methodists in 1835, Roman Catholics in 1845, and Mormons in 1865 followed these two groups of initial proselytizers.[18] From the 1850s on, France, the Netherlands, Great Britain, and the United States were also interested in acquiring the last available regions of the world for Westerners to expand their empires at this time: the islands of the South Pacific.[19] Germans started to develop strong interests in the harvesting, processing, and exporting of copra from Upolu in the 1870s. The Kingdom of Hawaiʻi also tried to form a confederation with Sāmoa in 1887, but those efforts ended after the Bayonet Constitution was forced on King Kalākaua later that same year.[20]

In 1899, three Western countries agreed to partition the area through the Berlin Treaty without consulting Sāmoans or any other native groups. Germany took control of the western Sāmoan islands, Great Britain gained authority over Tonga, the Solomons, and areas of West Africa, and the United States obtained authority over the eastern Sāmoan islands.[21] One year later, the U.S. Navy negotiated a Deed of Cession with Tutuila chiefs. On April 17, 1900, the U.S. Navy and twenty *mātai* (chiefs) of the island signed a document granting the U.S. government sovereign rights over the lands and waters of Tutuila, Aunuʻu Island, and the surrounding area, specifically "all other Islands, rocks, reefs, foreshores, and waters lying between the thirteenth degree and the fifteenth degree of south latitude and between the one hundred and seventy first degree and the one hundred sixty seventh degree of west longitude from the Meridian of Greenwich."[22]

This agreement also stated that "the Government of the United States of America shall respect and protect the individual rights of all people dwelling in Tutuila to their lands and other property.... The Chiefs of the towns will be entitled to retain their individual control of the separate towns, if that control is in accordance with the laws of the United States of America.... But the enactment of legislation and the General Control shall remain firm with the United States of America."[23] This verbiage maintained the right of the indigenous population to govern local society and manage land according to their traditional practices, as long as these conventions did not conflict with U.S. regulations.[24] However, the United States held ultimate political and legal rule over the area.

On July 16, 1904, Tuimanua, the king of the Manuʻa Islands, and his five chiefs signed a similar agreement for the northeastern portion of this archipelago, including "the whole of eastern portion of the Samoan Islands lying east of longitude 171 west of Greenwich and known as Tau, Olosega, Ofu, and Rose Island, and all other, the waters and property adjacent thereto."[25] This treaty stated that "the rights of the chiefs in each village and of all people concerning

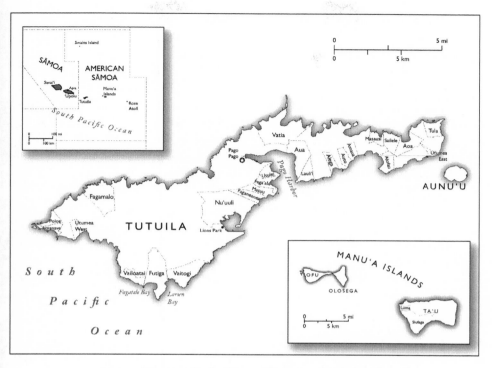

FIGURE I.02. Sāmoan islands. (Created for author by Michael Pesses.)

their property according to their customs shall be recognized."[26] Once again, the United States gained overall control with the stipulation that customary Sāmoan systems remained protected.

Together, these Deeds of Cession created tiered governance in the region that allowed the continuation of local indigenous practices and accepted general native subordination to U.S. governance. This shared political-legal authority, heavily steeped in Western methods of geographic calculation and nonnative notions of individual property rights, remains in effect today in this unincorporated territory of the United States.[27]

Why was the United States interested in shared authority in these islands and why did Sāmoans agree to hand over the sovereignty of their islands? In addition to participating in global empire building at the time, the U.S. government viewed Pago Pago Harbor as a key location for a coaling station between Asia and the Americas.[28] Some, like researcher Joseph Kennedy, believed that the

U.S. Navy did not want to take on responsibility for full control of the islands, therefore willingly agreed to joint authority over the region.[29] The United States was already fighting a bloody war for control in the Philippines.[30] With strong resistance to U.S. rule in that archipelago, as well as other Western powers in the region willing and ready to take their place, the U.S. Navy was open to a degree of shared governance with indigenous leaders in Sāmoa to gain their loyalty and cooperation. Joint authority also meant the U.S. Navy could keep other foreign investors out of the region while maintaining a South Pacific pathway to Asian markets. This arrangement allowed the United States to have overall authority that could remain limited indefinitely, but could also be expanded when needed at a moment's notice.

In fact, scholar Christina Duffy Burnett has claimed that "American imperialism has also consisted of efforts to impose limits on expansion: to draw lines around what counts as properly "national" territory," providing ways to reduce "the number of contexts in which the government must take up the responsibilities that come with such power."[31] Shared authority in American Sāmoa, unincorporated territorial status for Guam, the Philippines, Puerto Rico, and the U.S. Virgin Islands, informal protectorate status for Cuba, and purely extractive rights in the Guano Islands all demonstrate such an approach to U.S. expansionism. By avoiding full-fledged responsibility towards these locations, the U.S. government can reap all the benefits of exploiting these regions without the cost or burdens of providing citizen-level support and rights to the people living in these places.

Since Western powers had been vying for power in the region since the mid-1800s, and were likely to persist in the area, Sāmoan chiefs might have seen the United States as the best option among the determined empire builders from the west. Chiefs on Tutuila and Aunu'u were traditionally treated as vassals by the high chiefs of Upolu and Savai'i. 'Āiga from the eastern islands might have viewed the United States as a good protector from the tensions and conflicts with the western islands in the nineteenth century.[32] In 1872, High Chief Mauga gave the U.S. exclusive rights to use Pago Pago Harbor, and in 1873, Tutuila chiefs petitioned for the annexation of American Sāmoa by America. While the U.S. Congress never passed annexation, the U.S. Senate did ratify a treaty in 1878 giving the United States the right to establish a naval station at Pago Pago.[33] These negotiations set the foundation for future U.S. presence and control on Tutuila.

Kennedy also discussed how Sāmoans wanted to keep local governance but have U.S. protection without much sacrifice of their independent action in the years following the Deeds of Cession.[34] Regardless of the ultimate reasons for this political arrangement, the shared custody of power over American Sāmoa has led to some conflicts, disagreements, and disconnects between U.S. federal policies, guidelines, expectations, and regulations and indigenous Sāmoan interests, desires, culture, and values.[35] This work will explore the intricacies of combined governance through the lens of marine practices, labor issues, and ocean resources in the region since the mid-twentieth century.

Allowing traditional Sāmoan leadership and local control was acceptable to the U.S. federal government during the first half of the twentieth century because until World War II, this region was not considered an important area of U.S. jurisdiction. This territory lost its turn-of-the-century strategic military value due to a shift from coal to steam-powered naval vessels, as well as other American bases established in Hawai'i and the Philippines. After serving as a significant supply and mustering station for the Pacific theater of World War II, this Pacific archipelago once again fell to the back burner of federal government concern.

With the closing of the U.S. naval base at Pago Pago in 1951, American Sāmoans started migrating in large numbers to Hawai'i, the continental United States, and Guam to pursue cash-based wage labor jobs to support their families.[36] As Fa'anofo Lisaclaire Uperesa and others have shown, a strong historic and current belief exists that material success "is possible only through migration abroad and taking advantage of opportunities provided by the United States."[37] Outmigration continues today, with an average of 7,804 people leaving the region for work each year from 2006 to 2016, about 14 percent of the total population.[38] Such movement is used as opportunities to improve both the economic circumstances of migrants and their families at home who often receive financial support from those abroad. These remittances have provided an uncalculated but significant contribution to supporting *'āiga* and village economies in American Sāmoa.[39]

In 1963, a *Reader's Digest* article highlighted the poverty level conditions in this periphery of U.S. empire. Author Clarence Hall admonished the U.S. government for leaving this area to languish in deprived circumstances, describing how "government buildings were peeling and rotting on their foundations, beautiful Pago Pago Bay was marred and befouled by hideous over-water outhouses, rutty and teeth-jarring roads unrepaired for years. . . . Public schools are unequipped shacks."[40] In response, President John F. Kennedy authorized infrastructure improvement projects and social services that lasted through 1967. These projects included the development of radiotelephone services, extensive road repairs, educational television, the construction of a new conference building, hospital, and hotel, as well as the opening of a second tuna cannery. This temporary push to improve conditions in American Sāmoa ushered in the next major set of Western-based structural changes in the region.

From that point forward, the U.S. government encouraged the tuna canning industry in the region, discussed in chapter 2, and later started to pour federal grants and monies into the local economy. High tax and tariff breaks, as well as variable minimum wage and lax labor standards, encouraged the development of this commerce as a major source for the Gross Domestic Product, besides federal grants, in the territory. Since 2007, about 57 percent of territorial income has come from the tuna canning business, with an average of 30 percent coming from government funding.[41]

Despite such federal government influences in the region, as scholar Kirisitina Sailiata has written, the long-term continuation of indigenous practices can be seen as a unique form of American Sāmoan resistance to colonization.[42] Indigenous demands for more representation under federal rule have occurred in American Sāmoa since the Mau in 1920, which involved native protests against their poor treatment by the U.S. Navy.[43] Since that movement, Sāmoans have pushed for increased indigenous self-governance at various times, but have not sought complete separation from the United States. This native group established a territorial constitution in 1960, a full-time legislature in 1971, and the first elected governor in 1977. Until the 1980s, American Sāmoans exercised control over local environmental management. Local leaders also determined wage policies until 2007.

The full-time Sāmoan legislature *(Fono)*, emulates both Western and indigenous political structures. One component of the *Fono* involves eighteen popularly elected officials in the House of Representatives. The second section of the *Fono* is the Senate, which consists of fifteen members appointed by the "council of chiefs, in accordance with Samoan custom."[44] The allocations for both branches are based on traditional Sāmoan counties. While the names of each component of the legislature and the election of House representatives reflect U.S.-based governance models, the members of the Senate and district lines follow customary native Sāmoan *pule* (political authority).

The American Sāmoa Government (ASG) has struggled to keep the region's economy afloat since the establishment of the *Fono* in 1971. Every elected governor has faced administrative deficits. Several corporate efforts to establish businesses in the region were initiated but failed to stay operational long-term. These short-lived industries included a small assembly plant for Bulova watches, a Meadow Gold dairy manufacturing plant, a First National City Bank branch, and the Dory commercial fishing boat program that will be discussed in chapter 1. Proposals to start a third tuna cannery and an oil refinery were also brought forth but rejected by the ASG.[45] By 1975, manufacturing and production plants shut down due to the general worldwide recession.[46] Other impediments to the establishment of alternative industries in the 1970s included U.S. tariff agreements with developing countries and changes in territorial customs inspections.[47] By 1979, the five-year territorial economic development plan decided to focus ASG Department of Commerce efforts on the fishing industry and agriculture.

While American Sāmoa has always received some amount of federal funding since the Deeds of Cession, from 1999 through today the U.S. government has provided over $200 million annually in grants and subsidies to bolster this region's economy. In exchange, this funding requires American Sāmoan grantees to create economic, social, and environmental programs based on Western standards and nonnative forms of knowledge and decision making, as will be discussed in chapter 4.

Once the U.S. government started to invest large amounts of money into the region, the contours of the American Sāmoan–U.S. colonial relationship shifted. This native group became more dependent on U.S.-imported cash, food, and goods instead of subsistence fishing and farming. The United States also started to impose more regulations and management over the ecology and economy of the region. A disconnect between American ideals and indigenous ways of life developed. Sometimes the needs of a communal society with strong indigenous social and political hierarchies, as well as major economic dependence on the commercial fishing industry, conflict with federal initiatives for environmental and labor protection. Into the twenty-first century, the U.S. federal government has increased its role in developing policies that have not coincided with indigenous desires or needs, leading some American Sāmoans to become more anxious about their precarious position in relation to U.S. policies, a direct result of being U.S. colonials.

Shift in Marine Practices in American Sāmoa

Massive U.S. military presence in the Pacific during World War II quickly introduced and integrated American products and ways of living in American Sāmoa and other Pacific Islands.[48] After the war ended, U.S. troops and materials were quickly removed from these areas. However, American Sāmoans continued to "demand modern conveniences introduced by the military.... Everyone wanted a telephone line. Corned beef, bread, and butter became staples. *Palagi* [foreigner]-styled houses were replacing Sāmoan houses at an increasing rate."[49] In addition to newly developed desires for Western commodities, American Sāmoans wanted more wage-based jobs to pay for imported goods, better education, and improved health care. The colonial influence of a U.S.-style economy, culture, and lifestyle increased rapidly during this period.

Prior to U.S. rule in the region, American Sāmoans typically ate a self-sufficient diet based on seafood gathered from the ocean such as octopus, fish, shrimp, and lobster. Native groups also cultivated produce like bananas, mangoes, taro, papayas, and breadfruit on local plantations. According to Vaʻamua Henry Sesepasara, the Governor's Advisor on Fisheries and the ASG Department of Marine and Wildlife Resources (DMWR) director in 2018, "we eat what we catch. We don't play with our food. We eat almost anything we catch in the water. If it crawls, moves, swims in water, we eat it."[50] American Sāmoans interviewed for this project often identified the 1980s as the period when a shift occurred away from nutritional self-sufficiency to local commercial fishing and export-based eating.

According to Nate Ilaoa, the American Sāmoa coordinator for the Western Pacific Regional Fishery Management Council (Wespac), these days "if a family talks about buying fish, usually they pick up a can of mackerel or tuna."[51] However, as far back as 1926, researcher Alfred Judd noted that "today the natives are not fishing as they could."[52] Observer Frank Drees also described many cases of canned salmon and sardines at a funeral in Vaitogi in the mid-1930s.[53] From a more contemporary perspective, the 2010 U.S. Census showed that only 6.7 percent of the American Sāmoa population engaged in subsistence activities and 3.2 percent of the population worked in farming, fishing, and forestry occupations.[54] A 2016 report also found that 47 percent of American Sāmoans did not fish, 20 percent never swam, and 65 percent purchased seafood from stores or restaurants.[55]

Greater access to and reliance on cheaper and convenient canned or processed foods in grocery stores, as well as the influx of cash-based government jobs since 1999, enticed many American Sāmoans away from the more laborious and less glamorous tasks involved in manual fishing and crop cultivation. The increased use of Western technologies, like cable television, the internet, and related social media, as well as cell phones have also come to dominate the interest and attention of American Sāmoan youth.[56] These changes in consumption practices, away from frequent and regular marine practices and land cultivation towards a strong focus on and value for imported, off-island goods, directly reflects another impact of being U.S. colonials—incorporation into the culture of American consumer society.[57] According to Wespac Fishery analyst Marlowe Sabater, the Sāmoan islands has a great seafaring tradition, a reputation as navigator islands. American Sāmoans have lost that connection since becoming a territory.[58]

As a cash-based economy today, fishing is no longer a widespread tradition. While both the local American Sāmoa Government and U.S. federal groups have developed educational programs to encourage youth, as well as adults, to take up fishing and other ocean uses, some of which are discussed in chapter 4, most people in American Sāmoa do not believe angling will become a popular or dominant mode of living again. Fishers interviewed in 2016 stated that they have taught their children how to fish.[59] Many of these children enjoy the practice and some are even better fishers than their parents. But families without an active angler often do not pick up this practice.

Despite this decline in regular marine use by large portions of the population, as a set of islands in the middle of the Pacific, the ocean has always been an important and valuable commodity in American Sāmoa. Pacific Islanders scholars such as Epeli Hau'ofa and Alice Te Punga Somerville have written about the orientation of islander life to the water more than land.[60] The ocean is the source and center of physical and spiritual sustenance, as well as social, political, economic, and cultural exchanges. Water connects Pacific Islander people and places.

Consequently, control of ocean resources is fraught with multiple opinions and agendas. From fishing rights to conservation policies, different levels of U.S. and American Sāmoa leadership, as well as general society, have varied ideas about appropriate allocation and use of this supply. According to the National Marine Sanctuary of American Sāmoa website, "the American Samoa sanctuary is the most remote, is the only true tropical reef, and is thought to support the greatest diversity of marine life" in the entire national sanctuary system."[61] Consequently, some groups appreciate these regional waters for their scientific value. Others use the ocean as a source of income and profit. Some treat the ocean as sacred and deeply connected to cultural practices and customs, while others see the water as something to fear or something that does not factor into their daily lives. All impacted groups in American Sāmoa understand the importance of access to and the continued health of marine resources surrounding the territory. However, as the following chapters show, not everyone agrees on the type of regulations, policies, and projects needed for ocean stewardship.

Another major set of events that contributed to changes in commercial and recreational fishing practices, marine administration, and ocean knowledge gathering in American Sāmoa involved the creation of Wespac in 1976, the transition of the ASG Department of Marine and Wildlife Resources from a division of the American Sāmoa Governor's Office to a separate entity in 1985, and the formation of the National Marine Sanctuary of American Sāmoa in 1986. The following chapters examine how the establishment of these umbrella management organizations, as well as actions or inaction by the U.S. Congress, have created a modern administrative colonial state in American Sāmoa that has formalized, standardized, and bureaucratized ocean-related policies in the region according to Western ideas of conservation, environmentalism, science, protection, and ethics. In general, marine resource supervision works to protect the long-term health of the Pacific Ocean. However, different definitions of healthy ocean use exist, especially in American Sāmoa. These ideas range from wide swaths of no-take zones and complete preservation to temporary fishing policies that regularly evaluate the most effective and profitable methods to engage with local ocean resources. Issues of native rights to access ancestral waters also come into play.

Other Sāmoan Contexts

While much has been written about independent Sāmoa, a limited number of books, dissertations, and articles have been written about the history of U.S. involvement in American Sāmoa and the impact of U.S. colonialism on this indigenous group. While there was a naval history written on American Sāmoa in 1960, a coffee-table book published on the history of American Sāmoa in 2000, a general history of U.S.–American Sāmoan relations from 1900 to 1950 printed in 2009, and a high school level general history textbook printed in 2009, Sailiata's PhD dissertation is the only in-depth study of U.S.–American Sāmoa relations throughout the twentieth century.[62] To date, most academic studies of American Sāmoa have focused on the impact of Sāmoan culture on economic and social development, such as migration, language, education, and fisheries. Robert Franco wrote about Sāmoan perceptions of work in 1991 from an anthropological perspective.[63] Saʻiliemanu Lilomaiava-Doktor has written a dissertation and articles about Sāmoan population movement.[64] Faʻanofo Lisaclaire Uperesa has examined identity, migration, economics, and colonialism among American Sāmoan football players.[65] Holger Droessler wrote a dissertation in 2015 on U.S.–American Sāmoan relations from 1889 to 1919. Others have written dissertations on disaster recovery after the 2009 tsunami, as well as books and articles about marine ecology in American Sāmoa.[66]

Building on these works, this study supports the idea that indigenous knowledge, concepts, and ideologies should be integrated into analyses to better understand the perspectives and approaches of Pacific Island communities. The concept of *vā* (social space relations) can provide greater insight to American Sāmoan motivations, actions, and positionalities to the variety of marine policy situations discussed in this work. According to American Sāmoan historian Fofō Sunia, *vā* is "one of the most important components of the makeup of the Sāmoan culture, so important that it is considered 'sacred' in most situations. '*Vā*' is the distance between two bodies. The '*vā*' must always remain orderly, respectful and well kept. The '*vā*' must always be peaceful and harmonious."[67] All relations in Sāmoan culture are governed by this concept.

Scholar Albert Wendt described *vā* as "the space between, the betweenness, not empty space, not space that separates, but space that relates."[68] Lilomaiava-Doktor also explained how *vā* "connotes mutual respect in sociopolitical arrangements that nurture the relationships between people, places, and social environments."[69] The nurturing of *vā (tausi le vā)* involves *alofa* (love), *faʻaaloalo* (respect), and *tautua* (service).[70] Such moral guidelines outline culturally appropriate behaviors for both individuals and the extended family *(ʻāiga)* in all aspects of life ranging from social, economic, spiritual, cultural, and political components. Overall, such practices emphasize "cultural tools of conflict resolution in Island societies, where collective well-being is paramount."[71] Scholars have agreed that *vā* is a central concept to understanding social relationships in Sāmoan culture.[72]

However, *vā* requires time and effort. According to ʻAumua Mataʻitusi Simanu in an interview by Lilomaiava-Doktor:

> The whole Samoan way of life is premised on relationships and how we maintain this *vā* with others, including our superiors and workmates at work or any situation. It is always a good practice to consult and discuss your plans.... When people who have been caring for the land are notified, everyone is happy and will make sure the plan is executed and implemented to successful completion.... your cultural knowledge of what is appropriate in *faʻaaloalo* [respect] knowing the *vā fealoaʻi* [social respect], following protocols of communications will earn you respect.[73]

As will be shown in the following chapters, when proper protocols are followed and *vā fealoaʻi* is created, programs and initiatives are supported.

When such cultural expectations of "participation, obligation, and reciprocation" are not followed, policies and guidelines are resisted or outright protested against.[74] Sunia also commented how "if some disturbance arises between two families, you will hear the advice or admonition from others—'*teu le vā*,' meaning improve or be mindful of the harmony that should exist between you two."[75] Sincere responses must be provided to repair damaged relationships or reestablish harmony. Tui Atua Tupua Tamasese Ta'isi also explained how "conflict assumes when the *tau'oi* or boundaries within are transgressed or misunderstood. . . . disharmonies are resolved through the co-existence of remorse and forgiveness on the one hand, and the privileging of *alofa* (meaning love and compassion) and *'āiga* (or family) on the other."[76] Conscientious acknowledgement and deliberate monitoring of proper actions and understandings within Sāmoan culture become central to social relations in the region. To correct an offense, a combination of regret, sympathy, care, and kinship should be involved.

On a daily basis, American Sāmoans navigate indigenous concepts of moral, ethical, and respectful behaviors, as well as territorial and U.S. federal government regulations, policies, and expectations at the same time. Sometimes, decisions are made according to *vā,* and other times, Western ideals. American Sāmoans have not hesitated to express dissatisfaction when colonial policies do not mesh with their expectations or desires on appropriate conduct. This group has also embraced certain Western policies when useful or beneficial.

The priority of the family over any individual is key to *vā*. Historian Damon Salesa explained how "the central role of family in Pacific lives means that individuals are not the sole or even primary economic unit."[77] Consequently, "many Pacific people, when forced to choose between economic business success and family reputation or status, seem to put family first in order to enhance their 'social and cultural capital.'"[78] Understanding this fundamental approach to life, the incorporation of Sāmoan culture can lead to more appropriate and effective government policies and interactions with the local population. Researcher Miranda Cahn explained how rules not "congruent with indigenous ways... may jeopardize the success and sustainability" of programs.[79] According to scholar Susan Maiava, Sāmoan "self-esteem is related to family position and status, and to be a member of a well-respected family, socially well located, is a universal goal."[80] Ultimately, "improving and enhancing the *'āiga* culturally, socially and economically is the aim of *fa'a Sāmoa* (the Sāmoan way of life)."[81] Positive feelings and continued support stem from actions, policies, and programs that sustain and value *'āiga*.

Lilomaiava-Doktor defines *fa'a Sāmoa,* or the Sāmoan way of knowing, as "an intellectual tool for apprehending the world, how Sāmoans interact with each other, the church, outsiders, and the environment."[82] While a whole range of relations, actions, activities, and attitudes are involved in this practice, that also includes communal sharing, generosity, reciprocity, as well as maintaining harmony and balance, a general understanding exists among American Sāmoans over the essence and importance of such an approach to living.

The concept of bioregionalism is one way to meld concepts of *vā,* including *fa'a Sāmoa,* and postcolonial ecology. Byron Caminero-Santangelo analyzed Mitchell Thomashow's idea of bioregionalism, which entails

> a commitment to understand local ecology and human relationships" ("Toward" 125), as well as a sense of belonging based on such understanding. The bioregion itself is an ecopolitical unit integrating ecological and cultural relationships and determined by such factors as geography, ecosystem, indigenous culture, local knowledge, and environmental history. If capitalism in its various phases has made space out of place, stripping away prior signification (deterritorializing) and reshaping in order to facilitate control and exploitation, then the process of imagining or reimagining a "place" entailed by bioregionalism can be one means of countering threats of exploitation, environmental degradation, and disempowerment.[83]

Bioregionalism takes both human and ecological issues into account while also acknowledging the legacies of colonialism and indigenous knowledge in these regions. Thinking about the multiplicity of actors, motivations, goals, and perspectives in tandem can lead to new ways of understanding the history of marine practices in American Sāmoa and reimagining this space as central to U.S. economic, political, and environmental policies, as well as control over indigenous groups.

As Caminero-Santangelo has also stated, "This form of imaginative engagement encourages understanding of and commitment to one's place and community, as well as the places and communities of others, and it challenges the meanings imposed in the process of deterritorialization.... it encourages careful attention both to ecology and to human relationships as a means for care and stewardship."[84] A focus on bioregionalism involves a deep analysis of both local and global relations, various sides of any issue, as well as diverse ways to think about ecology policy from a community and an environmental perspective.

This work studies the bioregion of American Sāmoa marine spaces to provide clear information on the development of specific post–World War II fishery related policies and their impacts on American Sāmoans, U.S. citizens, American Sāmoa, and the United States. U.S. colonial status results in multiple agency jurisdictions over local waters. This variety of entities has diverse opinions and approaches for each issue, as well as particular, complicated, and extensive Western-based bureaucratic administration and enforcement procedures.

Both *vā* and bioregionalism can help in the analysis of marine practices in American Sāmoa and point to future ways to develop and maintain appropriate and effective policies and guidelines moving forward for "resource use, stewardship, and sovereignty."[85] Balance is a concept and goal expressed when discussing both ideas. And as Jacoby has urged, such attempts are "first steps toward an environmental policy that protects not only nature but also the human communities with which it is intimately entangled."[86] An ecology and indigenous rights-based approach can lead to alternative possibilities and relationships.

Wendt, Hau'ofa, and Sailiata have each argued that strategic negotiations within U.S. federal formations are needed for the future. This analysis of federal ocean-use policies (and related issues like wage rates) assesses past policymaking so American Sāmoans, U.S. citizens, and the U.S. federal government can have solid historical knowledge to help decide on how to move forward with future marine practices and other areas of shared authority in well-informed and creative new ways.

Chapter Breakdown

Information for this book stems from over one hundred interviews with individuals connected to marine programs or policies in American Sāmoa at all levels, including U.S. federal government agencies, territorial government officials and staff, local businesspeople and workers, as well as community leaders, students, teachers, fishers, and other members of the general public with an interests in these issues. The selected bibliography provides a sampling of those interviewed. Other sources integrated into this work include historic and contemporary documents such as government reports and local newspapers. In particular, online portals such as Talanei.com (discussed in chapter 1), *Sāmoa News* (discussed in chapter 2), and regulations.gov (discussed in chapter 3) provide windows into voices of those vested in American Sāmoan issues on the internet. As will be discussed in the conclusion, contemporary Sāmoan communities across the globe are highly connected through the web and social media. Even if it is impossible to verify the location or residence of online commentators, as Macpherson and Macpherson have explained, relatives abroad are still important parts of the local village. The opinions of all *'āiga* members count, regardless of where a person is living throughout the diaspora.[87] The hope is that this variety of sources will provide a diverse picture of the marine bioregion of the unincorporated territory of American Sāmoa.

Each chapter of this book highlights a type of ocean-use policy or marine-related practice in American Sāmoa regulated by either the territorial or federal government. Historic and current U.S. colonial control—as well as the importance of *vā* and *fa'a Sāmoa*—are highlighted in each case study to better understand this bioregion. Chapter 1 examines the development and experiences of two major local commercial fishing groups (small-scale indigenous alia fishers and large-vessel local longliners), as well as the impact of federal regulations on fishing access in nearby waters. The contours of commercial fishing in American Sāmoa are consequences of past and contemporary U.S. authority and initiatives in the region. Some local fishers find U.S. programs and regulations useful and beneficial for their businesses while others believe recent changes in policies violated *vā fealoa'i*. Varied Sāmoan perspectives demonstrate the diversification of native society in the face of globalization, the complications involved in shared indigenous and federal governance over the waters surrounding this area, as well as the reliance of fishers on colonial structures to protect their indigenous rights to engage in a cash-based economy.

Chapter 2 considers the American Sāmoa tuna canneries that, until 2009, provided one-third of all canned tuna to the United States. The imposition of U.S. labor standards in this unincorporated territory by the U.S. Congress in 2006 ignored the historic ground-level reality of the canning industry in this Pacific region that has benefited from the variable application of federal employment and trade regulations. Tuna businesses set up shop in American Sāmoa due to the cheap labor and tax exemptions provided by the U.S. federal government. A pool of wageworkers for canneries developed during the shift from self-sufficient subsistence fishing and agriculture systems to a cash economy focused on import purchasing. Manual laborers have accepted menial pay and resisted unionization throughout the history of the canning industry in the region, partially because their employers have followed *vā fealoa'i*. By providing free foodstuffs during holidays and accommodating absences for major family events like funerals, such attention to proper and respectful social relations has appeased workers enough to keep them working in these difficult and low-wage jobs.

Chapter 3 analyzes the creation and expansion of the National Marine Sanctuary of American Sāmoa. While local indigenous leaders took advantage of their U.S. colonial status and initiated the establishment of this nationally protected area in 1986, the process to extend federal jurisdiction to five additional areas over 13,580.75 more square miles of water in 2012 did not involve enough *vā fealoaʻi*. Consequent vocal resistance to the augmentation of the sanctuary led to much negativity and long-term skepticism for government ecology initiatives. Per the Deeds of Cession, areas of American Sāmoa that Americans currently deem as unspoiled or environmentally important to preserve have been or continue to be owned by indigenous groups. However, native presence and rights have started to take a back seat in contemporary ecological and scientific rhetoric for preserving a pristine nature environment. Such erasures can hide the longer colonial history and continued occupation, control, and alteration of the Pacific region by outsiders.

Chapter 4 highlights two local marine-based projects created by the American Sāmoa Government Department of Marine and Wildlife Resources: Village Marine Protected Areas and the on-the-ground data collection of shore-based and offshore fishing activities in local waters. Successful programs have acknowledged and integrated Sāmoan cultural practices and expectations like *vā* into the development, implementation, and maintenance of ocean-related initiatives. However, the federal monies that fund these projects also impose nonnative forms of knowledge making and ocean supervision on the community, demonstrating historic and contemporary colonial influences on local marine policies, programs, and procedures in American Sāmoa.

While scientists and environmentalist venerate parts of the Pacific as some of the last virgin environments in the world that need protection and regulation by the U.S. government, places like American Sāmoa and Hawaiʻi have long been populated by native groups that have successfully and productively tended to the ecology of their homelands through their own indigenous practices and knowledges for centuries before Western control.[88] Experiences that highlight the historic insights and current roles that native groups can actively play in useful and effective marine policy development are often ignored in discussions of ecological conservation and preservation.

These Western-based scientific and green conversations also mask America's "excessive consumption, pollution, and waste as well neocolonial forms of globalization, militarism, and development."[89] Discussions of overfishing to protect the profitable tuna industry discussed in chapter 1, minimum wage addressed in chapter 2, and marine sanctuaries and marine monuments analyzed in chapter 3 position the U.S. federal government as the best guardian for the future and long-term health and security of the Pacific region. However, the needs and actions of the United States and other Western nation-states have caused most global environmental destruction and economic disparities.[90] Environmental consequences from industrialized nations' overconsumption and pollution, such as rising sea levels and changing weather patterns from greenhouse gases, burden Pacific Islanders with the need to create environmental and ocean policies for the long-term survival of their marine regions. Neoliberal capitalism that pushes for free market trade, tax and manufacturing advantages, and the highest possible profits also positions Pacific Islander laborers at the bottom of the economic and social hierarchies of production. Such ecological and economic structures continue to subjugate Pacific Islander U.S. colonials, as well as Caribbean U.S. colonials, to Western needs and priorities.

Additionally, Mansel Blackford highlighted "the growing importance since World War II, and especially since the 1960s, of consumerism in environmentalism. Many Americans have come to view clean air, clean water, and so on almost as birthrights like consumer goods. More than that, Americans have come to see nature itself as a consumer product to be put to good use, as in national parks for sightseeing."[91] U.S. environmental principles and practices are grounded in neoliberal capitalist desires for positive experiences for one's own entertainment and fulfillment. Ideal activities from this perspective often involve adventure, recreation, pleasure, and awe-inspiring experiences. This seemingly universal desire to enjoy the environment fundamentally differs from the reliance of many Pacific Islanders on ecology for everyday living and functions. Sometimes American Sāmoans are even scared of the environment, which can pose dangers such as drowning and devastation from tsunamis. For some, the ocean needs to be feared and respected, better kept at a distance for safety.

Despite the diversity of interests included in each of these chapters, all of these issues center on the fact that as U.S. colonials, American Sāmoans are ultimately subjected to U.S. federal regulations. American Sāmoans are born as U.S. nationals, or wards of the United States. They have the right to freely travel within U.S. jurisdiction, as well as become U.S. citizens within two years of declaration. American Sāmoans are raised with both American and Sāmoan cultural and social customs, as well as regulated by U.S. and American Sāmoa economic and political structures. Native and nonnative standards and expectations interweave in policymaking as well as ground-level decisions and practices.

This combination of both indigenous and U.S. colonial status complicates authority over topics like marine practices. Both the National Oceanic and Atmospheric Administration (NOAA) and the American Sāmoa Department of Marine and Wildlife Resources have jurisdiction in local waters. Sometimes their policies coincide and other times their priorities conflict.[92] Chapters 1 and 4 demonstrate the pros and cons of shared authority over ocean-use policies while chapters 2 and 3 detail key moments when federal goals dominated policy development in American Sāmoa. In all of these cases, native groups have not hesitated to voice their discontent and frustration with government policies that appear to encroach upon their indigenous rights to or expectations for properly enacted local management, relations, and control.

American Sāmoa–specific policies also have an invisible but major impact on national and global policies. Decisions to expand fishing vessel permits in U.S. Pacific waters in 2016 and backlash from the expansion of the National Marine Sanctuary of American Sāmoa in 2012 have significantly altered the contours of both the international tuna fishing industry and NOAA community engagement. American daily consumption of canned tuna, campaigns for minimum wage, and efforts to increase environmental protections are enabled or hindered by ecological and economic regulations imposed on this unincorporated territory of the United States. Like postcolonial ecology studies' encouragement to "uphold a sense of alterity while still engaging a global imaginary," this work presents multiple indigenous and governmental perspectives to gain a fuller picture of life and living in the unincorporated U.S. territory of American Sāmoa as U.S. colonials, as well as the many reverberations of such status beyond its waters throughout the Pacific, the United States, and global marine and indigenous environments—in essence, the bioregion of American Sāmoa fisheries.[93]

Native Commercial Fishing and Indigenous Debates over Regulations in the U.S. Pacific

Multiple entities have a stake in the waters around American Sāmoa. At the federal level, the National Oceanic and Atmospheric Administration (NOAA), an arm of the U.S. Department of Commerce, has overall jurisdiction for waters surrounding American Sāmoa, specifically under the office of NOAA Fisheries. NOAA Fisheries, also known as the National Marine Fisheries Service (NMFS), controls the ocean from three to two hundred miles offshore, known as American Sāmoa's Exclusive Economic Zone (EEZ). The NMFS also manages the use of the high seas through international treaties and agreements. The goal of NOAA Fisheries is "stewardship of the nation's ocean resources and their habitat. . . . productive and sustainable fisheries, safe sources of seafood, the recovery and conservation of protected resources, and healthy ecosystems—all backed by sound science and an ecosystem-based approach to management."[1] The NMFS aims to protect ocean resources for human consumption and long-term preservation grounded in scientific research. The Western Pacific Regional Fishery Management Council (Wespac) is the local arm of NOAA Fisheries in American Sāmoa and the wider U.S. Pacific.[2] While Wespac can make policy recommendations, only the NMFS can create laws. However, regulations cannot be changed without being reviewed by the Council.

In American Sāmoa, the local government's Department of Marine and Wildlife Services (DMWR) creates its own regulations for ocean use from the shore to three miles out. As an unincorporated territory of the United States, Federal Public Law 93-435 designated the American Sāmoa Government (ASG) as the administrator of all submerged lands from the mean high tide line out to the limit of the territorial sea, including mineral rights.[3] This Western-based shared structure of ocean control due to U.S. colonial status has resulted in several debates and complications over fishing policies.

With the boom of commercial angling in the Pacific since the 1980s, fishing regulations have increased in the waters around American Sāmoa. Some say open admission for all types of fishers will result in overfishing. Others believe there are plenty of fish in the ocean for everyone. This chapter examines the two major types of indigenous commercial fishing that developed in the second half of the twentieth century and are intimately involved in debates over angling policies: small-scale alia fishing boats and mid-sized ships, known as large-vessel longliners. Overall, the U.S. federal government encouraged a transition from subsistence fishing and other traditional livelihoods to a cash-based export economy and Western-style fishing techniques in this region. Since 1976, the NMFS, not the local indigenous population, has controlled the management of who gets permission to use most of the ocean spaces surrounding the unincorporated U.S. territory of American Sāmoa.

Often, the general public is unaware of the processes that fish in their local restaurants and supermarkets go through to end up on their dining tables. This chapter provides details on the chain of events, people, and regulations involved in the fishing industry to highlight the connection between global food consumption demands and the historic, as well as current, colonial implications of this commercial venture in the U.S. Pacific. While NOAA agencies position themselves as the best guardians to prevent overfishing, Western seafood consumption is also a main contributor to the problem. From January to September 2017, approximately 152 million tons of fish were caught for human consumption.[4] In the twenty-first century, Asia, Europe, and the United States have been major consumers of seafood. In this context, American Sāmoan fishers work hard to make a living and provide for their families through Western-style commercial fishing for the cash-based market economy introduced and supported by the U.S. federal government.

As subjects of the United States, these indigenous anglers call upon colonial management structures to protect their livelihoods while also vocally protesting federal infringements on their native rights to fish in their local, ancestral waters. Even though NOAA Fisheries tries to accommodate native desires while maintaining overall control, the diversity of positionalities among American Sāmoan fishers has placed one group against the other. Violations of *vā fealoaʻi* (respectfully maintaining proper social relations) have also created tensions between alia fishers and federal government representatives. Policies developed in this region impact nonnative fishers in the U.S. Pacific as well, adding yet another layer of influence on this total bioregion (all ecological and cultural relationships) of international fishing and fish consumption.

Historical Forms of Fishing

Fishing has always been a part of Sāmoan culture. Texts by Augustin Krämer, Te Rangi Hiroa (also known as Peter Buck), and Lowell Holmes, as well as research by Karen Armstrong, David Herdrich, and Arielle Levine, have all outlined traditional practices based on the communal village system.[5] According to Armstrong, Herdrich, and Levine, "there were common fishing techniques—gleaning, diving, rod and line, netting and trapping (including communal fish drives), and boat fishing—throughout the Samoan islands but there were also slight differences in practices according to particular village rules and techniques related to the habits of the marine resources."[6] Regardless of the angling tools used, fishing was central to life in the Sāmoan islands.

In a global context, anthropologist Brian Fagan stated, "How little the methods and technology have changed over thousands of years. The net, the spear, the hook and line, and the trap were the fishing tools of prehistory; they are still the tools today. What mattered were experience, careful observation, knowledge of the environment, and familiarity with the potential catch. This was the closely held expertise that passed from generation to generation, rarely to others."[7] Developed knowledge of the local waterscape and behaviors of birds were passed on from generation to generation within fishing families across the world as well as in American Sāmoa.

For example, Afoa Lutu, a former alia fisherman and an American Sāmoa *Fono* senator, talked about using visual cues to find traditional fishing spots. He started fishing in the late 1980s and explained how fish was plentiful at the time. He stated how American Sāmoan fishers are navigators who "learn to use the moon and stars around South bank. There's nothing around it. We used stars before modern instruments were available. Mountains and other points for navigation" as well.[8] Detailed knowledge about the contours of the physical environment has always been key to fishing success.

Others interviewed also mentioned the use of a flock of birds over banks to indicate the location of fish, another traditional Sāmoan fishing skill.[9] Some fondly remembered group bonito boat fishing that involved following sea birds in *va'aalos* (offshore canoes) to hunt for sea life, including sharks. According to scholars Craig Severance and Robert Franco, "for a long time before Western contact, and up until the 1950s in Tutuila, and even into the 1960s and 1970s in Manu'a, American Samoan fishermen pursued <u>atu</u> [bonito] in offshore water using specialized canoes and gear as an expression of the strength and skill of the crew and <u>tautai</u>" (the recognized village fishing expert).[10] For centuries, this type of ocean activity was engrained in native masculinity, indigenous social and political hierarchies, as well as community functions in Sāmoan villages.

Prior to the introduction of motorized boats in 1972, Sāmoans paddled out in *paopaos* (small outrigger canoes) to fish, usually going out three to four miles and maxing out at about five miles from shore. According to Vaʻamua Henry Sesepasara, the Governor's Advisor on Fisheries and DMWR director, about 90 percent of the catch from these manually powered traditional vessels went to cultural use.[11] Cultural use includes providing fish for weddings, funerals, the bestowment of chiefly titles, church fundraisers, and other community gatherings. Involvement in these activities were part of *vā fealoaʻi* and *faʻa Sāmoa* (the Sāmoan way of life) discussed in the introduction.

In American Sāmoa, the annual highlight of fishing involved the once-a-year catches of *atule* (bigeye scad) and *palolo* (sea worms). *Atule* were "often caught by using a communal effort—*lauloa*—of driving the fish towards a trap with branches" while *palolo* were traditionally "caught in small funnel-shaped baskets."[12] These seasonal runs required group participation and represented the social blessings, prosperity, as well as the unity and identity of a village: in other words proper *vā* (social relations).

The type of fish gathered has also remained constant over the years. According to P. Craig, A. Green, and F. Tuilagi in 2008, "the current composition of fish harvested was also similar to that previously found in a nearby archeological excavation dated 1,000–3,000 years ago. These findings indicate that the harvest has been sustainable over the millennia."[13] Fagan also explained how "subsistence fishing, what one might informally call fishing for one's dinner, is almost as old as humanity."[14] Angling for familiar species has been a cornerstone for long-term and persistent marine lifeways in Sāmoa and across the globe.

While the kind of fish has been steady over the years, the style of fishing started to shift in the mid-twentieth century. According to Arielle Levine and Stewart Allen, "by the 1950s, many of the small boats in American Sāmoa were equipped with outboard engines, modern steel hooks were used rather than pearl shell, and monofilament fishing lines had replaced hand woven sennit lines."[15] Outboard engines enabled fishers "to travel farther offshore in shorter time periods. With this technological boost came additional costs in the form of fuel and engine maintenance. Fishermen offset these costs by selling portions of their catch for a profit. These changes initiated a divergence from traditional fishing activities to more of a commercial enterprise."[16] By 1961, only approximately ten traditional-style canoes regularly fished around the main island of Tutuila.

In addition to diversified fishing techniques, the American Sāmoa Government requested the predecessor to NOAA, the Bureau of Commercial Fisheries, to conduct a study on ways to increase local fishery production in the region in 1961. This survey, known as the Marr Report, resulted in multiple projects that introduced Western fishing styles, as well as spurred the growth of local commercial fishing. New types of bottom-fishing and deep sea fishing, as well as new techniques such as fish exporting, long-lining, and fish farming were all tried and supported by the U.S. federal government from 1961 to 1987 to expand for-profit fishing in the region.[17]

Types of Commercial Fishing in American Sāmoa

"Fisheries" is a term that can describe multiple aspects of ocean use. In one sense, a fishery can be a regional concept, meaning the actual latitude and longitude of fishing grounds or the distance of a section of water from land (fishing from shore, just offshore, or in international waters). A fishery can also refer to a type of angling, whether trolling, bottom-fishing, long-lining, or purse seining, all discussed in this chapter. A fishery can be a classification of fish: reef, bottom-feeder, or migratory. Fisheries can also be the level of water that fish are caught at, such as the top level of water, the center column of water (known as pelagic), and the ocean floor. All of these definitions come into play in the deliberations and discussions over marine practices in American Sāmoa.

With fishing already a part of indigenous life in American Sāmoa, the U.S. federal government's encouragement of commercial fishing for local and global markets through the use of Western techniques and technology could provide a profitable and easy transition for some indigenous fishers into the cash-based market economy, especially with the growth and dominance of tuna canneries on Tutuila after World War II (also supported by the U.S. federal government).[18] Two types of Western-style local commercial fishing predominate in the waters surrounding American Sāmoa: bottom-fishing and pelagic fishing. While some fishers associate bottom-fishing with subsistence fishing and long-lining with commercial fishing, bottom-fishing can also be used for commercial fishing.[19] Bottom-fishing generally yields commercial fresh fish and pelagic fishing mostly produces flash-frozen fish for canning.

Bottom-fishing involves the use of weighted lines with a hook to catch fish that feed close to the ocean floor. Bottomfish in American Sāmoa typically include snapper, jobfish, bream, grouper, and amberjack. Historically, bottom-fishing was profitable during three different periods in American Sāmoa: 1982 to 1988 (garnering up to 50 percent of the commercial market share during that

Alia Bottomfishing Vessel

Catamarans of about 30 feet (9 meters) in length used for small scale bottomfishing. A hooked line is weighted to sink to the ocean bottom. Alias typically crewed by two to three people.

Longline Fishing Vessel

Large scale fishing in which a line has bouys and potentially thousands of baited hooks. Vessel is 89 feet (27 meters) long with a crew of seven.

Purse Seiner

A large scale fishing technique in which a net is held vertically in the water with weights and floats. A line is pulled to draw the net closed before lifting the fish out of the water. Vessels range from 150-280 feet (45-85 meters)

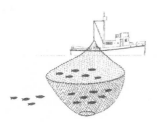

FIGURE I.OI. Major fishing and boat styles in American Sāmoa. (Created for author by Michael Pesses and illustrated for author by Joanna Sokua.)

period), 1994 to 1997, and 2000 to 2002.[20] However, this kind of catch in the region has never been sustainable long-term due to "limited nearshore bottom-fish habitat."[21] Fisheries scientist David Itano found that "the promotion of domestic bottom fishing in American Samoa has been so successful that some of the local bottom fish grounds have become significantly depleted."[22] Over time, the availability of fresh fish from nearby Independent Sāmoa, as well as more profitable yields from pelagic longline fishing for canneries, also contributed to the reduction of bottom-fishing efforts in American Sāmoa.

In this unincorporated territory of the United States, pelagic fishing usually occurs through trolling or long-lining methods. Trolling was the main pelagic fishing method in American Sāmoa until long-lining started in 1995. Trolling involves one or more lines with lures or bait being dragged from behind a boat to simulate a school of small fish to attract bigger fish. Yellowfin and skipjack tuna have made up most of the trolling landings in the region. According to Levine and Allen, "In 1986, when trolling was the only pelagic fishing method, 53 trolling boats landed 137,100 pounds of skipjack tuna and 54,622 pounds of yellowfin tuna. In 1996 when longlining was just getting started, these two species comprised 75% of the trolling landings. . . . By 2001, when longlining became the dominant fishing method in American Sāmoa, the number of trolling boats and their total catch dropped dramatically. Only 18 boats were engaging in trolling."[23] This fishing method dominated the industry in the region for over fifteen years until the newer, more intense, and more effective process of long-lining developed. Today in American Sāmoa, fishers mostly engage in trolling for personal use.

Starting in 1996 and continuing through today, long-lining has been the leading form of local commercial fishing in this unincorporated U.S. territory. Since the introduction of this Western technique, "the fleet grew rapidly with the addition of new alias up to about 38 feet in length and, more significantly, with the addition of other larger monohull vessels that fished much longer trips. The primary target species for longline vessels is albacore tuna for delivery to the canneries" along with yellowfin tuna, bigeye tuna, wahoo, blue marlin, mahimahi, and some other incidentally caught species.[24] Both alias and large-vessel longliners use long-lining in American Sāmoa.

Long-lining has been popular among local fishers "because they catch more fish with less effort and gas consumption."[25] This particular fishing method involves "a mainline longer than 1 nautical mile suspended horizontally in the water column, anchored, floating, or attached to a vessel, and from which branch or dropper lines with hooks are attached."[26] While many sizes of ships use this fishing technique, "longline fishing using *alia* vessels is generally a small scale operation, typically setting approximately 350 hooks per set and hauling the gear with hand-operated reels."[27] In contrast, a larger longliner boat will have 1,600 to 2,000 hooks and mechanized reels.

According to Levine and Allen, five longline vessels began fishing in American Samoa in 1995. The researchers found that "2001 was marked by a peak in the number of longline vessels fishing in American Samoa, and an abrupt shift towards tuna as the dominant species caught. The number of larger boats had swelled to 32 and the number of alias grew to 35, and the average number of hooks per set climbed to 1200 (for alias and large boats combined). The large monohulls now accounted for 88% of the catch."[28] The year 2002

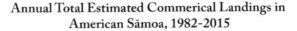

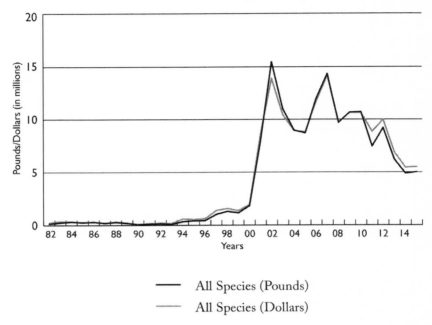

FIGURE 1.02. (Created for author by Michael Pesses.)

was the peak of fish landings in American Sāmoa at 15,482,079 pounds worth $13,924,701.[29] While the most lucrative year for fishing in American Sāmoa was 2007, with 14,366,471 pounds landed at $14,205,971, other high-revenue years over $10 million included 2003, 2006, 2009, and 2010.[30]

In a global historical context, American Sāmoa did not get involved in the commercial fishing industry until other fisheries had become depleted. According to Fagan, "since the Industrial Revolution the strategy of intensified fishing to feed more people has mushroomed into a major international industry" and by the eighteenth century, signs of overfishing were developing.[31] The development of new fishing technologies also increased the reduction of fish stocks and the destruction of marine environments in the Atlantic and the North Pacific. "With the adoption of steam power in the 1830s and 1840s and then, a century ago, the diesel-powered trawler, fishermen could stay far offshore for much longer periods, icing their catch as they worked. . . . With the development of modern-day trawls and purse seines, encircling nets first used in the 1850s, fishing became . . . an efficient way of exploiting the ocean on an industrial scale."[32] More ships were sailing farther into the ocean to catch more fish to feed the ever-rising market demand for seafood consumption.

Fagan also highlighted how "after World War II fishing became a fully industrial business, with Japan leading the way."[33] Wartime technology developments such as radar and sonar were now being used to locate fish.[34] Mansel Blackford also described how "Hydraulic power blocks, which came into use in the 1950s, assisted in pulling some nets on board the vessels. No longer did all the work in lifting nets have to be done by hand."[35] Such mechanization resulted in a massive increase in fishing intensity and effectiveness. According to Blackford, "between 1970 and 1995, the number of commercial fishing vessels increased from 451,000 to 885,000, and their aggregate size from 11.6 million to 23 million gross registered tons."[36] Such increases in angling placed global fisheries on an unsustainable path of resource extraction.

At the same time that commercial fishing was increasing in the Pacific, the world was becoming more concerned with environmental issues, such as pollution and overfishing. Western nations started to develop regulations to address various forms of ecological degradation. Spurred by Rachel Carson's book *Silent Spring,* published in 1962, an environmental movement developed in the United States. The National Environmental Policy Act, which created a federal policy to "encourage productive and enjoyable harmony between man and his environment; to promote efforts which will prevent or eliminate damage to the environment and biosphere and stimulate the health and welfare of man; to enrich the understanding of the ecological systems and natural resources important to the Nation; and to establish a Council on Environmental Quality," was passed in 1969.[37] The U.S. Environmental Protection Agency (EPA) was formed in 1970. This administration's charge includes "a variety of federal research, monitoring, standard-setting and enforcement activities to ensure environmental protection. Since its inception, EPA has been working for a cleaner, healthier environment for the American people."[38] Ironically, most of the environmental destruction targeted by this administrative unit was actually caused by historic U.S. resource needs, policies, and consumption.

In the fishing realm, between 1976 and 1977, the United States, Canada, the Soviet Union, and North Korea all declared Exclusive Economic Zones (EEZs).

For two hundred nautical miles from their territorial seas, each nation claimed sovereign rights over the natural resources within those waters, as well as the ability to regulate activity in those areas. Today, EEZs, "which include most continental shelves, contain an estimated 75–90 percent of the world's commercial fish."[39] However, these initial moves to control vast swaths of ocean often involved nationalist protectionist motivations rather than ecologically minded goals.

For example, the United States' EEZ was created at a time when the "U.S. economy in 1976–77 was just emerging from a deep recession, and the FCMA [Fisheries Conservation and Management Act] won noncontroversial congressional approval mainly as a jobs bill."[40] Politicians supported this legislation to manage fish and other species in the EEZ, because such regulations would create a variety of jobs through various aspects of the fishing industry, from fishers and processors to distributors and industry support services, like gas, bait, and repairs. In fact, the Fisheries Conservation and Management Act, also known as the Magnuson-Stevens Act, did not prioritize the conservation of fishery resources until the passage of the Sustainable Fisheries Act in 1996.

This amendment aimed to sustain "participation of fishery dependent communities and minimize economic impacts to those communities and minimize by catch and its mortality. . . . identify overfished species and take action to rebuild those stocks. . . . establishes a fishing capacity reduction program [and] mandates research on fishery management/conservation and the economics/ social characteristics of the fisheries."[41] Until this shift in approach for the U.S. Fish and Wildlife Service (USFW), as will be discussed later in this chapter, decisions made by the Regional Fishery Councils often benefited larger, for-profit fishing industry businesses. American Sāmoa's local commercial fishing industry developed within this wider international and historic context of long-term overfishing and new efforts to regulate and control future angling.

In the 1980s, confrontations between American fishers and Pacific coast Latin American countries also developed. Boat seizures, the firing of weapons, and fines for regulation violations escalated in the Exclusive Economic Zones of Ecuador, Chile, and Peru.[42] Such tensions encouraged U.S. tuna fishers to relocate to the western Pacific, where two-hundred-mile EEZs were harder to enforce over long distances for Pacific Island nations. The United States also had its own Exclusive Economic Zone waters around their Pacific territories, like American Sāmoa.

Alia Efforts

With fishing in eastern Pacific waters restricted from the United States, and Americans having access to the EEZs in their colonized parts of the Pacific, angling efforts within U.S. waters became more important for the U.S. fishing industry. The first official attempt to commercialize fishing in the unincorporated territory of American Sāmoa occurred with the Dory Project in the 1970s. According to Blackford, American fishers used dories since the first commercial fishing efforts in Alaska in 1888. These anglers "dropped long, baited lines to the sea bottom and soaked them there for several hours to attract halibut. They pulled up the lines hand-over-hand or through hand-cranked rollers, took the fish off the hooks, and rowed or sailed back to their schooners, where they cleaned and iced the halibut before returning to port. Hours were long, and work was physically demanding."[43]

Close to one hundred years later in American Sāmoa, the territorial government encouraged this same style of commercial bottom-fishing among native people to help supply Tutuila's tuna canneries. In 1972, the American Sāmoa Office of Economic Opportunity started the Dory Project, which provided "easy credit and loans to fishermen to develop offshore fisheries. The project developed a boat-building facility that produced 23 vessels over a 3-year period. These dories were made available to local residents interested in commercial fishing on the understanding that the cost of materials and construction costs would be paid back to the government at a low rate of interest generated by fish sales."[44]

This initiative ultimately failed due to the inability of fishers to keep up with the costs of constant boat repairs. Itano stated that "a wide range of mechanical problems beset several dory owners and many of the dories were out of service for extended periods of time. . . . After the first few years, the lack of routine maintenance on many of the dories took a heavy toll on dories that eventually became unserviceable and some were out of service due to repossession for failure to pay the vessel loans."[45] Wespac American Sāmoa Advisory Council member William Sword also explained how dory boats were small and mostly good for bottom-fishing.[46] These vessels could not handle rough seas and the fishing gear involved hard labor because of manually operated cranks. Only twenty-three boats were purchased in total and all were defunct by 1980.[47]

According to Levine and Allen, "in the 1980s, dories were replaced by alia catamarans, larger, more powerful boats that could stay multiple days at sea. Alias were usually 28 to 32 feet long and powered by an outboard engine."[48] This particular design came from independent Sāmoa. Navigation on these double-hulled aluminum boats with fiberglass or wood superstructures "was visual, using landmarks. Fishing gear was stored on deck, including a hand-crank reel which could hold between two and ten miles of monofilament mainline."[49] Despite new vessel and fishing gear technology, American Sāmoan fishers still relied on observation and past experiences with angling in the area. As Fagan explained, the art of "knowing when and where to look" has always been an important skill for small-scale fishing success throughout time and across the globe.[50]

A variety of definitions exist for small-scale fisheries. According to marine science scholar Theodore Koboski, "while vessel size was typically an indicator of a small-scale fishery, differences in the types of technological complexity, capital investment, and market structure within small-scale fisheries" should also be taken into account.[51] Alias have been central to the commercial small-scale fishery in American Sāmoa that supplies both the canneries in Tutuila and fresh fish for local consumption. Equipment on alias remain relatively modest, with costs for maintenance and market fluctuations often having negative impacts on continued participation in commercial fishing.

In the beginning of alia fishing in American Sāmoa, trolling and bottom-fishing were the preferred catch methods, with spearfishing, netting, and vertical long-lining used occasionally. In 1995, "some alia captains began using horizontal longline gear."[52] This change in fishing technique, though still mostly manual, significantly increased catch rates for these indigenous small-scale fishers. According to a Wespac report, alia long-lining "trips were 1 day long (about 8 hours). Setting the equipment generally began in the early morning and hauling was generally in the midday to mid-afternoon. The catch was stored in boxes built into the hull of the boat or in portable coolers or freezer chests."[53] In 2005, the alia fleet on Tutuila usually consisted of three-man crews who fished eleven hours per trip and caught about 173 pounds of fish on average. The Manuʻa-based fleet typically had two-man crews, fished about five hours, and landed around eighty-one pounds of fish.[54]

According to Koboski, "The typical alia vessel held just about one ton of albacore tuna (the target species of the alia fleet), and fish were stored on the boat in each hull of the catamaran. Once the vessel was back at port, the fish were transferred to freezers, usually located at the fisherman's place of residence. One fisherman reported having as many as seven deep freezers to store his catch. Once the freezers reached capacity, the fishermen would transport their catch to the canneries on the island, where it was sold."[55] The entire process involves less technology compared to large-vessel long-lining vessels and purse seiners.

At the time of this research, Alvin "Eo" Mokoma was the most active alia fisher in American Sāmoa. He started long-lining from alia boats in 1995.[56] Mokoma worked his way up to owning four boats, all of which he ran until the 2009 tsunami. Two of his boats were destroyed during this catastrophe. In the summer of 2016, he used one of his remaining boats for commercial long-lining and the other for bottom-fishing for personal use. Mokoma discussed how "if I make a penny from my small alia, then I'm happy." He, like many others interviewed, acknowledged that being "a fisherman is not easy. You have to look for fish, it's not an easy job."[57] To be effective, a fisher has to love fishing, crave the ocean, and know go where the fish go.

Ma'a Maea, who was the secretary of the Pago Alia Fishing Association in 2015, was another alia fisherman interviewed. He enjoyed long-lining because this method was "very exciting, a nice way to catch a wild animal or fish. It's like doing a trick. All set up, ties, right performance, technique, art to bring fish. It's a modern form of art."[58] Setting out the lines and the bait involved a certain level of skill and knowledge for success. In addition to the personal challenge of angling, Maea discussed the social and cultural significance of fishing in Sāmoan life. Seafood has been a key aspect of major events such as weddings, title bestowments, funerals, and feasts. He believed it was his "duty as fisherman to provide these resources. It is a distinct honor for fishermen, family look up to you to play this role."[59] Maea was proud of the responsibility he fulfilled to feed his extended family and his community, as well as maintain ancient cultural traditions and proper *vā*.

Christinna Lutu-Sanchez, longline boat owner and daughter of Afoa Lutu, explained how her family started commercial fishing with alias. "At one time we had eight alias fishing. It was great, fishing was really good.... Everyone was longlining."[60] After long-lining began among alias in 1995, commercial fish landings and revenue increased. The first five longline vessels that fished that year landed an estimated fifty-eight thousand pounds of albacore.[61] In 1997, thirty-three vessels held permits for longline fishing, and twenty-one of those were actively fishing in the region primarily catching 681,000 pounds of albacore tuna.[62]

With alias dominating long-lining from 1995 to 1997, the arrival of the first, much larger monohull longline vessel in 1997 expanded the growth of commercial fishing in American Sāmoa. Intensified extraction from the American Sāmoan fishery began just as U.S. Fish and Wildlife was starting to work on fish conservation in general. Since commercial angling in this Pacific region was relatively new, USFW was not concerned with fish stock depletion. Initially, the Service did not create any regulations to manage commercial fishing practices in the area.

Large-Vessel Longliners

Large-vessel longliners, at eighty-nine feet long, usually have a crew of seven and a full array of electronic navigation and communications equipment. The hydraulic powered reel can hold twenty to thirty miles of monofilament mainline and 1,600 to 2,000 hooks suspended from sixty floats. The crew sets and hauls the gear each day the vessel is actively fishing. Each ship usually makes three-to four-week trips, sometimes as far away as Tonga, and each ship can hold up to forty-four tons of frozen albacore that can be brought back and sold to the canneries in American Sāmoa after each trip.[63]

According to Levine and Allen, "in 1999, two other large monohulled longline vessels, similar to the first, arrived in American Sāmoa and began longline fishing. Then in 2000 and 2001, large monohulled longline boats began arriving from places such as San Diego, Korea, Taiwan, Hawai'i, New Zealand, and Australia. In 2002, about thirty-six large vessels were operating from Pago Pago. The rapid fleet expansion caused the fishing effort to increase from about 1 million hooks per year at the end of 2000 to 5.6 million hooks by the end of 2001."[64] The year 2001 became the peak in the number of longline vessels fishing in American Sāmoa. The number of larger boats increased to thirty-two and the number of alias climbed to thirty-five.[65] Both alias and large monohull ships were profiting and prospering at that time. But this peak also represented the point at which large-vessel longliners started to dominate commercial fishing in the area. In 2001, there was a major shift toward tuna as the main species landed. The large monohulls made up 88 percent of the catch of 7,125,000 pounds of albacore, 417,000 pounds of yellowfin tuna, and 165,000 pounds of bigeye tuna. That year, the annual net revenue averaged about $177,000 per vessel.[66] By 2003, seafood provided 15.5 percent of animal protein in global diets, with American Sāmoa fishers providing a significant contribution to the canned tuna market.[67]

In 2005, fifty-four fishing vessels were active in American Sāmoa waters. Fifty-one of these boats were based in Tutuila and three docked in the Manu'a Islands. Many of these vessels used more than one type of fishing method. Forty-one of the Tutuila boats (including twenty-seven vessels, which were over fifty feet in length) engaged in some long-lining. Of the fifty-four total boats, thirteen went trolling and bottom-fishing, and four used other types of fishing. According to a NOAA report, "essentially, all of the longlining was based out of Tutuila and the majority of their catch was sold to the canneries on island."[68] Supplying local tuna factories motivated the development of this style of fishing.

In 2016, Krista Corry ran one of the first large-vessel longliners in American Sāmoa. Her father, Vince Haleck, started fishing in 1997. Corry took over management of the family business in 2010, but her father still owned the boats. Their company, Tuna Ventures Inc., owned three longliners in 2016: the *Fetuolemoana* carried up to twenty-four tons, the *Sivaimoana* held twenty-two tons, and the *Manaolemoana* stored between twenty-eight and thirty tons of fish. According to Corry, her longliner boats went out for thirty to forty-five days, about 150 miles out, and caught about one thousand fish at a time. Her ships set more than three thousand hooks a day. The crew was like a family, watching out for each other. On her ships, crewmembers came from Western Sāmoa, Tonga, American Sāmoa, and Indonesia. When she started to run the family business, the fishing industry was in a downturn. She discussed how "the fishing industry is very difficult. We try our best to do with what we have. . . . We are figuring out ways to survive, not only for our company but for the guys' families. . . . We're doing our best to hang on."[69] Lutu-Sanchez also explained how "it's been a really rough last several years."[70] She lamented the "misconception that boat owners are millionaires. If there is no fish, there is no money."[71] Overall, fishing is hard work for everyone involved, regardless of boat size and the amount of available technology.

While longlining can be lucrative, this type of fishing is also a complicated and expensive endeavor. Like any boat, repairs are constant. Refrigeration is key to the process. An engineer is always needed onboard. With two generators, two compressors, a six-cylinder engine, and an electric-powered reel, anything could break and stop the fishing process at any moment. Corry recounted one fishing trip when the hydraulic system that draws up fishing line broke. The crew had already put out the line so they had to manually pull up twenty-six miles of monofilament. She explained how "every time the boys got tired, the captain yelled 'What boat are we from?' And the crew would respond 'Mana!' Mana means power."[72] Pride in their boat and their job motivated crewmembers to push through the painful and difficult task. So while these larger monohulled boats generate bigger catch amounts than alias, these vessels still involve a relatively small and locally based crew. Lutu-Sanchez also explained how "this is our home."[73] American Sāmoan longliner companies and their workers are part of the local economy and society, taking their rest, getting their supplies, and conducting their repairs in American Sāmoa. Some owners also live and raise their families in this region, their ancestral home.

To protect their interests, local longline owners formed an association called

Tautai-O-Sāmoa Longline & Fishing Association. The group's president, Lutu-Sanchez, explained how this organization "represents close to 40 longliners—including U.S.-flagged longliners and foreign vessels—and all operate out of American Samoa. The only difference is that the U.S.-flagged fleet fish in the U.S./American Samoa EEZ and the other fish in other Pacific islands EEZs, such as the Cook Islands."[74] As significant suppliers for the tuna canneries in American Sāmoa, this coalition of U.S. and Pacific boat owners from multiple regions have common interests in the regulation of marine practices for fishing in the region.

Regulating Fishing in the U.S. South Pacific

In the United States, there are eight Fishery Management Councils that have been in charge of different regions of U.S. jurisdiction since their establishment through the Fisheries Conservation and Management Act of 1976. The general mandates for these councils, under the purview of the U.S. Fish and Wildlife Service, are to create "measures to control foreign fishing in US waters, to allow overfished stocks to recover, and to monitor, conserve and manage fishery resources in a manner that maximizes long-term benefits to the nation."[75] Councils regulated outside fishing and prioritized the preservation of fisheries for future use.

However, scholars like Blackford have found that "the goal of most international and national fishery laws . . . has been to make fishing profitable and sustainable. The laws and the commissions set up to administer them have very much been in the mainstream American Progressive tradition of putting nature to efficient use. The goal was not to preserve oceanic nature in a pristine state, except in the establishment of a relatively few preserves."[76] Continued access to resources has always been central to the U.S. conservation movement since the late nineteenth century, as will be discussed in chapter 3.

Marine policy scholar Thomas Okey also stated there is an "overwhelming dominance of extractive interests" in these councils that have led to unrealistic fishing quotas which do not protect fish species or reduce overfishing.[77] This tension between the stated goals of the councils and actual actions through the years has occurred in all colonized regions of the U.S. Pacific, including American Sāmoa. In fact, continuous fish stock depletion under this overall administration ultimately led Congress to pass legislation in 2006 to mandate an end to overfishing in U.S. waters by 2011.[78]

The Western Pacific Council covers Hawai'i, American Sāmoa, Guam, and the Northern Mariana Islands, as well as "fisheries in the Pacific Ocean seaward of such states and of the commonwealth, territories and possessions."[79] The council system includes council members, council staff, advisory bodies, and the public that can participate in the decision-making process. There are thirteen voting members and three nonvoting members. Eight members are private citizens with some familiarity with commercial and/or noncommercial fisheries and/or marine conservation appointed by the secretary of commerce from a list of suggestions provided by the governors of the regions served by the council. The five other members are government representatives from each Pacific region covered by the council. Three nonvoting members assist with decision making from the perspectives of the U.S. Coast Guard (for enforcement and safety issues), the U.S. Department of State (for information on international implications), and the U.S. Fish and Wildlife Service (for advice on flora and fauna impacts).

According to the official guide to the council, "Council members must balance competing interests while trying to make decisions for the overall benefit of the nation."[80] Council staff coordinates meetings and provides information to all constituents. Advisory bodies provide feedback on topics being addressed by the council. The three main bodies include the Scientific and Statistical Committee, Advisory Panels (composed of subpanels of marine-concerned individuals from each covered Pacific region), and Regional Ecosystem Advisory Committees that focus on marine ecosystem impacts.

The Council meets three times a year where issues are brought up and discussed. The public is allowed to comment on any agenda item. But as Blackford pointed out, "as a practical matter, this system favored well-established fishers and seafood processors, who had the time and funds to attend meetings. Council Meetings typically lasted for several days, but sometimes for a week or longer" often held in Hawaiʻi, but sometimes in Guam and American Sāmoa.[81] A small-scale fisher in the Pacific region would likely not be able to afford to attend a Council meeting held outside their home region. Once an issue has been investigated and commented on by advisory bodies, and public comment has been taken, the Council deliberates and may vote on a topic. Decisions, which must comply with multiple federal acts and other applicable laws, are then forwarded to the secretary of commerce for a second review, more public comment, and final approval. Once finalized and approved, the National Marine Fisheries Service implements the new regulations.

Since its creation, Wespac has approved longline closures in the Commonwealth of the Northern Marianas, specified annual catch limits in all regions under its jurisdiction, established management measures for noncommercial and recreational fishing within National Monuments in the Pacific, and prohibited commercial fishing within Pacific National Monuments.[82] However, purse seiner activity, the largest and most extractive form of commercial fishing, has not been specifically regulated in this region.

Okey explained this disconnect as "the general pattern in the US ... councils dominated by industry (user group) representatives make the decisions about exploitation of public (marine fishery) resources. This has been referred to as 'capture' of the regulatory or management process by industry."[83] Consequently, "a natural tendency of capital-minded fisheries sectors is to maximize short-term profit at the expense of sustainability (and social and ecological considerations) thereby degrading the public value of the exploited resources."[84] Maximum catch for their own ships or companies, as opposed to maintaining or protecting fishery resources, took priority in many Council members' decisions. Blackford also highlighted how "catch quotas that were much too high to be sustained, against the advice of its own marine scientists" also dominated Council policies until the twenty-first century.[85] Both scholars found that indigenous issues are often ignored or subsumed to large commercial fishing interests in the Council process.

In contrast to these typical stories, NMFS regulations have prioritized fishers based out of American Sāmoa since 2002. Due to the peak of angling vessels from all over the globe in this area during this time period, on March 1, 2002, NOAA Fisheries created a Large Vessel Prohibited Area (LVPA) that physically separated smaller commercial American Sāmoa indigenous alia efforts from large-vessel long-lining endeavors. At the time, close to forty alias actively fished in local waters. Boats larger than fifty feet were prohibited from fishing within fifty nautical miles of American Sāmoa "to protect the islands' local, small-scale fishery."[86] However, any large-vessel pelagic ships that already operated in American Sāmoa on or before November 13, 1997, were also allowed to continue fishing in the zone.

The LVPA accomplished the goal of safeguarding smaller artisanal native commercial fishing in nearby waters. Wespac chose to protect this aspect of fisheries in American Sāmoa because the Council recognized that this particular group of fishers provided "important socio-cultural and economic benefits to the American Samoa fishing community."[87] Wespac acknowledged the symbolic and financial importance that native marine practices had in the region, through the encouragement of American Sāmoan fishers themselves. However, these laws also further subjected American Sāmoans to U.S. authority and control.

To protect fish stocks in American Sāmoa waters and also encourage larger-

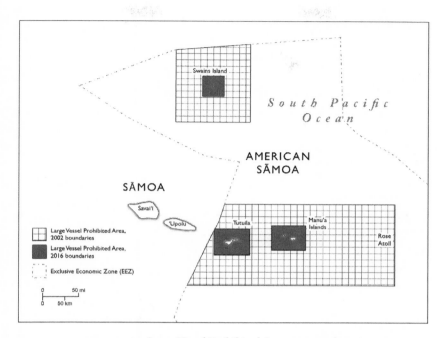

FIGURE 1.03. Large Vessel Prohibited Area: 2002 and 2016.
(Created for author by Michael Pesses.)

scale fishing specifically based in American Sāmoa, the NMFS created an American Sāmoa Longline Limited Entry (ASLLE) program that went into effect on August 1, 2005.[88] This permit allowed a limited number of longline owners operating out of American Sāmoa to fish in the region's Exclusive Economic Zone. This initiative "intended to establish management measures that would stabilize effort in the fishery to avoid a "boom and bust" cycle of fishery development that could disrupt community participation and limit opportunity for substantial participation in the fishery by indigenous islanders."[89] As a result of this policy, a maximum of sixty permits became available for ships from American Sāmoa using longline gear to catch pelagic or migratory fish between three and two hundred nautical miles from shore. These permits are available to four vessel sizes: Class A boats are forty feet or smaller, Class B (and B-1) ships are between forty-one feet and fifty feet, Class C (and C-1) vessels are fifty-one feet to seventy feet, and Class D (and D-1) boats are longer than seventy feet.[90] These permits have never been fully used up. In 2018, forty-six of the sixty permits were being used.[91]

Lutu-Sanchez explained how she helped spearhead both of these regulations to specifically protect smaller American Sāmoan fishing boats. At the time of creation, alia long-lining was at a peak. By limiting the number of longline vessels that could fish in the American Sāmoa EEZ, alias had more access to migratory fish in the area. Lutu-Sanchez also discussed how the ASLLE program was created because "we thought there would be up to 200 alias owned by American Sāmoans. We had high hopes and we really thought it was going to happen. We are not happy" that alias did not continue to succeed.[92] During the creation of these regulations in 2002, both alia and large monohulled American Sāmoan fishers agreed with and supported federal government measures to control angling in these waters.

However, after 2005, alia long-lining drastically reduced. That year the "total fishing effort was decreasing, and the era of the alias was ending. There were 30 monohulled vessels and only 6 alias."[93] Several reasons contributed to this decline. First, longliners started to sell extra catch that was not purchased by the canneries to local stores and restaurants, directly competing with alias for income in the regional market. According to Wespac American Sāmoa representative Nate Ilaoa, "stores prefer longline fish because it is stored in frozen brine, so it's higher quality" product."[94] Daily imports of fish from Independent Sāmoa also started to drive the price of fish down in American Sāmoa. Levine and Allen additionally found that "an increased reliance on imported store-bought food has discouraged development of locally based offshore fishing for the local market" and "these factors, as well as an increase in fuel prices and vessel and engine breakdown and repair problems, combined to make small scale alia operations challenging and largely unprofitable in American Samoa."[95]

In addition to cost and price factors, Koboski found a decrease in catch numbers and an increase in fishing risk to be other key reasons for the decline in commercial alia angling. Alia fishers he interviewed stated that bigger boats "were catching all the tuna offshore before they could come in. They were suffocating the inshore area."[96] Consequently, alia boats had to travel farther than their vessels were built to handle to reach more fish, posing safety hazards in more distant and rough seas with equipment and structures built to stay closer to shore. The high cost of bait and required vessel safety equipment, as well as lower albacore catch rates stopped many commercial alia fishers from going out on a regular basis.[97] Additionally, many alia crewmembers came from Independent Sāmoa. Increasing enforcement of immigration laws also made it harder to get willing and qualified fishers to work on boats.

To bolster fishing out of American Sāmoa and preempt overfishing of local resources, Wespac recommended the prohibition of purse seiner vessels within seventy-five nautical miles of American Sāmoa in 2011. According to the International Seafood Sustainability Foundation, "purse seine fishing vessels catch nearly 62% of the 4.2 million tons of tuna caught globally every year. Globally it is estimated that 1,664 purse seine vessels are authorized to fish for tuna"[98] These industrial-scale fishing vessels cast huge nets up to 6,500 feet in length and 650 feet in depth.[99] Purse seiners also involve a lot of equipment compared to alias and longliners. According to the Food and Agriculture Organization of the United Nations, "industrial tuna purse seiners are usually large vessels which length ranges between 45 and 85 meters, sometimes over. . . . Those seiners are facilitated with a large skiff, often with a few speed boats, and with a helicopter. Also equipped with brine freezing fish wells."[100] Purse seiners catch the most fish and use the most resources, such as fuel and the creation of greenhouse gases, to supply the tuna canning industry.

According to Levine and Allen, "while purse seiners did not fish frequently in American Samoa's waters, the Council determined that the recent increase in the number of these vessels had the potential to disproportionately impact the local fishery."[101] Since no American Sāmoan has ever owned a purse seiner, the seventy-five-mile regulation would have continued the historical pattern of National Marine Fisheries Service regulations protecting smaller-scale native fishing efforts out of American Sāmoa. However, this law did not pass because the proposed measures were inconsistent with the Magnuson-Stevens Fishery Management and Conservation Act that "requires conservation and management measures to be based on the best scientific information available, and requires that fishery actions be founded on thorough analyses that allow NMFS to conclude that the selected alternative will accomplish necessary and appropriate conservation and management objectives."[102] Without clear scientific evidence to prove such a regulation would "prevent localized stock depletion, as well as reduce catch competition and gear conflicts," NOAA Fisheries could not limit the activity of purse seiners in American Sāmoa EEZ waters.[103] As scholars Jon Barnett and John Campbell explained, the lack of substantial and validated Western-style data in Pacific Island regions often prevents the development of policies and regulations to address immediate and long-term environmental issues.[104] Such reliance on precise technical data ignores historic and non-Western forms of indigenous knowledges and skills in local ecologies, as well as subsumes native fishing rights to western logics, categorizations, and oversight that is difficult to establish and maintain in these underfunded and understudied regions.

Since 2006, Wespac has specified annual catch limits to prevent the depletion of targeted fish species. The goal of these ceilings is "to ensure long-term fishery sustainability by ending and preventing overfishing, and by rebuilding over-fished stocks."[105] These Western-style regulations include maximum sustainable yield (the most catch that can be engaged in on a continual basis without destroying the fishery), annual catch limits, and accountability measures.

Some scholars question the usefulness of concepts such as maximum sustainable yields. According to Callum Roberts,

> the greatest surplus yield, termed maximum sustainable yield, could be obtained, according to the fishery models, by reducing a population to half of its unexploited size. Since then, the concept has exerted a hegemonic grip over fisheries science that is proving extremely difficult to loosen, despite serious shortcomings. . . . The goal of sustaining yield over the long-term has proven elusive and is too often sacrificed for short-term gain. . . . estimates of target population sizes needed to achieve maximum sustainable yield being set too low, thus leading to a greater risk of population collapses.[106]

Despite half a specific fish population being maintained, many other species critical to a healthy and stable fishery are often caught in the process and not counted. In today's highly regulated world of fishing, if a vessel does not have a quota for a particular species, the boat must discard all others caught, regardless of whether the catch could still be used for eating or for fish meal.[107] Even if they are returned to the ocean, this bycatch of noncataloged species often die in the process, further depleting the fishery. Despite such realities of high amounts of sea life death from one fishing net, the calculation of 50 percent maximum sustainable yield for one specific type of fish has become accepted and naturalized as sufficient to create and maintain fishery stability.

Such an approach has not worked. According to the 2018 State of the World Fisheries and Aquaculture report provided by the Food and Agriculture Organization of the United Nations in 2015, "the world's marine fisheries had 33.1 percent of stocks classified as overfished."[108] In addition to this status, bycatch or "discarded fish are not recorded in fishery statistics. But they are just as dead as those landed."[109] Consequently, Western-style fishery statistics are fallible and have prevented the creation of true sustainability in global waters. Ultimately, the leaders making decisions on fishing rules are "bound to fail because they have vested interests that maximize short-term returns for themselves at the expense of long term sustainability for the general public."[110] The logic, motives, or actions of fishery decision makers who were connected to large-scale fishing businesses usually did not coincide with government goals for conservation or sustainability.

An indigenous marine management perspective could provide one path to move away from segmented, narrow-minded, and unsuccessful Western accounting methods to prevent overfishing. In American Sāmoa and many other global indigenous cultures, all parts of anything caught from the ocean are used. Sea life holds an equal status, if not sacred status, in the hierarchy of life and is treated respectfully. If seafood stocks seem low, temporary prohibitions on angling are put into place by local leaders. As described by Tui Atua Tupua Tamasese Ta'isi, "All matter, human, water, animal, plant and biosphere are.... divine creations connected by genealogy. They share the same biological beginnings.... the respect or *faaaloalo* that must be shown by man to all things is a respect for the sacred essence, the sacred origins of their beginnings. This is the cornerstone of Samoan indigenous religious thought." [111] Such beliefs are central to the creation and maintenance of harmony between Sāmoans and the environment. Tui Atua also explained how "ancient Samoa protocols were developed to ensure that the environment was preserved.... During times of re-growth certain trees and plants were prohibited from being cut or picked."[112] Sāmoan culture has age-old policies and practices to protect and manage their ecology.

In fact, as Roberts described, "the idea of creating refuges from fishing has a long pedigree ... Across the Pacific, from Papua New Guinea to Hawai'i, islanders traditionally placed some areas of reef off limits to fishing. In most places these were "rested" for a time before being fished again to supply some feast, rather than given permanent protection. But the penalties applied for taking fish could be severe. In Hawai'i, offenders were clubbed to death for violating such kapu areas." [113] Once the marine environment seems to have recovered, fishing resumes. Barnett and Campbell also claimed that "small island states have alternative knowledge and specificity that could enhance or work better on the ground than blanket, generalized environmental policies."[114] With more equitable representation by noncommercial interests on the fishery councils, especially native groups (as recommended by Okey), more effective alternatives for ocean-use policy could develop.

A focus on "optimum yields, which considered social and economic community issues, especially job creation and destruction," over maximum sustainable yields, "which looked only at biological matters" is another alternative, more balanced way to rethink fishery management from a Western perspective.[115] The current study and standard use of isolated quantitative numbers for a limited number of species ignores the interconnectedness and dynamics of all entities within an ecosystem.

From a bioregional perspective, one must look at the overall impact and well-being of all key players when creating marine policies. According to Fagan, "People have caught fish for more than a million years, yet only in the past century and a half, with the growth of industrialized fisheries, has the quest become unsustainable. Now that insatiable demand from rising populations is coming into ever-greater conflict with decimated fisheries," fishery councils are trying to figure out how to move forward.[116] At the same time, "Fish having become the most traded commodity in the world, the fish business employs millions of people worldwide. Careful management and the creation of ocean reserves are thus vital to jobs and trade as well as to nutrition."[117] Multiple groups, including the seafood-consuming public, have a stake in the success of the global fishing industry and long-term sustainability. However, one must also remember that any federal marine regulation continues to subject American Sāmoans to U.S. control and authority. Until 2015, indigenous fishers did not oppose such colonial marine management.

Policy Changes

In 2013, the longline fleet out of American Sāmoa was 100 percent monohulled and accounted for "about 80% of the fishing effort reported in 2012. There were only 22 active vessels, 12% less than 2012. A total of 177,627 fish were caught (all species combined), which was 38% less than in 2012."[118] Overall, boats were going out less frequently in the 2010s. Ships were setting more hooks in one day to try and catch more fish more quickly and shorten the amount of days for each trip, hoping to reduce costs in fuel, labor, and fishing permits. Despite such efforts, the total amount of catch also fell during this period. Increased competition from foreign fishing vessels not subject to ecologically minded U.S. fishing quotas and size regulations, often purse seiners, also impacted the local fleet.[119] Such shifts in the abundance and profitability of fishing in the waters surrounding American Sāmoa motivated discussions to change ocean-use policies in American Sāmoa, starting in 2014.

With the encouragement of local large-vessel longliner owners in American Sāmoa, Wespac proposed the opening of the Large Vessel Prohibited Area to mid-size U.S.-flagged boats starting at twelve nautical miles from shore. Two public meetings were held in American Sāmoa on May 3, 2014, and January 28, 2015. The Council's eventual proposal to reduce the restricted zone was the first time this entity did not abide by the sentiments of their local Pacific representatives. Such a move could be considered a violation of *vā fealoaʻi* (social respect) because Council members Taimalelagi Dr. Claire Claire Poumele, director of the American Sāmoa Port Authority, and Dr. Ruth S. Matagi-Tofiga, director of the American Sāmoa Department of Marine and Wildlife Resources, voted against reducing the Large Vessel Prohibited Area in 2015.[120] The other regional Council representative abstained from the vote.

Despite this lack of support, Wespac chair Ed Ebisui Jr. said that "reducing the LVPA from its current 50 nautical mile limit to 12 nautical miles would reduce operational costs of the longline vessels and allow the American Samoa longline fleet to continue to provide an important domestic source of albacore to local canneries, while still protecting important areas for other coastal resource users, including troll and recreational fisheries."[121] Wespac believed this change represented a fair compromise for both small-scale alia and longliner fishing needs. NOAA Pacific Islands Regional Administrator Michael Tosatto also stated that the Large Vessel Prohibited Area reduction "supported the people who are fishing now."[122] Lutu-Sanchez explained how "the request to change the LVPA was to follow the fish. If we are fishing in the north and catch some fish, if they go south, we can still catch them there.[123] Corry also stated that the twelve-mile protected area is the norm in other Pacific regions, except for Fiji and Tonga.[124]

The Council also pursued this adjustment in zone size because scientific assessments of the South Pacific deemed local fish stocks healthy. The Scientific and Statistical Committee stated in October 2015 that "none of the bottomfish stocks in the U.S. Pacific Island territories are currently overfished or experiencing overfishing."[125] This group predicted that American Sāmoa would be 13 percent below the allowable federal overfishing levels of 50 percent in 2017.[126] Based on these statistics, small-scale alia boats should have plenty of bottomfish to catch within the twelve-mile Large Vessel Prohibited Area reduction. But as already discussed, isolated statistics for a limited number of species can ignore the larger impact of fishing on the total ecosystem, including bycatch and social and economic impacts.

The Magnuson-Stevens Fishery Conservation and Management Act mandates that NOAA Fisheries policies "promote fishing efficiency and . . . not discriminate among fisheries."[127] While protecting boat owners in American Sāmoa has always been a part of NMFS regulations, the designation of a fifty-mile Large Vessel Prohibited Area for the exclusive use of smaller American Sāmoa alia boats was difficult to justify with Western-based statistics in the 2010s. By

2015, there was only one commercial alia fisher actively long-lining for a living on a regular basis. There were about nineteen other alias boats with licenses, but these ships focused on bottom-fishing or trolling.[128] These fishers went out more irregularly and their catch was mostly used for personal consumption and *fa'a Sāmoa* obligations. These alia usually sold fish when they needed to pay for their monthly expenses.

American Sāmoa Governor Lolo Matalasi Moliga countered diminutive portrayals of a small alia fleet by "explaining that even if there is only one small vessel fishing with long-lines in the protected area, there are approximately 29 others that bottom-fish or troll within the fishery—having converted from long-line fishing."[129] The governor wanted to protect angling access for any small-scale local indigenous fisher who went out for profit or not. When the access of native peoples to their traditional functions seemed threated, members of the local population readily spoke out against U.S. colonial authority and policies.

In fact, the proposed modification of the Large Vessel Prohibited Area angered several alia owners and American Sāmoa Government officials. At a Wespac Council meeting in October 2015, the president of the Pago Alia Fishing Association, Fuega Moliga, made a statement on behalf of this organization that works to protect the interests of small-scale artisanal fishers. He said "that's one thing that's getting on our nerves—people making decisions on us without us having input. . . . I hate to see President Obama declare the Pacific Ocean a sanctuary . . . [he] doesn't understand our needs, we solely depend on the ocean."[130] In this situation, the conflict between local needs and federal policies becomes clear. Alia fishers hail from a historic tradition of angling the waters surrounding American Sāmoa to support their families and cultural practices. Rules that threaten such access are strongly opposed, especially if this group of fishers is not actively involved in the decision-making process, part of *vā fealoa'i*. NOAA policies, on the other hand, examine global ecosystem issues from Western scientific, economic, and bureaucratic perspectives when developing fishing regulations.

Some individuals posted about Fuega's comments online at Talanei.com, an online local news source in American Sāmoa connected to the local radio station. Two of three commentators were unsympathetic to the Fishing Association's position, with one stating how "opening the 50 mile zone does not stop you from fishing there. Alias are free to fish anywhere in the entire 200 mile zone."[131] One factor this commentator did not acknowledge is that alia boats have a maximum distance of about thirty miles at which they can safely fish from shore.[132] The other commentator said, "Stop crying and go fishing."[133] Both sentiments alluded to the negligible amount of alia fishing in American Sāmoa. If more people were angling, then the case for maintaining the fifty-mile Large Vessel Prohibited Area would be stronger to federal lawmakers. While alia owners are focusing on a fundamental indigenous rights-based argument for maintaining traditional fishing grounds, not everyone in American Sāmoa supported their efforts to stop the reduction of the small-scale fishing zone for both commercial and personal use. The debates over zone changes became quite heated among American Sāmoans.

Wespac believed a change to the LVPA was appropriate for current circumstances of lower commercial catch rates for larger long-lining vessels and lack of overfishing in the region. Alia fishers, in contrast, focused on the infringement upon their ancestral rights and the lack of acknowledgment and regard for their positionality in policies that directly impacted their lives, an absence of *vā fealoaʻi*. Koboski also commented how "in American Samoa, where devotion to the family and the community is so strong, the depletion of albacore as a resource is seen as an affront to future generations of Samoan fishermen. In the interviews, the conservation of the resource was repeatedly mentioned as an important component to the healthfulness of the fishery."[134] As discussed in the introduction, the centrality of family in *faʻa Sāmoa* and the priority of raising and maintaining the status of one's *ʻāiga* (family) are critical aspects of indigenous social, political, and economic life in the region.

While one person I interviewed claimed the public meetings in American Sāmoa were more informational, not open to alternative opinions, and even hostile to expressions of resistance or disapproval, the NMFS stated that "there appeared to be more support for the reduction of the LPVA at the 2015 meetings, given that the longline fishermen were for the most part local American Samoans."[135] No mention was made in the draft regulatory amendment of any strong opposition to the exemption in the on-site public meetings.

On March 18, 2015, Westpac approved a temporary exemption to the LVPA, allowing longliner boats to fish from twelve nautical miles offshore. This change would be evaluated every year for effectiveness and impact. Within one week of this decision, the *Fono* passed a joint resolution to request that the Council "maintain the current 50 miles of the LVPA."[136] Governor Moliga also asked the American Sāmoa attorney general to look into legal options to maintain the original size of the restricted zone. In July 2015, the *Fono* took another step in opposing the amendment by passing a resolution against the reduction of the LVPA. The American Sāmoa legislature stated that the shift in regional coverage "will not protect some of the most productive fishing grounds from fishing vessels larger than 50 feet."[137] In September that same year, Governor Moliga wrote a letter of protest to the U.S. secretary of commerce. He explained that decreasing the Large Vessel Prohibited Area "will create competition and gear conflict."[138]

In response to these concerns, Corry stated that she has not heard of any large-vessel longliner coming into contact with local alias, especially since mono-hulled lines are set much deeper. She stated that her ships "haven't seen alias that far out, mostly four to five miles, not more than ten miles."[139] Lutu-Sanchez also claimed "there is no gear conflict" because these longliners are much farther out than alias usually travel.[140] For these reasons, plus the fact that only one alia boat fished on a regular basis, longline owners believed the restricted zone was an underutilized area and resource.

In contrast, those who opposed the shrinking of the Large Vessel Prohibited Area worried that alia fish stocks would dwindle when larger boats with a bigger capacity started to angle in the same waters. Maea explained how a longliner could get "tons of fish catch by one line, five to seven miles long, they are going to catch tons of fish. Local alia are lucky to catch ten yellowfin" at a time.[141] The scale of a catch was a major concern for alia boat owners, the *Fono,* and the American Sāmoa governor when discussing changes to the restricted zone. In contrast, local large-vessel longline owner Edgar Feliciano believed the reduction of the Prohibited Area was not detrimental to alia fishing because bottom-fishing uses different methods and targets different species of fish.[142] Corry concurred that "we target albacore" while alias focus on bottomfish."[143] These conflicting opinions have riddled indigenous debates over reducing the restricted zone.

Many large-vessel longline owners in American Sāmoa believed the conversations surrounding the reduction of the Large Vessel Prohibited Area involved a lot of lobbying and misrepresentations that presented them in a negative light. Corry stated that "it's all perception and misinformation. . . . I think there needs to be more public information and awareness" especially about the differences and similarities among local longliners, much larger purse seiner boats, and Chinese fishing boats.[144] Large-vessel longliners are medium-sized U.S.-flagged boats, not the very large purse seiners often seen in Pago harbor or the foreign Asian boats also increasing in the area. Several large-vessel longliners are American Sāmoan businesses whose employers and employees live, work, and spend their money in the region with their families. Asserting her company's native roots and the contributions of all longliner boats to the local economy, Lutu-Sanchez stated that "we all operate out of here, we all fuel our boats here, buy bait locally, buy all supplies, food, lube oil, gear, and equipment here in American Samoa and do all repairs here in American Samoa."[145] American Sāmoan large-vessel longliners can, should, and have had native rights to fish in the Large Vessel Prohibited Area. Both indigenous alia and large-vessel longliner owners have steadfastly fought for their ability to maintain such traditional access to their ancestral waters under U.S. colonial rule.

While alia and large-vessel longliner owners generally agreed on U.S. federal policies in 2002, strong lines were drawn between these American Sāmoan fishers by 2015. As sociologists Cluny Macpherson and La'avasa Macpherson found, in a globalized environment "Sāmoan society is becoming increasingly plural and less able, or willing, to agree on how to confront and manage these forces."[146] Fishers have adapted to changing economic and ecological circumstances through the centuries, most recently shifting to Western vessel and fishing technologies, as well as angling for a market economy and global consumption. Intensified fishing competition and growing angling regulations, as well as shrinking fish stocks have led to divisions among American Sāmoan fishers.

Furthermore, as postcolonial ecologist Byron Caminero-Santangelo discussed, there is no singular indigenous identity and culture is not fixed or static. In fact, "the local, the natural, and the indigenous must be seen as emerging and reemerging from specific, messy interrelationships with their supposed opposites."[147] Focusing on the total bioregion can help explain why some American Sāmoans reacted differently from others to the changes in fishing zone parameters. Most alia fishers primarily angle for personal, familial, and cultural reasons. Commercial supply and profit is a huge benefit, but not a requirement for their livelihood as small-scale artisanal fishers. Large-vessel longliners focus on supplying fish for commercial markets and rely on sales of their catch to survive. While functioning at different output and production scales, both groups want to protect their native angling rights and provide for their families in the short and long term. As angling has become more arduous and less profitable in the twenty-first century, desires to protect one's own form of fishing over others become more vocal and strong.

In the final ruling on the extension, the NMFS stated that they were "satisfied that three full Council meetings, the January 15, 2015, public meetings, and the 30-day public comment period on the proposed rule provided the public with adequate notice and opportunity to be heard."[148] NMFS also claimed that they "took particular care to ensure that the views of American Samoa stakeholders, including fishermen, fishing communities, and the American Samoa government, were solicited and taken into account throughout the development of this action.[149] From the federal government perspective, *vā fealoaʻi* was created and maintained in this decision-making process.

During the final public comment period, which ran from August 25 to September 24, 2015, the NMFS "received comments from over 270 individuals, commercial and recreational fishermen, businesses, Territorial government offices (including the Governor of American Samoa and the American Samoa Department of Marine and Wildlife Resources), Federal agencies, and non-governmental organizations."[150] Several comments and most NMFS responses echoed the pro-reduction perspectives of large-vessel long-lining ships, such as the need to provide food, jobs, and support for the local American Sāmoan economy, the equal right of these boats to fish in local waters, the underutilization of the protected zone, as well as the cost savings and safety benefits of having larger vessels in the local area.

In opposition to the reduction, several commenters questioned the impact of large-vessel long-lining on coral reefs, endangered species, gear conflict with other anglers, water pollution, and fish catch competition with alias and recreational fishers. In each case of opposition, the NMFS had a strong response that continued to justify and support the view of the LVPA reduction as a rational, logical, and reasonable policy. Satisfied that they fulfilled federal expectations for public comment and response, the NMFS passed this exemption on January 29, 2016.

As with the expansion of the National Marine Sanctuary, discussed in chapter 3, some members of the American Sāmoan community believed this Western-style, impersonal, English language, written-based, and bureaucratic federal government public comment system and process did not take Sāmoan *vā fealoaʻi* into consideration. As discussed in chapter 4, the traditional Sāmoan village consensus-building process involves meeting the different constituents in each impacted village in separate meetings: the village council, women, and untitled men. After these groups are informed of a proposal, the council advises the high chief, who makes a decision for the whole community to follow. This slow and deliberate process can often take many months. Bypassing this process, public comments gathered and submitted to the NMFS mostly came from individuals or organizations. The NMFS made no attempt to go into community villages and work within the customary Sāmoan decision-making process and hierarchy.

On February 3, 2016, the final ruling in the LVPA reduction went into effect. This legislation stated that "this action allows fishing in an additional 16,817 nm [nautical miles] of Federal waters, allowing large longline vessels to distribute fishing effort over a larger area. This may reduce catch competition among the larger vessels and promote economic efficiency by reducing transit costs. This action is intended to improve the efficiency and economic viability of the American Samoa longline fleet, while ensuring that fishing by the longline and small vessel fleets remains sustainable on an ongoing basis."[151] Despite protests from the American Sāmoa Government and local alia owners, NOAA Fisheries pushed forward with this law, supporting the needs of the larger longline vessel owners.

Just over a month later, on March 4, 2016, the American Sāmoa Government filed a lawsuit to overturn the ruling based on guarantees provided in the Deeds of Cession, the Magnuson-Stevens Act, and other administrative procedure acts. The twenty-one-page complaint claimed that allowing "large long-liners to fish within the ceded areas that were designated as protected properties ignores and violates the U.S. obligation under the Deeds of Cession to safeguard and respect the property rights of the native people of Samoa to their customs and practices including cultural fishing."[152] Overall, the suit claimed that the United States has a "fiduciary duty to protect the lands; preserve the traditions, customs, language and culture; Samoan way of life; and the waters surrounding the islands."[153] This legal approach argued that the federal government cannot make a decision that violates U.S. promises to the people of American Sāmoa, as outlined in the Deeds.

Two motions and a counter-motion, as well as two replies, were filed for this case between June 2016 and January 2017. A U.S. District Court hearing was held in Honolulu, Hawai'i on February 13, 2017. On March 20, 2017, more than a year after the first filing of the suit, U.S. District Court Judge Leslie E. Kobayashi supported the American Sāmoa Government, ruling that "in light of the long-standing significance of fishing to the fa'a Samoa, Plaintiff has a quasi-sovereign interest in protecting the American Samoan's cultural fishing rights to preserve their culture for the benefit of the American Samoan people as a whole."[154] Based on these fundamental indigenous rights to cultural preservation guaranteed by the Deeds of Cession, the 2016 LVPA rule was deemed "arbitrary and capricious" as well as "invalid."[155]

Governor Moliga praised the ruling, expressing how "I hope this case serves as a reminder to the federal government that we have rights and they should not be easily dismissed."[156] Attorney General Talauega Eleasalo Ale, who participated in the February hearing, also emphasized how "this decision is the first federal case law to articulate the meaning of the deeds as it relates to our direct dealings with the federal government. . . . It establishes a critical pathway towards clarifying our relationship with the federal government, as well as our status as a people and culture within the American family."[157] This ruling provides an important precedent for future questions over the rights of American Sāmoans within the U.S. colonial system and structure.

On May 10, 2017, NOAA filed a motion for reconsideration to question "the legal standing for American Samoa to bring this claim" and whether "the appropriate remedy for the court" was applied to this case.[158] NOAA legal counsel Frederick W. Tucher believed the court should have asked for supplemental briefings to justify its ruling instead of overruling NOAA's authority to create regulations in these waters.[159] NOAA Fisheries hopes the reconsideration will "remand it [the LVPA] back to NMFS to address customary fishing in accordance with the Deeds of Cession. . . . NMFS expects that it can complete a new rulemaking to correct its error within fifteen months."[160] This continuation of litigation demonstrated the strong desire of NOAA to maintain its ultimate authority and policy-making control over the waters surrounding American Sāmoa.

According to Tosatto, in the year since the reduction went into effect, the smaller Large Vessel Prohibited Area "provided benefits to American Samoan longliners while producing no adverse impacts on catch rates for other American Samoan fishery participants"[161] The NMFS also presented data showing how catch rates "were higher not only for longline vessels, but also for other pelagic troll vessels."[162] Additionally, "NMFS has not received any complaints or reports from pelagic trollers, bottomfish fishermen, alias, or recreational fishermen of gear conflict or catch competition with longliners."[163] In the context of these positive statistics, NOAA Fisheries believed it could justify the appropriateness of the 2016 Large Vessel Prohibited Area rule change and maintain their position as the wise and deserving decision makers over the waters in the South Pacific.

Tautai o Sāmoa also appealed to Judge Kobayashi on June 2, 2017, to reconsider her ruling. This large-vessel longliner association petitioned the U.S. Interior Department, the American Sāmoa Government, and the federal court "to restore our rights to fish in these waters that you [Kobayashi] have all agreed should be accessible to indigenous peoples of American Samoa."[164] In their letter, the group asked why the court "would deny that we have the same rights as other American Samoans, and why are we discriminated against while favoring others?. . . . A truly impartial decision from you would be to allow anyone with American Samoa heritage to fish in American Samoa waters during this ordeal until it is decided who the supreme owner of these waters is, as it looks like this fight will continue until it reaches the U.S. Supreme Court."[165] While the March

2017 ruling provided a legal victory for general American Sāmoan indigenous rights in the U.S. colonial system, the LVPA rule continues to be beleaguered by the fact that different members of the indigenous group stand on opposite sides of this issue.

While *Territory of American Samoa v. National Marine Fisheries Service* effectively secured native fishing rights and guaranteed the prioritization of indigenous protections in all U.S. actions in the region, a more nuanced understanding of who is native and what they want is needed. This specific federal ocean-use policy requires finding a balanced compromise among the needs of small-scale and medium-sized local fishing vessels in American Sāmoa while guaranteeing native rights to fish local waters for both groups, all part of maintaining *vā* (social relations) in Sāmoan society.

The battle over the restricted zone size has the potential to continue for many years. In March 2018, the case went into mediation. In June 2018, Wespac recommended another four-year exemption and "annual monitoring of the American Samoa longline and troll catch rates, small vessel participation and local fisheries development initiatives."[166] The American Sāmoan government continued to oppose the exemption to the Large Vessel Prohibited Area.

Regardless of the ultimate resolution to this lawsuit, historic and current U.S. colonial status has directly impacted both indigenous American Sāmoans and NOAA policies. This native group, composed of multiple views and perspectives, boldly challenges the federal system on a regular basis to defend their rights to fish local waters. However, American Sāmoans are also looking to the federal government to address and resolve these issues within existing colonial structures of Wespac and the U.S. judicial system. The U.S. government bureaucracy strongly believes in its guardian responsibilities to control and manage this region and its resources, discussed more in chapter 3. In the end, the major question is "how to continue fishing in a depleted ocean while also conserving it."[167]

In American Sāmoa, "fishing has transformed over the years into a commercial endeavor while still preserving traditional elements that contribute to the perpetuation of the local culture."[168] In addition to addressing native rights, some scholars view small-scale fisheries as one way to address issues of poverty, economic development, and food security.[169]

Internationally, small-scale fisheries account for over 50 percent of the world's catch and employ 90 percent of people engaged in fisheries.[170] Because artisanal fishing can be a key to long-term food security, the issues facing these anglers should be taken seriously both at local and global levels.

The next chapter explores another invisible aspect of accessing the resource-rich fishing waters surrounding American Sāmoa and the complications of indigenous desires versus federal control in the unique combination of large-scale fisheries, commercial tuna canneries, continental U.S. politics and consumption, the local native economy, and the *vā fealoaʻi* of Sāmoan laborers in the context of *faʻa Sāmoa*.

CHAPTER 2

Minimal Returns

Colonial Minimum Wage Issues
and the Global Tuna Canning Industry

Until 2009, the StarKist Samoa cannery was the largest tuna factory in the world. Chicken of the Sea was the second-largest fish processor and exporter across the globe.[1] Both of these canneries were located in American Sāmoa. Their products, whether packaged for high-end stores like Whole Foods, grocery chains like Trader Joe's, or big-box stores like Walmart, were labeled "Made in the USA" because American Sāmoa is an unincorporated territory of the United States. But as an unincorporated territory of the U.S., federal labor laws do not apply equally, such as minimum wage and maximum work hours. This allowable divergence in work standards due to colonized status, as well as tax and tariff breaks, cheaper freight, lower insurance, and close access to fishing waters, has made American Sāmoa an attractive liminal political-legal and economic space for the tuna industry since the first cannery opened in 1953. Fish processing in American Sāmoa is a generally invisible aspect of U.S. and global seafood consumption. While chapter 1 discussed the various methods used to obtain seafood for tuna factories and fresh local consumption, this chapter focuses on the politics and economics behind the massive enterprise of canning tuna for the world.

According to food journalist Andrew Smith, fish canning started in the United States on the east coast in 1818 and the first can of tuna was produced in 1903.[2] Canned tuna became popular during World War I as a cheap source of protein, and by the end of World War II the United States had the largest tuna fleet in the world. Smith explained how "by the late 1940s, Americans ate more tuna than any other fish or seafood."[3] Tens of thousands of people worked either directly or indirectly for the tuna industry. Today, Americans consume 29 percent of the canned tuna produced worldwide (almost all is imported to the

United States) and 84 percent of tuna comes from the western Pacific.[4] Foreign domination of the industry in the twenty-first century stems from cheaper wages paid outside of the United States for both fishing and processing.

In 2007, as part of the push for minimum wage increases in the continental United States, Congress passed a federal law that required a fifty-cent wage increase every year until American Sāmoa wages were at the same level as states of the union. When the first mandatory increase was implemented in 2007, the minimum wage for cannery workers in American Sāmoa was raised from $3.26 to $3.76. That same year, the lowest legal wage in the fifty states was $5.85. By 2009, the federal U.S. minimum wage was $7.25, where it remained in 2018. After three fifty-cent increases in a row to $4.76, Chicken of the Sea announced the closure of its American Sāmoa cannery in 2009 and StarKist reduced its labor force by eight hundred people. Employment in American Sāmoa fell by 19 percent and cannery work decreased by 55 percent. This chapter examines the debates surrounding the minimum wage issue in the colonized space of American Sāmoa, as well as the historic and contemporary impacts that variable labor standards for this large-scale for-profit fishery have had on this Pacific Island region and United States politics and businesses.

Living in an American possession, U.S. colonials are subjects, not full-fledged members of the union with complete rights and privileges of citizenship.[5] The economic needs of corporate fish canneries have historically been accommodated over worker welfare throughout U.S. rule in this region. This chapter will examine U.S. government prioritization of the monocrop industry of tuna canning in American Sāmoa, resulting variations in Fair Labor Standards, and the current lack of accommodation for indigenous appeals for tailored policies. Like in chapter 1, the functions of commercial marine practices and related labor regulations in American Sāmoa have increasingly been shaped by nonnative economic objectives that do not always coincide with indigenous goals, lifestyles, and traditions. Through tuna canning industry issues, American Sāmoans have been and continue to be colonially subjected, regulated, and controlled by the federal government. However, workers have remained loyal to this large-scale fishery due to on-the-ground social welfare employee benefits that acknowledge *vā* (social relations) obligations and incorporate forms of *fa'a Sāmoa* (the Sāmoan way of life) in their treatment of laborers.

As discussed in chapter 1, wage labor in American Sāmoa was a product of a World War II cash-based economy introduced to the region by Americans and supported by the U.S. federal government in the postwar period through the establishment of the fishing industry in the area. The controversy over wage increases for cannery workers in the twenty-first century demonstrates the continuation of multiple interests and ideas connected to labor and wages in both American Sāmoa and the United States. In addition to impassioned statements by American Sāmoa government representatives, businesspeople, and the general public, politicians in the U.S. Congress actively participated in these discussions for the interests of their own constituents or political parties, often from opposite perspectives. While historically accommodated, the fiscal needs of this monocrop marine-based industry in the unincorporated territory of American Sāmoa has started to take a secondary position to larger federal issues of fair wages, jobs for U.S. citizens, and national security. As liminal U.S. colonials, the ground-level economics of American Sāmoans have always been subject to global tuna industry needs. In the twenty-first century, this indigenous group is now also being subsumed to the political goals of the fifty states.

Since the 1900 Deed of Cession agreement between the eastern Sāmoan *mātai* chiefs and the U.S. Navy, American Sāmoans have maintained unique control over their local jurisdiction. However, the U.S. Congress has the ability to impose rules on or veto actions by territorial governments, known as plenary power.[6] In 2007, Congress used this overarching authority to address the issue of wage discrepancies between U.S. territories and U.S. states.

However, the inclusion of American Sāmoa in 2007 legislation was not a clear-cut issue. Initially, only the Commonwealth of the Northern Mariana Islands was targeted for wage standardization due to recent news coverage of poor working conditions in garment factories in that region.[7] But according to a *Washington Times* article, "that would have left American Samoa as the only territory outside the federal minimum-wage rules.... Republicans said that smelled fishy, since Del Monte, the parent company of StarKist's cannery, had headquarters in San Francisco, in the district Mrs. Pelosi [the Speaker of the House represented].... In the ensuing days, Mrs. Pelosi insisted American Sāmoa be added, in order to equalize the law."[8] Despite these efforts to apply minimum wage standards throughout territories in the Pacific, American Sāmoa was not included in the 2007 Fair Minimum Wage Standard Law.

A few months later, Republican representative Mark Steven Kirk from Illinois added minimum wage hikes for American Sāmoa as an amendment to the "U.S. Troop Readiness, Veterans' Care, Katrina Recovery, and Iraq Accountability Appropriations Act." Once again, the larger party politics of the U.S. Congress, specifically Republicans' attacks on Speaker of the House Nancy Pelosi, resulted in the inclusion of American Sāmoa in the minimum wage debate, not any request from American Sāmoans themselves. As a rider attached to a much larger appropriations bill, increases in American Sāmoa minimum wage became law without any specific debate or discussion on the Congressional floor about its impact on this colonized region or its people.

In reaction to the partisan inclusion of American Sāmoa into this legislation, "democratic leaders promised to try to remove the amendment later in the legislative process but [according to the same *Times* article] never followed through."[9] This political back-and-forth over the inclusion of American Sāmoa in minimum wage hikes highlights the precarious position U.S. colonials occupy under U.S. empire. While American Sāmoans generally have authority over local issues, the federal government holds ultimate control over the region. Important issues such as wage policies for tuna workers can consequently become subject to the maneuverings of party politics in Washington, D.C., that do not take into account the ground-level effect of such legislation on the local American Sāmoan economy and people.

As an unincorporated territory, American Sāmoa has had one nonvoting representative in the U.S. Congress since 1981. This delegate has the right to speak in Congress, but does not get to vote on legislation. Therefore, these U.S. colonials do not have the right to elect any leader who wields ultimate control over their region, such as the U.S. president or members of Congress. This status in terms of political representation is also true for the other U.S. territories of Guam, the Northern Marianas, Puerto Rico, and the U.S. Virgin Islands.

In 2010, the American Sāmoa Congressional representative Eni Faleomavaega reacted to the 2007 appropriations amendment by stating that Representative Kirk "knows nothing about American Sāmoa and did not have the courtesy to contact my office."[10] Despite Faleomavaega's request that Democrats remove American Sāmoa from the legislation, the bill passed with this region included. In 2015, American Sāmoa Congressional representative Aumua Amata Coleman Radewagen called the inclusion of her home region in the 2007 legislation "an over sight."[11] Overall, American Sāmoan government representatives did not support changes to local minimum wage regulations due to the threat such raises would pose to the fishing industry in the region. But their colonial voices were not listened to. Instead, both state-level pushes for minimum wage increases and partisan politics propelled this legislation through Congress.

Ironically, if there was no controversy over labor standards in the Northern Marianas, these Pacific regions might never have been included in state-level minimum wage legislation; especially since no federal labor laws had developed in these areas since 1956. As territories on the periphery of the U.S. empire, these islands are often far off the radar, if not invisible to American politicians. But when a controversial subject develops in the continental U.S., like the campaign for a living wage or nuclear threats from North Korea, these colonial territories come under full scrutiny and become subject to legislative decisions of the U.S. Congress. As the case studies in this book demonstrate, Western standards and goals do not always coincide with or impact indigenous groups in the same way as American citizens in states of the union.

History of the Tuna Industry in American Sāmoa

Tuna canning in American Sāmoa started within a decade of the rise in international canned fish consumption. According to Mansel Blackford, by 1944, canned tuna and canned salmon provided much of the seafood consumed at the time.[12] Callum Roberts also stated how the "development of canning technology and the discovery that tinned tuna preserves wonderfully well created a product for which there was a ready market" in the interwar years.[13] By the early twenty-first century, "the seafood industry was a thoroughly industrialized, globalized operation. About three-quarters of all seafood products were destined for direct human consumption. . . . Of the seafood eaten by humans, 49 percent went to market fresh, but 51 percent was processed. About half of the processed seafood was frozen, with much of the remainder canned. A whopping 37 percent of this total production entered international trade."[14] Since 1953, American Sāmoa has contributed to this major source of world protein through massive marine monocropping and production.

The Rockefeller Company set up the first fish cannery on Tutuila in 1953. Van Camp Seafood, a division of Ralston-Purina during that period, purchased the facility in 1954, which eventually became Chicken of the Sea in 1976. Thai Union, the seventh-largest supplier of seafood to the U.S. market in 2006, purchased Chicken of the Sea in 2000.[15] After three federally mandated wage hikes in two years, this production line shut down in 2009. The Italian company TriMarine, the third-largest seafood provider for the United States in 2007, opened a cannery at this same location in April 2015, but closed operations in December 2016 after experiencing two government required pay increases in a year and a half.

The American Sāmoa Government (ASG) approved the opening of a second fish processing plant by H.J. Heinz Company in September 1962. The first shipment of canned tuna from this StarKist factory left Pago Pago harbor on October 4, 1963. In 2003, the canning arm of this company spun off into Del Monte Foods Company. In 2008, the Korean company Dongwon bought StarKist,

FIGURE 2.01. StarKist Samoa cannery. (Author photo.)

which was the ninth-largest supplier for the U.S. market in 2006. Despite re-
ductions in labor force and work hours in the face of continual federal wage
hikes, this facility continues to operate in 2018.

   The shift from U.S.-owned fish processing companies to other countries
showed how by the end of the twentieth century, "seafood companies have increasingly operated across national boundaries by entering into joint ventures,
as Japanese processors did with American fishers, moves unintentionally encouraged by the U.S. declaration of a 200-mile economic exclusive zone."[16] With
restrictions on who could fish where, discussed in chapter 1, different nations
partnered with each other to gain better access to fishing grounds. Also evidenced by the twenty-first-century change of ownership for both Chicken of the
Sea and StarKist in American Sāmoa, "processors acquired foreign subsidiaries
to be close to their major overseas markets."[17] After purchasing StarKist Samoa,
Dongwon also took control of the can-producing factory across the street,
demonstrating "vertical integration, [where] company officers join the various
stages in their businesses, from raw materials to production through sales."[18]
Such control over all phases of the manufacturing process was occurring in other
industries at the same time, like the auto industry with joint ventures by Ford
and Mazda in the 1980s.[19] American Sāmoa was an ideal location for being close

to tuna fishing grounds as well as controlling both fishing and processing in American territory.

The U.S. federal government fostered the development of the tuna processing industry to expand the economy of American Sāmoa in the post–World War II era through variable labor standards, generous tax and tariff breaks, and subsidies for supplies, transportation, and insurance. According to Richard Barnet and John Cavanagh, "poor countries with unorganized work forces are attractive production sites for global companies, whatever flag they fly. Higher profits, labor peace, access to natural resources of the region and to local markets are powerful incentives" for factory locations.[20] Cheap labor combined with U.S. and territorial tax subsidies and exemptions, plentiful fish nearby, tuna treaties, as well as low insurance, fuel, labor, and freight costs to facilitate the profitability of tuna canneries in this colonized Pacific region.

Allen Stayman has studied how "the United States has embraced a pragmatic and flexible approach to building stable relations" in U.S. territories which included "extended special trade, tax, wage, financial assistance, and other privileges to support the growth of the Islands' less-competitive market economies."[21] In American Sāmoa, U.S. tax credits since 1976 have resulted in exemptions equivalent to that of U.S. corporate income taxes.[22] Tariff relief made this unincorporated territory of the United States even more attractive. According to a Department of Labor report in 2007, "shipments of canned tuna or other products from American Samoa into the United States are not subject to tariff rates. . . . because American Samoa is a territory of the U.S. and is not considered to be an exporter."[23] Conducting business in a region that was part of the United States but not a full-fledged member of the union provided economic benefits on both sides of this political-legal liminality for the tuna industry. For tax purposes, American Sāmoan products were considered domestic. But for national labor regulations, like minimum wage, this area did not have to maintain the same standards.

Since the beginning of cannery involvement in the region, the ASG has also collaborated with tuna industry leadership and Washington, D.C., officials to develop local tax breaks, tariff cuts, and other incentives to maintain factories in the area. For example, the territorial administration allows significant exemptions from its own corporate tax laws that could result in up to 44 percent savings on corporate income.[24] In 1962, the federally appointed governor of American Sāmoa, Idaho native H. Rex Lee, stated how "the Government of American Samoa is fully prepared to cooperate fully with any fishing fleet delivering fish to the Star-Kist plant in Pago Pago."[25] This commitment to the economic success of U.S. fish companies, and as a by-product the American Sāmoa economy, has continued among local leaders in the region into the twenty-first century. In fact, a fear over the loss of this main industry in the region has and continues to shape the opinions and actions of these leaders.

Carrying the "Made in the USA" label provided even more enticement for canneries to function in American Sāmoa, particularly because the U.S. military only purchases tuna canned within U.S. jurisdiction. The Buy American Act of 1993 "attempts to protect domestic jobs by providing a required preference for American goods in direct government purchases."[26] The Berry Amendment to this legislation in 2014 "is a 'super percentage' status which requires the Department of Defense, when purchasing certain goods, to purchase goods that are 100% American in origin."[27] Western Pacific Regional Fishery Management Council (Wespac) Fisheries program officer Mark Mitsuyasu believed the future success of canneries in American Sāmoa depends on how valuable the "Made in the USA" label remains for companies. "It was an advantage, it still is an advantage."[28] While labor may be cheaper in Southeast Asia or South America, gaining a monopoly on tuna supplies for the U.S. military makes production in this generally invisible colonial space a major benefit. In fact, according to Barnet and Cavanagh, "by 1991 more than half of all U.S. exports and imports were transfers of components and services within the same global corporation, most of them flying the American flag."[29] But as tuna canning in American Sāmoa shows, production under U.S. jurisdiction does not necessarily mean fair wage jobs for U.S. citizens. The liminal space of U.S. territories and possessions provides economic and political loopholes for businesses.

However, for fish canneries to stay in American Sāmoa long term, these corporations "need to see predictable costs."[30] This idea of the economic bottom line for businesses was echoed by many interviewed.[31] According to StarKist production manager Carlos Gonzalez, there are two important factors for factory profitability: 1) fish prices and 2) fuel prices.[32] If either of these two aspects goes up, the profit for the company goes down. Dan Sullivan, vice president of production for TriMarine in 2015, also remarked that the price of fish, labor costs, and freight costs were all critical inducements for opening and maintaining a factory location in the area.[33]

One disadvantage Sullivan identified for American Sāmoa as a cannery site involved the fact that the region was subject to a multitude of federal regulations, such as those monitored by the Environmental Protection Agency, the U.S. Food and Drug Administration, U.S. Health Advisors, and the U.S. Coast Guard. Complying with the numerous and costly rules for health and safety standards overseen by each of these bureaucracies results in more expended effort and higher costs to a company's bottom line.

In 2015, StarKist spokesperson Michelle Faist stated that "American Samoa has had three things in its favor—duty free access to the U.S. market that is now nearly irrelevant, a wage system reflective of the local economy rather than the mainland economy, and a reliable supply of direct-delivered fish... all of these factors have been negatively impacted in the last six months" due to minimum wage increases, fishing limits, and the Pacific Trade Treaty that eliminated tariffs among member nations.[34] Such tuna industry rhetoric about tenuous stability in the fiscally colonized space of American Sāmoa has occurred since their opening in the 1950s.

According to Barnet and Cavanagh, "Corporations dream of escaping the laws of any nations that restrict the free movement of goods, info, and profits. But at the same time global companies everywhere look to their home governments to protect their existing markets and to provide muscle for penetrating new markets, to keep labor and environmental costs down, and to subsidize their operations in various ways."[35] This general dual desire of businesses to obtain legal and monetary advantages in both a free market and through home government regulations typifies the actions and motivations of the tuna industry as well. But "government treatment of their home-based corporations can result in competitive advantages or disadvantages" as seen with the benefits of tax and tariff relief versus the burden of national health and environmental requirements in American Sāmoa.[36] Tuna canneries, like the sugar industry in Hawai'i and the oil refining industry in the U.S. Virgin Islands, have always tried to create an overall advantage from this variety of pros and cons for setting up shop in an unincorporated territory of the United States.[37]

History of Wage Rates in American Sāmoa

The fish processing industry has historically threatened to leave American Sāmoa if minimum wage became too high. In 1956, the U.S. Congress debated legislation to exempt American Sāmoa from the wage and hour provisions of the Fair Labor Standards Act of 1938. In March 1956, Vaiinupo J. Ala'ilima, King Malietoa's great-great-grandson and an employee of the Army Corps of Engineers, testified at a House Education and Welfare subcommittee in Washington, D.C., to plead against any policy that kept wages down to attract industries to American Sāmoa. He believed the application of the national minimum wage standard of one dollar an hour would "protect our people from being exploited for cheap labor and likewise slow down the industrialization of our little country.[38] However, the Van Camp Seafood Company insinuated throughout these Congressional hearings that it might need to leave the islands if required to pay one dollar an hour.[39] As the only industry in American Sāmoa, which was already operating at a loss, Van Camp employed three hundred island women for their tuna packing plant.

The cannery's acknowledgment of a potential shutdown in the face of increased wages raised deep concerns for both American and Sāmoan leadership. Congressional leaders feared that the departure of this main source of income for the area would tank the local economy.[40] Indigenous leaders also submitted a resolution urging an exemption from the Fair Labor Standards Act for similar reasons.[41]

At a hearing for the U.S. Senate Committee on Labor and Public Welfare in May of that same year William D. Moore, overseas operations manager for the Van Camp Seafood Company, stated that "a minimum wage of $1 per hour, as required under present laws, is unrealistic, unwarranted, and unquestionably will have a deleterious effect upon the economic and social structure of the islands."[42] Van Camp did not think American Sāmoans should be compensated at the same level as continental U.S. workers due to lower productivity, stereotypically explained by the high humidity of the tropical region.[43] Consequently, the company paid American Sāmoan cannery workers twenty-seven cents per hour. Linton Collins, legal counsel for Van Camp, also stated that "the company has found that it takes from 3 to 5 Samoan workers to perform what 1 continental worker in the United States will do. It is, therefore, felt that this justifies a lower rate for Samoans."[44] While Alaʻilima wanted to protect the dignity and worth of native workers, the racist rhetoric of Van Camp leaders highlighted the prioritization of corporate profit goals and the lower valuation of U.S. colonial labor.

Because government officials were more concerned with losing this vital industry in the region than fair treatment of indigenous laborers, the U.S. Congress chose to not raise wages. As Senator John F. Kennedy expressed in the final discussion of this legislation in July 1956, exclusion from the labor standards act would be "essential if the Samoan economy is to continue to operate."[45] Consequently, Van Camp successfully obtained an amendment to the Fair Labor Standards Act that exempted the tuna industry from paying workers in American Sāmoa the federal minimum wage. Such an exception from national work requirements highlights one major impact that colonial status has had on

American Sāmoans. Both the monetary and figurative values of their colonial labor were minimized for the benefit of the large-scale for-profit tuna industry.

Before the U.S. Congress imposed the required wage increase on American Sāmoa in 2007, pay rates were handled by a Special Industry Committee composed of voting representatives from the canneries, the private sector, and the government. This committee formed as part of Van Camp's 1956 request for an exception to the Fair Labor Standards Act. The American Sāmoa Special Industry Committee met intermittently until 2007 to assess the economy "and to make recommendations for a sub-minimum wage in certain industries."[46] This group was supposed to take the specific ground-level reality of daily life in American Sāmoa into account when discussing possible pay rate increases, especially for cannery workers. Ultimately, this entity favored the profit-oriented interests of fish exports from the region over wage increases, similar to the capture of fishery council members discussed in chapter 1.[47] Only once, in 1986 when employees testified to the Special Industry Committee for a pay raise, did tuna workers' pay match U.S. minimum rates of $3.35 per hour.[48] But the next year, due to the complaints lodged by the fish processing industry, wages decreased back to $2.82. From 1999 to 2007, tuna canning pay only increased once, from $3.17 to $3.26 an hour.[49]

In 2008, Delegate Faleomavaega felt the Special Industry Committee was biased and useless. In a U.S. Senate Committee hearing he stated how "the industry committee structure for American Samoa was intended to be an interim measure but it remained in effect until last year when it was abolished by the enactment of P.L. 110–28 [2007 wage increase legislation]. I supported its abolishment because special industry committees were a sham and an insult to the intelligence of every hourly worker in American Samoa."[50] Congressman Faleomavaega did not feel that this assessment group provided a fair evaluation of the economic possibilities for better treatment of fish workers in American Sāmoa. Instead, the needs of the tuna canneries were prioritized. In 2010, Democratic House representative George Miller from California also stated how "in decades past, the use of a special industry committee to periodically review and set the minimum wage in American Samoa proved ineffective, unfairly depressing wage levels below what was economically feasible."[51] Both politicians believed the fish industry could have paid higher rates over time, but the wage committee consistently chose not to upset and potentially lose the business of tuna processing companies.[52]

While there was no Special Industry Committee in the Hawaiian Islands, the monopoly of the Hawaiian Sugar Planters Association during the first half of the twentieth century also set the wages for the entire sugar industry in this colonized Pacific archipelago. Wages were standardized throughout the region and workers who broke their contracts, or caused trouble by trying to organize for higher pay, were blackballed from the industry.[53]

While federal officials in Washington, D.C., spoke negatively about the Special Industry Committee, several years after the dissolution of this entity, some in American Sāmoa supported the reestablishment of a similar type of group. Territorial leaders and businesspeople interviewed in 2014 and 2015 spoke positively about this historic process that decided if a pay increase was necessary as well as sustainable in this unincorporated territory. Togiola Tulafono, the American Sāmoa governor from 2003 to 2013, stated that the industry committee was a good concept because it "constantly looked at the economy of American Sāmoa and wage increases were not something forced upon us."[54] Tulafono believed that if the government does not "fix structure of wages and people are fairly compensated" this approach can "sustain industries."[55] ASG human resources director Sonny Thompson also believed that an industry committee could help American Sāmoa "meet what we can afford."[56] He even recommended a prorated increase. Private businessperson Patricia Letuli stated that the government should go "back to letting our own locals look at businesses and government, how we want to structure wage rate."[57] According to these leaders, a dedicated organization that takes local colonial circumstances and issues into account seemed to be the best solution to balance the different sides involved in pay rates.

Such rhetoric continued in 2017 with Representative Amata introducing legislation for the restoration of this group.[58] The American Sāmoa governor and director of the American Samoa Department of Commerce supported this bill.[59] As U.S. colonials, American Sāmoan leaders have historically negotiated a delicate balance between cooperation with fish corporations and the federal government, which each funded one of the two major aspects of the regional economy. The historic belief in, and action based on, the heavy dependence of the area on the tuna industry persists into the twenty-first century.

Current cannery leadership also uses the specter of increased wages as a reason to leave American Sāmoa. In May 2015, both canneries functioning at the time, StarKist and TriMarine, as well as the American Sāmoa Chamber of Commerce, vocalized their opposition to a 2015 wage increase. According to TriMarine's chief operations officer Joe Hamby, "Tri Marine has invested significantly in Sāmoa Tuna Processors and increasing labor costs with a higher minimum wage would make the company's already difficult job even tougher. We are just starting. Increasing costs will obviously have a very negative impact on our young business. We simply can't afford a wage hike."[60] In fact, a U.S. Department of Labor report explained that in order to replicate a similar effect of the American Sāmoa minimum wage increase schedule, "the U.S. minimum wage would need to be raised to more than $16.50 per hour."[61] This statement puts the enormous impact of wage increases on American Sāmoa into a continental U.S. perspective. Pay increases clearly displease the fish industry and has historically been accommodated by both the territorial and federal government. This pattern started to shift in the twenty-first century.

Various Local Perspectives

Online, a hot debate developed when the local newspaper *Sāmoa News* published an article on minimum wage hikes. The imposition of Western standards in American Sāmoa garnered much passion and some conflicting opinions. In May 2015, there were fifty-seven posts by fifteen different people debating whether or not U.S. minimum wage standards should be applied in the region. The majority of the commentators believed fish canneries were exploiting workers and being greedy. Tofaeono Hollywood stated how "it is about time for the American Samoa government officials to campaign to end exploitation of Samoa employees on an hourly rate of just $5.26 to increase to a humane rate as Mainland U.S."[62] There were twenty-two other pro-minimum wage hike comments in addition to this one.

However, fourteen online posts worried that raising the minimum wage would result in the loss of this major industry and job creator. Troyboy expressed that "raising the minimum wage is not a job creating idea. It will be a job killer. It will only benefit those who are currently working. Some will probably start losing their jobs when employers counter with lay-offs. . . . We don't even pay rent like the U.S. Our bills are not as high as the U.S and yet we want to make the same money Americans are making?"[63] While not all of the people posting about business considerations were against fair wages, this particular group of commentators believed that maintaining low wages was part of rational corporate decision making and realistic economic policies for the ground-level situation in American Sāmoa. Such concepts were grounded in Western concepts about business.

Several posts also discussed the lower cost of living in American Sāmoa compared to the continental United States. Troyboy's statement about not paying rent refers to the fact that all land in the region is owned by American Sāmoans. According to Representative Amata, "in American Sāmoa, the cost of living is

drastically different. Due to how the lands are owned and managed in American
Sāmoa there's actually no such thing as rent or mortgage items that often com-
prise up to one half of a person's monthly expenses. Because our people do not
have an expense for housing, $4.76 an hour goes much further than it would here
in the States."[64] While cash wages are needed to pay for electricity and imported
items, families in American Sāmoa can survive without such conveniences and
live off *'āiga* land. One U.S. dollar in American Sāmoa can be stretched further
in an extended clan system that has access to communal sharing and sustainability through plantation farming and sea life gathering than the average family
household in the continental United States.

These indigenous factors were some of the reasons Representative Amata expressed how "the playing fields in the United States and American Sāmoa are
too drastically different to place on the same wage scale. And to keep American
Sāmoa tied to the current standard is dangerous and irresponsible."[65] Daily life
in American Sāmoa is quite different from the continental United States. Imposing Western criteria on this region ignores the reality of native lifestyles in
the area. Representative Amata's comment also reiterated the constant fear of
some in American Sāmoa that an incommensurate increase in wages could drive
away the fish canneries.

Another commentator in the online *Sāmoa News* debate suggested the development of a survey that would "ask all the people that work there [canneries] as
well as all the minimum wage earners at the government and other private businesses. See what they have to say. Compare the results from each entity. After
all, this is about them."[66] This post received two comments. Steve agreed that "a
scientific study like you mentioned is the way to go. People on this blog probably
do not represent the majority. Come to think of it I always earned above minimum wage even in High School and college."[67] In contrast to this positive response, the controversial and heated nature of this issue came out when another
commentator Niuveve responded by saying, "Not about stupid surveys-follow
the law of the land. . . . I make choices for the people-feel better. Don't go away
mad—just go away."[68] This post highlighted the frustration some in American
Sāmoa feel at the constant use of Western-style surveys, reports, consultants, and
paperwork (particularly by the government) to address problems in the region.
Scientific and sociological studies have frequently been conducted in the islands,
taking up the time and resources of the local community. But direct action rarely
developed from these efforts.

Scholar James C. Scott discussed how government observation and categorization of native peoples ultimately helps political leaders wield control over a

community.[69] In the case of American Sāmoa, information gathering and re-search could placate the public by identifying problems and demonstrating a desire to investigate issues, as well as provide education and awareness to the people. However, this gathered knowledge has often not resulted in massive changes in government policy or direction. Some would prefer outside surveyors just leave and not return. Information gathering in American Sāmoa is discussed more in chapter 4.

Niuveve's post also highlights how some in American Sāmoa prioritize in-digenous cultural values and practices over Western knowledge making and logic. This commentator's focus on "the law of the land" directly references con-ventional Sāmoan political and social structures where people in the community take care of one another in times of need, part of *vā* and *faʻa Sāmoa*. According to Karen Armstrong, David Herdrich, and Arielle Levine, "The basic units of Sāmoan social structure were (and are) the family and village. Unlike Western society, the family was the central unit rather than the individual, and unlike Western capitalist society, the emphasis was on reciprocity rather than indi-vidual accumulation. . . . The generous distribution of food marked—and still marks—every occasion, and from the 19th century into the early 20th century, fish and marine produce were central items in the circulating baskets of food."[70] Due to strong *ʻāiga* ties in American Sāmoa, no one should go hungry or be homeless.

Researcher Felix Kessing also stated that "high virtues are to be polite, kind and generous to relatives, friends and dependents. . . . prestige comes through generous distribution, not accumulation, of wealth."[71] Such expectations of reci-procity, or *vā* among community members are fundamental to Sāmoan culture and native views on providing appropriate support for their families. Under these same principles of *faʻa Sāmoa,* employers should also treat Sāmoan work-ers in a caring and compassionate way. So whether in the 1950s or the 2010s, pay rates that support one's family in exchange for labor have always been a point of concern between indigenous peoples and tuna canneries in American Sāmoa.

While most people interviewed for this project recognized the need to find other industries to support the local economy, some believed tuna canning was the best industry for what they viewed as an isolated region in the Pacific. Ac-cording to the ASG director of Human and Social Resources and former can-nery employee Taeaoafua Dr. Meki Solomona, "Canneries are a viable economic asset that needs to be retained. . . . American Sāmoa does not have a lot to offer, but we have tons of fish. How to maximize that opportunity for our people[?]. . . . I'd rather keep what's here and work on it than bring other" industries in.[72] Representative Amata further stated that "the tuna canning industry is all we

have. There's no Coca Cola or IBM. We have no Silicon Valley there to provide massive revenue and employment opportunity to the territory. There aren't
numerous military and government facilities that provide sources of economic
growth. We are not surrounded by fellow states that enable us to expand to other
markets. All we have is the tuna industry and we are grateful."[73] While American Sāmoan politicians easily spoke out against the imposition of the Western
Pacific Regional Fishery Council and the National Marine Fisheries Service
(NMFS) on indigenous fishing rights in chapter 1, a deferential and dependent
tone represents the dominant perspective of several American Sāmoan political
leaders towards the corporate tuna industry.

If the economics of American Sāmoa were more similar to that of American
states, minimum wage might be more sustainable or have less of a detrimental
impact. But that is not the case in the unincorporated territory of American
Sāmoa. These leaders believed concentrated efforts were needed to maintain the
tuna industry in the islands. As discussed in chapter 1, fishing and subsistence
from the local ocean were already parts of Sāmoan culture, making canning a
logical business for this particular location.

Some in American Sāmoa believed the application of minimum wage increases was a prime example of the region being unfairly treated like a full-fledged
state of the union. In August 2015, the American Sāmoa Commerce Department identified $5.67 as the minimum wage needed for a family of six to live in
the territory.[74] This amount was $1.58 less than the final amount targeted by the
federal wage hike legislation, but also fifty-one cents lower than the territorial
minimum wage in 2017.

In addition to different standards of living on island, Letuli stated continental "minimum wage is not fair to this island" because the rate was not compatible
to other Pacific Islander nations.[75] For example, minimum wage in neighboring
Independent Sāmoa was the U.S. equivalent of fifty cents while nearby Fiji's
basic wage was about ninety-one U.S. cents an hour. There was no minimum
wage in Tonga. Workers in American Sāmoa earned considerably more than
laborers in comparable positions on adjacent island nations. In that context,
some American Sāmoa leaders thought that the fairest thing to do, in terms
of overall Pacific Islander labor relations, involved keeping jobs in the region
instead of driving the fish industry away from American Sāmoa. Due to these
circumstances, Solomona stated how "in Seattle 15 cents might make sense. No
way that 10 to 15 cent raises is manageable in American Sāmoa. Please allow us
to make those decisions to maintain these huge companies."[76] Solomona did
not support matching continental U.S. rates because the leveling of pay did not

take the economic realities of the unincorporated territory of American Sāmoa into account.

Only one of five commentators to the *Sāmoa News* article about the impact of the 2015 wage hikes in American Sāmoa discussed how the pay increase was unnecessary due to the lower cost of living in American Sāmoa. Joe Taeao claimed that "technically, this minimum wage increase is hogwash. Our minimum wage in American Samoa should factor in surrounding island nations. Since we import most of our goods; with many produced in China; our issue is not inflation and increase in cost of living but more towards people wanting higher wages."[77] While Taeao also pushed for diversification of industries in American Sāmoa, he did not believe a blanket application of the continental U.S. standard of living was appropriate in the region.

In contrast, the other four commentators on the site expressed that "those who own the canneries ARE NOT WILLING TO MEET THE DEMANDS OF THE MINIMUM WAGE HIKE. Their bottom-line is the number one concern and they will not give in to the notion of paying higher wages. They are in American Samoa to make money—period. . . . Since the 1950s this industry has taken over $60 billion worth of fish from our oceans and they have NEVER PAID LIVING WAGES to their workers"[78] Pomasame and other commentators bemoaned the exploitation of native people and the greediness of the tuna industry.

Just like the Large-Vessel Prohibited Area debate discussed in chapter 1, American Sāmoans have a diversity of opinions about the minimum wage issue. Individuals, regardless of their position, willingly expressed their dissatisfaction with U.S. federal actions that did not take their ground-level indigenous and colonial reality into account. While some understood Western-style logics for business function and profitability, others emphasized the particularities of daily life in American Sāmoa from a native perspective.

Worker Experiences

While many acknowledge the economic benefits of the tuna industry, no one denies the arduous nature of work in the factories. Tuna canning is an extremely labor-intensive process. First, frozen fish are off-loaded from large purse seiner ships or longline vessels at the dock. Unloaders hunch over the fish onboard with machete-type instruments, chucking and sorting the frozen products into metal bins below according to size. Once separated, the fish go through an initial cleaning process, basically the manual removal of the head and the tail. These

fish are then wheeled by hand into a cold storage freezer until the canning line is
ready for that particular species. Once the type of fish to be canned for the shift
is determined (like albacore, wahoo, yellowfin, skipjack, or bigeye), the appropriate bins are removed by workers from cold storage and thawed out, or precooked,
by traveling through a semi-automated line of hot water baths or steam cham-
bers. The softened fish are then mechanically transported to the fish processing
floor, an expansive warehouse room where rectangular tables are set up in long
rows. Women standing on their feet for eight-hour shifts at a time remove fish
scales and skin, as well as debone the fish, all by hand. The cleaned fish are then
tossed by the laborers onto a conveyor belt that transports the fillets down the
line to be canned, either as solid tuna or through the chopper into chunk tuna.
In American Sāmoa, drivers forklift canisters from the container-making factory across the street. When put into the canning line, these metal cylinders first
go through a heated sanitation step, then get mechanically filled with fish. Oil
or water, depending on the type of tuna being processed, is subsequently added.
Then a machine seals the lid onto the can. The canisters are heated to sanitize
the containers one more time and finish cooking the fish. Then the products go
through the automated labeler and are stacked onto pallets that are manually
shrink wrapped for transport and loaded by workers into shipping containers
bound for the United States and beyond. Cannery work is physically demanding, repetitive, dangerous, smelly, and exhausting.

On average, with one hundred people on a line, a facility can produce three
hundred to six hundred containers a minute, which amounts to about 540,000
canisters per day, or almost six shipping containers a day.[79] At the peak of tuna
canning in 2005, the industry exported $446,382,000 in processed fish.[80] This
amount was 98 percent of all total exported goods from American Sāmoa. While
the market share of global tuna supply from American Sāmoa has declined since
the wage increases of 2007, this region's economic dependence on this industry
continues through 2016.[81]

The canning process for salmon is similar to tuna. However, the Alaskan
salmon industry used the laborsaving device the "Iron Chink" to mechanically
cut the tail and heads off fish. While early supporters of this technology believed
the machine resulted in the replacement (hence cost savings) of ten to twenty
workers, hand cleaning always results in the least amount of fish waste. A combination of hand and mechanized cleaning developed from the 1920s, enabled by
the homogenous size of fish from salmon runs.[82] Despite such a technological in-
novation in seafood processing, canneries in American Sāmoa continued to use
manual labor since wages were low, hand cleaning resulted in more fish product

to can, and tuna fish sizes were more variable. Regardless of these differences in tuna and salmon industry automation, cannery work was always laborious and involved some level of intense manual work.

The monocrop agriculture of sugar cane cultivation in the colonized space of Hawai'i was also physically difficult, requiring hard manual labor all day in the dusty fields of volcanic soil, prickly cane stalks, and the hot sun. In the colonized Hawaiian Islands, heavy industrial exploitation of workers occurred through the post–World War II period, when laborers finally surmounted race-based divisions created by the sugar industry and unionized across race and ethnicity.[83] Such labor organizing for higher wages, the transition of Hawai'i from a U.S. territory to a state of the union, and a growing sugar beet industry in the continental United States all contributed to the decline of the sugar industry in this Pacific archipelago.[84]

While the idea of higher wages initially seemed attractive to cannery workers in American Sāmoa, the constant fear over losing their jobs eventually convinced laborers to not support further wage increases. According to Brett Butler, general manager for the StarKist Sāmoa cannery from 2005 to 2014, 85 percent of StarKist Sāmoa's workforce in the twenty-first century came from Independent Sāmoa.[85] This distribution was similar for the other cannery in the territory. All foreign workers must be sponsored by an American Sāmoan, typically an extended family member who sometimes garnishes part of the individual's wages or expects additional free domestic assistance in the home, such as cooking and cleaning. Some of these laborers have very little education and few economic options. Hourly workers get paid every week at a much higher rate than wages in their home region. According to Solomona, "now a good number of those are from outside, they come here for opportunities. Minimum wage, American money... jobs for people who never gone to school to those with a Ph.D. in science... opportunity for everyone, not everyone seeks college degrees. If [they] flunk out of high school, they can work as long as they are 18 years old."[86] As non-indigenous laborers with temporary status in the region, these workers have chosen not to make a fuss over raising the minimum wage in exchange for a steady job and a relatively good income over the years for this region of the world.

According to a *Sāmoa News* article, "in the 1970s, a union was formed at Samoa Packing, however, its existence was short-lived reportedly because of difficulties in collecting membership dues from members." [87] Teamsters also tried to organize cannery workers in 1984, 1985, 1993, and 1994 but failed each time. Cannery leadership usually held meetings the day or night before workforce voting on unionization to remind laborers about the financial burden of union

FIGURE 2.02. StarKist employees returning to work.
(Photo by Samoa News/Ausage Fausia.)

fees. Since pay was already low, the thought of regularly giving away a portion of their small paycheck deterred many workers from joining year after year.

However, as a result of these campaigns the fish industry usually increased social welfare benefits at the factory. For example, after unionization efforts in 1994, StarKist offered "paid vacation for employees calculated on years of services and hours at work and life insurance that provides for families of employees who die from work related accidents to receive up to $10,000. There is also a funeral benefit entitling employees to receive $350.00, ten cases of wahoo and two large fish, when a member of their immediate family dies. In addition, StarKist Sāmoa operates a pension plan fully funded by the company which retiring employees benefit from."[88] Scholars have examined the role industrial welfare programs play in maintaining worker loyalty and diffusing labor protests or unionization without drastically improving wages or the work environment.[89] Similarly in American Sāmoa, these gestures, both big and small, were often greatly appreciated by workers as employer recognition of and assistance in maintaining *vā* and *fa'a Sāmoa*. Subsidies that acknowledged cultural and family obligations to provide money, food, and time off for special occasions (such as funerals) effectively raised laborer satisfaction, deflected organizing efforts, and reduced demands for pay increases.

By 2014, workers surveyed by the federal government accounting office "generally opposed further minimum wage increases, expressing concerns that any increase would result in lost jobs or a complete closure of Star-Kist."[90] The reality of downsizing and the reduction of hours, as well as the constant threat of cannery transfer to a cheaper labor location persuaded workers to accept current, stable pay rates, a familiar scenario of economic intimidation historically used by corporations worldwide. In 2015, StarKist employee Line Tauatama stated that "we want the minimum wage to come but when we think of the one economy we have here that we might as well save what we've got right now to feed our families, put food on the table and do all such things. I will take whatever it's gonna take."[91] A steady job to provide for one's family has always been priority for workers over increasing wages in American Sāmoa. Employer acknowledgment of *vā fealoaʻi* (social respect) obligations and accommodations to meet the cultural expectations of *faʻa Sāmoa* also made the dirty job good enough.

Recent Legislation

After the first three wage hikes from 2007 to 2009, the U.S. Congress agreed to delay further increases from 2009 to 2011 for both American Sāmoa and the Commonwealth of the Northern Mariana Islands due to the increased unemployment that occurred since pay changes were implemented. By 2009, American Sāmoa employment was down 17 percent and jobs in the Marianas were down 24 percent.[92] According to Representative Doc Hastings of Washington State, who led the Republican efforts for this legislation in the House, "the Democrat Congress voted to pass a minimum-wage increase for these territories in 2007, and therefore, it was only appropriate that they vote again to fix it. . . . In doing so, Democrats were admitting that they were wrong to impose this policy that cost real people their jobs."[93] Even though Hastings referenced the negative impact that wage hikes had on workers in these island territories, the overall tone of his comments focused more on exposing the failure of Democratic legislation and Congressional party politics than the needs and issues facing peoples of the Pacific.

In 2011, the U.S. Congress passed the Insular Areas Act that modified the minimum wage increase in American Sāmoa from a yearly basis to a triennial basis and halted any pay hikes from 2012 to 2014.[94] This act also stopped any wage increases between 2012 and 2014. Representative Miller from California stated that "precisely because American Samoa has a unique, isolated, and relatively undiversified economy and because the path to the full federal minimum wage for this territory is a necessarily long one, Congress must be flexible over time with the minimum wage schedule in response to changing economic conditions. Congress must also maintain the clear requirement that the minimum wage in American Samoa be on a schedule to reach Mainland levels."[95] This American politician understood the specificities of American Sāmoa while also maintaining the desire to eventually raise wages in the region.

The Insular Areas Act also gave the Department of Energy the ability to monitor the stability of a toxic waste facility on Runit Island in the Marshall Islands, currently a sovereign nation subject to U.S. security and defense measures.[96] The joining of military refuse and labor policies into one overall piece of legislation for liminal Pacific islands demonstrates how national security issues rank just as high, if not higher than labor topics for the U.S. federal government in colonized spaces of the Pacific in the twenty-first century. Since 9/11, Congress tightened authority over native-controlled immigration policies in the Northern Marianas "to assure proper border control in the post–September 11 security environment."[97] With the threat of North Korean nuclear testing near Guam in 2017, the historic and current strategic military and geopolitical positionality of these U.S.-controlled archipelagos also comes to light.

Delegate Faleomavaega stated that, "I take no happiness in the successful passage of this bill because I still stand for fair wages for American Samoa's workers. . . . So between now and 2015, it will be up to the American Samoa government and our corporate partners, including StarKist and Tri-Marine, to find new ways of succeeding without further compromising the wages of our fish cleaners because I cannot promise that I will support any more delays after this."[98] Again, the tension between giving workers fair compensation and maintaining the main nongovernment industry in the islands surfaced in Faleomavaega's comments. Local leaders are trying to find a balance between the needs on both sides of this issue in the colonially controlled and regulated space of American Sāmoa. Ultimately, these U.S. colonials have been and continue to be subject to the whims and desires of the U.S. Congress.

With the pay increase delays ending on September 30, 2015, Representative Amata introduced three different bills to address the minimum wage issue in American Sāmoa. One proposal would have allowed the American Sāmoa Government to make future decisions on pay hikes. The second proposal requested another delay to wage increases. The third bill stated any future pay increase decisions would be based on government reports that investigated the impact of raises on the region. Eventually legislation was amended and passed to reduce the annual American Sāmoan minimum wage increase from fifty cents to forty cents. Georgia Senator Johnny Isakson pushed for this rate due to the larger political economic interests of his constituents.

After closing its operations in American Sāmoa in 2009, Chicken of the Sea moved the final step of its tuna processing procedure to Lyons, Georgia. At this location, Chicken of the Sea employed a much smaller number of skilled workers to operate high-tech canning machinery and still label their product as "Made in the USA." Two hundred people in Georgia are paid fair wages to engage in the final stage of packaging fish. However, that same fish were initially cleaned and processed by low-wage workers in Southeast Asia, who are paid less than a dollar an hour, versus the total 2,147 former employees in American Sāmoa who previously took care of the entire process for below continental U.S. minimum wage.[99] Consequently, politicians from Georgia have a strong motivation to continue the increases in American Sāmoa wage rates, keep tuna canning out of this Pacific region, and secure their state's foothold in the final stage of fish processing for Chicken of the Sea.

According to Delegate Amata, "this new interest from the Georgia delegation translates to a tougher fight on any tuna canning issue in the future."[100] This statement was reinforced when, after the forty-cent increase was passed, a spokesperson for Senator Isakson said "the artificially lower wages in American Samoa—well below the federal minimum wage level of $7.25 per hour—provide employers in the territory a competitive advantage over Georgia job creators."[101] Even though the Georgia senator succeeded in increasing the American Sāmoa minimum wage for the first time since 2008 to $5.16 an hour, his representative still focused on the unfair benefit that the lower wage rates provided for colonial laborers in this unincorporated Pacific region over continental workers. As seen in chapter 1, state politics related to U.S. citizen job protection within the fish industry came into play in Congressional actions in American Sāmoa. In the mid-1970s, the Fisheries Conservation and Management Act was primarily passed by Congress as a jobs bill. In the early twenty-first century, jobs for full-fledged U.S. citizens, not the needs and interests of U.S. colonial American Sāmoans, were a critical component to stateside debates over minimum wage hikes in this colonized Pacific region.

While Delegate Amata was glad that workers in American Sāmoa received a wage increase, she remained "concerned regarding the long-term stability of the canning industry on the island, as this increase, while welcomed for the people, will place an even greater strain on our local industry, which is already under attack from all sides."[102] In principle, Amata and others might back minimum wage increases. However, in practice most in the region understand that wage hikes could ultimately push away the tuna industry and result in higher unemployment in American Sāmoa.

According to the American Sāmoa governor's executive assistant Iulogologo Joseph Pereira, "the Governor walks a fine line in trying to strike a balance between the survival of the canneries and the survival of our people. We can't give up the fight because our people's lives are at stake."[103] Higher pay for workers is a positive. But such increases come with larger economic consequences for the fish industry in the region. This economic versus ethical dilemma directly stems from the liminal colonial status of American Sāmoans in relation to the U.S. government.

The continued debate and discussion over minimum wage in American Sāmoa has been compounded by the general push to raise the minimum wage in states of the union.[104] In general, Republicans have not supported this move, while Democrats have spearheaded efforts for a living wage. In 2010, North Carolina Republican representative Patrick T. McHenry expressed how "we said this increase would be harmful in 2007, and the Democrats did it anyway. . . . It proves our point that the federal government setting wage rates is destructive to job creation, whether it's in American Samoa or western North Carolina."[105] The failure of minimum wage increases to improve the lives of Pacific Islanders in U.S. territories bolstered Republican rhetoric against higher pay, especially when Delegate Amata stated that "while well intended, the Fair Minimum Wage Standards Act has placed the economic well-being of American Sāmoa in great jeopardy." The increase "would surely be the proverbial nail in the coffin for the local economy."[106] With U.S. colonial politicians themselves fighting against pay hikes, Republican efforts to block minimum wage increases on the continent were reinforced.

Overall, the application of national pay standards due to federal party politics since 2007 has had a generally detrimental effect on the local island economy. Since wage increases began in 2009, cannery employment has gone down by almost 50 percent. In reaction to the second forty-cent increase in two years, the Samoa Tuna Processors plant closed its canning operations on December 16, 2016, only eighteen months after opening and resulting in the loss of seven hundred jobs. In June 2017, Representative Amata proposed another bill in Congress to halt the next pay increase scheduled for the end of the year, keep minimum wage at $5.16, and revert back to the Special Industry Committee to make future wage hike decisions. Congress took no action on this bill and the next forty-cent wage increase occurred on September 30, 2018.

Online discussions continued among a handful of commentators about paying workers fairly, the failure of the local government to make change, as well as the fear of losing the fish industry.[107] Cannery workers still expressed a desire for higher wages, but also did not want to risk losing their jobs.[108] Common themes of local needs being ignored by the federal government and the burdens of this demanding fish industry on native peoples ran through all of these perspectives. Colonial status and control have historically and contemporarily subjected American Sāmoans to this wage labor quandary.

American Sāmoa leaders have also been consistently frustrated with the lack of consideration from U.S. politicians for the particularities of this unincorporated Pacific territory. Governor's assistant Pereira stated in 2015 that the "expectations of our fears of economic gloom and doom have eventuated. We have been vociferous in our attempts to articulate over the years the consequences that will result if the competitive advantage of the two canneries was to be eroded."[109] Tri-Marine's Hamby also stated that "if the voices of the American Samoan people aren't being heard by NMFS regulators and policy makers in Washington, DC the future of American Samoan's tuna dependent economy looks bleak."[110] All of these voices express anxiety over the liminal status of American Sāmoans in relation to U.S. programs, a direct impact of being regulated and controlled as U.S. colonials. At what point, if any, will or should the economic stability of American Sāmoa, or the wishes of the American Sāmoan people, take precedent over federal minimum wage hikes?

In the post–World War II era, this unincorporated territory of the United States transitioned from subsistence livelihoods to a cash-based economy focused on the single export of tuna and headed down a road of accommodating the corporate fish industry to make ends meet. Tuna canneries have historically threated to leave in the face of pay increases. While two canneries have closed in the twenty-first century, one facility has been stable since the 1960s. In a global market where the canning of fish at the cheapest price and maintaining a major source of Gross Domestic Product matters more than paying humans a judicious wage, the demands and economic priorities of United States and world consumers and businesses take precedent over the welfare of cannery workers.

It is true that the cost of living in American Sāmoa is not as high as the United States. The same wage standards are not necessarily logical from an empirical perspective. However, some increases are reasonable. Issues of dependency on a single-market economy and U.S. federal funding, as well as federal party politics and corporate interests heavily influence the development of these policies in the liminal economically colonized space of American Sāmoa. Therefore, the minimum wage issue, like many other local versus federal matters discussed in this book, is complicated and difficult to work through. Multiple indigenous and American perspectives exist as part of this bioregion, or totality of ecological and cultural relationships.

These often invisible strains of colonial rule, such as differential pay rates for cannery workers, are important and central policies in the lives of American Sāmoans, as well as those living in the continental United States and beyond. As long as American Sāmoa remains a colonized region of America, these questions are not going to disappear. Instead, such tensions must be discussed and dealt with in an open and direct way moving forward. The next chapter discusses another example of the complicated intersections of federal policies and native expectations of *vā fealoa'i* through the creation and expansion of the National Marine Sanctuary of American Sāmoa. In all of these cases, historical and contemporary searches for appropriate and workable balances between and among indigenous and colonial relations occurs.

CHAPTER 3

The Devolution of Marine Sanctuary
Development in American Sāmoa

In 1982, the American Sāmoa Government (ASG) initiated efforts to protect a bay on Tutuila as part of the U.S. national marine sanctuary system. When Fagatele Bay became a protected zone in 1986, the region was the smallest underwater federal sanctuary in the entire program, one-fourth of a square mile overseen by the National Oceanic and Atmospheric Administration's (NOAA) Office of National Marine Sanctuaries (ONMS). In 2012, the sanctuary expanded to six total areas covering 13,581 square miles. Now the largest but lesser known of the fourteen protected regions across U.S. jurisdiction, the National Marine Sanctuary of American Sāmoa is considered by the U.S. government to be the most remote underwater government preserve, the most diverse sanctuary in terms of marine life, and the only true tropical reef in the federal system. While the establishment of a national marine sanctuary in American Sāmoa was initiated by the ASG in the 1980s, not all American Sāmoans supported sanctuary expansion in 2012.

Multiple interests exist in the twenty-first century over ocean use within this national marine sanctuary (NMS). Some focus on the value of preserving these waters for scientific research and the long-term health of local and global ecosystems. Others feel the use of and control over this vital marine area should have remained under the control of the local community. Themes of imposed U.S. ideas and expectations, as well as the need to acknowledge Sāmoan traditional culture both came into play with the development and controversies over the national marine sanctuary in American Sāmoa. But just like the Large Vessel Prohibited Area (LVPA) examined in chapter 1, minimum wage explored in chapter 2, and national grant funding that will be discussed in chapter 4, overall federal management in this region is a consequence of being U.S. colonials. Living in an unincorporated territory of the United States means that these wards

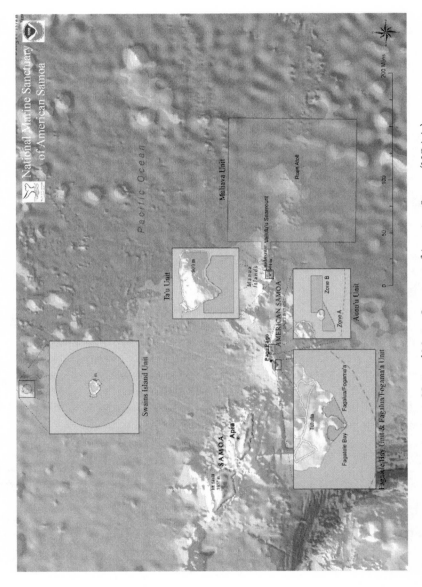

FIGURE 3.01. National Marine Sanctuary of American Sāmoa. (NOAA.)

FIGURE 3.02. Fagatele Bay. (Photo by Joseph Paulin.)

have historically and are currently subject to and ultimately controlled by the rulings of bureaucratic institutions in Washington, D.C.

However, as U.S. colonials, American Sāmoans can also take unique advantage of federal programs. This indigenous group successfully lobbied to protect their ocean resources through the marine sanctuary system and ended up shaping U.S. environmental policy. But once these waters became part of this national agency, activities and people within this ecosystem became indefinitely beholden to specific U.S. government mandates and requirements. As historian Mark David Spence has claimed about American Indians and the creation of national parks, "wilderness preservation went hand in hand with native dispossession."[1] The permanent nature of the National Marine Sanctuary of American Sāmoa reflects a similar connection between U.S. conservation and loss of indigenous control over lands and waters.

This chapter highlights the impact that U.S. colonial native groups have had on the national marine sanctuary system, both through their active support and later their vocal protests of ecological initiatives. While the creation of federally protected waters initially aligned with indigenous customs and mores, such as *vā fealoaʻi* (social respect), the later phase of expansion utilized a top-down approach that resulted in a storm of debates and lack of wide community support. Over time, national marine sanctuary development in American Sāmoa devolved from a collaborative decision-making process to a detached bureaucratized and dispossessive procedure disdained by many in the local community.

Establishment of the Sanctuary

The establishment of the marine sanctuary area in American Sāmoa demonstrated one way that U.S. colonials could use their dependent status with the United States to advance their own environmental management concerns. In March 1982, American Sāmoa governor Peter T. Coleman drafted a proposal for the National Oceanic and Atmospheric Administration (NOAA) to nominate Fagatele Bay as a candidate for marine sanctuary designation. Coleman encouraged the creation of this protected area to safeguard and preserve the bay's natural resources and pristine character, to expand public and scientific awareness and understanding of marine ecosystems in the Pacific, and to allow environmentally conscious subsistence and public recreational uses of the bay.[2] As Spence has explained, wilderness has historically been seen "as scenic playground. . . . a symbol, and sacred remnant of God's original handiwork," and "outdoor enthusiasts viewed wilderness as an uninhabited Eden that should be set aside for the benefit and pleasure of vacationing Americans."[3] Coleman used such American ideas about nature and conservation that started in the late nineteenth century to present his case for a sanctuary in the most legible and acceptable rhetoric for the U.S. federal government system.

One major reason a territorial campaign developed to protect Fagatele Bay stemmed from the devastation of local reefs by attacks from the coral-eating crown-of-thorns starfish *(Acanthaster planci)* from 1978 to 1979.[4] According to the National Ocean Service, land-based pollution and runoff of nutrients like nitrogen and phosphorus cause most crown-of-thorns outbreaks.[5] During this time period, American Sāmoa engaged in a massive public works project to build roads on Tutuila.

By April 1982, scientific researchers found that "most of the former living coral colonies were dead. . . . [and] Coral coverage . . . has been reduced to 1.7 percent from a previous estimate of 70 to 90 percent in 1979."[6] Such reef destruction resulted in the native push for a marine sanctuary. According to Bill Thomas, former research director of the Fagatele National Marine Sanctuary program, the American Sāmoa "sanctuary started as an in situ lab for crown of thorns recovery" and was supported by a lot of local leaders at the time.[7] Fagatele served as a case study area to see how long coral would take to recoup from this predatory starfish.

The designation of this bay as a national marine sanctuary followed a typical federal bureaucratic process of mandated announcements, community meetings, and planning reports. In April 1982, Fagatele Bay was placed on the List of

FIGURE 3.03. Crown-of-thorns starfish injection. (Photo by Greg McFall—NOAA.)

Recommended Areas to come under federal protection. In May, an Issue Paper was prepared and a public workshop was held in American Sāmoa to obtain community responses to the sanctuary proposal. From that workshop and other meetings with American Sāmoa officials and federal agencies, Fagatele became an Active Candidate for sanctuary status in August 1982. A draft management plan and environmental impact statement was then created and distributed on October 27, 1983. A public hearing in American Sāmoa was held for the plan on January 18, 1984. Of the thirteen comments received, seven individuals supported the sanctuary proposal, as well as expressed concern over the enforcement of sanctuary regulations.[8] In response, NOAA stated that assistance from the American Sāmoa Government and public education of rules would be sufficient to handle violations in federally protected waters.

Another major set of comments from the public hearing centered on the proposed sanctuary boundary. Community members asked NOAA to "allow commercial fishing in the outer portion of the bay. Over the years, this area has been used as a refuge from rough seas and a fishing ground while waiting for the heavy seas to pass."[9] Due to this local sentiment, the next draft of the management plan separated the sanctuary boundary into zones and permitted commercial fishing in the outside half of the bay. This adjustment to the rules became a typical accommodation that the Office of National Marine Sanctuaries provided to the people of American Sāmoa throughout the history of this sanctuary. NOAA recognized "the importance of fishing to the Samoan way of life and the multi-use aspects of the sanctuary. . . . After careful evaluation of this potential sanctuary, NOAA has concluded that a tiered structure that would allow commercial fishing in the outer portions of the bay could benefit both the sanctuary and users of the sanctuary."[10] Indigenous fishing practices usually received acknowledgment and permission in federally protected waters, as long as the angling was not significantly detrimental to marine preservation and conservation efforts. In the case of Fagatele, fishing in the outer bay was deemed non-impactful to inner reef protection.

Other feedback to the draft management plan stated that existing local and federal agencies already worked to protect marine resources in the area. One commentator expressed how "a marine sanctuary would only add an unnecessary and expensive layer of Federal bureaucracy."[11] As an unincorporated territory of the United States, the waters surrounding American Sāmoa involve multiple levels of jurisdiction including the local Department of Marine and Wildlife Resources (DMWR) and NOAA Fisheries, as discussed in chapter 1. The addition of a marine sanctuary would increase the amount of regulations and oversight for waters that already had government stewards. Others also believed traditional indigenous ocean management systems already protected and controlled water use sufficiently.

NOAA addressed these concerns by explaining that a national marine sanctuary would provide a comprehensive supervisory structure that specifically focused on this important marine site. NOAA believed overarching administration by the Office of National Marine Sanctuaries could better direct both research and explicit conservation efforts for the short-and long-term health of the bay. As historian Karl Jacoby stated, "Concentrating decision making in the hands of a few highly trained officials ensured that natural resources were administered in the most enlightened manner possible."[12] Such a belief in the superiority of government management was typical of U.S. federal conservation since the nineteenth century, as will be discussed later in this chapter.

Additional respondents worried that greater federal authority in the region would infringe upon traditional Sāmoan lifestyles. NOAA responded by stating the agency "has continually maintained that 'Fa'a Samoa,' the Samoan way, will be of utmost consideration during the evaluation process. It is recognized that strong cultural ties are reflected in daily life in American Samoa. NOAA will do its utmost in assuring that the Samoan way of life, as it pertains to the sanctuary, is maintained and incorporated into sanctuary management."[13] On their web-site, the National Marine Sanctuary of American Samoa explains *fa'a samoa* as placing "great importance on the dignity and achievements of the group rather than on individual achievements. The traditional communal lifestyle revolves around the *aiga*, or family. *Aiga* are headed by leading matai (chief) or Sa'o, who manage the communal economy, protect and distribute family lands, are respon-sible for the welfare of all in their *aiga,* and represent the family in councils."[14] NOAA believed the best way to respect *fa'a samoa* (Sāmoan customs and tradi-tions) was to request feedback from the American Sāmoa government, village chiefs, and other local groups.

However, to fully include indigenous social and political structures in the running of the sanctuary, policies also needed to engage in the typical native decision-making process that involves meeting with each major segment of the village, presenting proposals to the village council, and allowing the high chief to make the final decision for the community. Thomas expressed how American Sāmoa was the "first sanctuary to take into account traditional management sys-tems."[15] While Western-style public awareness and feedback-collecting meetings can help develop community support for federal programs based on national government standards, active use of indigenous communication methods and attention to proper *vā* (social relations) should be included for any government initiative to succeed in American Sāmoa. A lack of in-depth village participa-tion in the planning process became an issue when sanctuary expansion was discussed twenty-three years later in 2009.

The revised version of the Fagatele Bay sanctuary management plan was pub-lished on December 4, 1984, and comments were accepted until February 4, 1985. In the final plan, published in June 1984, collaboration between local and federal agencies, increased research, and public information became the main priorities of the federally protected area. Due to feedback requesting more local involvement, the final report also emphasized the importance of community outreach through education and awareness activities like a comprehensive in-terpretive program with exhibits and audiovisual programs. With no opposition from the U.S. Congress, Fagatele Bay became a national marine sanctuary of the United States on July 31, 1986.

Throughout the establishment of the national marine sanctuary in American Sāmoa in the 1980s, federal and indigenous environmental goals for protecting ocean resources overlapped. The ASG initiated the designation process and Gov-ernor Coleman's proposal provided the foundational language for the manage-ment plan that legally shifted jurisdiction of this area from local administration to federal protection. NOAA also worked closely with the indigenous landowners adjacent to the body of water, allowed fishing in the outer bay, and promised to provide a positive and useful structure for marine education and conservation.

Most of the people I interviewed did not see the 1986 marine sanctuary designation as controversial. In fact, members of the Fuimaono family, who owns the land adjacent to Fagatele Bay, nostalgically remembered the positive relationships previous leaders in their family had with federal and sanctuary officials. Even before the creation of the protected area, Paramount Chief A. U. Fuimaono, who was also the first elected American Sāmoa Congressional Delegate, was close with D.C. officials. His family recounted how Fuimaono would "bring them [federal leaders] to swim in Fagatele Bay."[16] The Fuimaono family also expressed how sanctuary staff worked well with them in the early years, coming together to make and maintain access trails, as well as monitor bay use, in a collaborative and respectful way. A. U. Fuimaono even received a volunteer achievement award from NOAA for his dedicated service to the sanctuary in 2007. Regular cooperation and teamwork exemplified federal and native interactions attuned to *fa'a Sāmoa* during and soon after the establishment of the sanctuary.

Running the Sanctuary

The collaboration between NOAA and the ASG that started with the establishment of the sanctuary continued with the management of the area. While NOAA has the main responsibility for monitoring activity in this federally protected area, overseeing scientific research projects, and offering educational programming, the American Sāmoa Department of Commerce is tasked with helping NOAA, predominately through coordination of community outreach and local consensus building through divisions like the Coastal Management program. Today, the American Sāmoa Coastal Management program promotes "development while safeguarding the territory's natural resources."[17] Effective resource management and public outreach have been the foci of this agency.

In 1995, NOAA also established a Joint Enforcement Agreement with the American Sāmoa Department of Marine and Wildlife Resources to empower local officers to enforce federal sanctuary regulations. NOAA conducted training sessions to help these territorial representatives develop their skills to administer federal rules. These workshops included interviewing practice exercises, boating and safety drills, and education in the records reporting process. Hiring locals to enforce federal regulations occurred throughout the history of conservation in the United States. As Jacoby discussed, in the early 1900s the

Adirondack Park in New York hired "policemen of the woods" from among the "experienced woodsmen" of the Adirondacks."[18] Locals were also hired as guides to help at Yellowstone National Park.

While NOAA reported only one complaint about illegal fishing in Fagatele Bay from 2005 to 2011, the seclusion of this protected area does not lend itself to intense government monitoring. Department of Marine and Wildlife Resources officers rely on community reporting to learn about violations. Despite one NOAA special agent and one NOAA enforcement officer assigned to American Sāmoa since 2012, Peter Eves, head of the DMWR's enforcement team, believes most violations are not seen and therefore remain undocumented.[19] While huge fines can be imposed on offenders of sanctuary rules, without enough staff to investigative infractions in a timely manner, citations are rarely issued.

According to Eves, the individuals who are more likely to be cited are American Sāmoans who might breach rules from near shore practices that are often traditional. These rules become more of a deterrent to cultural ocean use than non-Sāmoan vessels disobeying dumping or fishing regulations in deep-sea waters. Fines can reach up to $140,000 per event per day, as well as related costs to and damages from the infraction.[20] Sanctuary enforcement remained a difficult task in 2017. Jacoby discussed similar enforcement issues in the early U.S. conservation movement, echoing Eves' ideas of native people bearing the brunt of federal environmental laws, as well as the difficulty of patrolling and enforcing rules in hard to access locations without enough staff.[21]

To increase contact with the public, sanctuary supervisor Gene Brighouse created a community-based advisory group called the Sanctuary Advisory Council in 2005. This council has seventeen voting members who are appointed by the sanctuary supervisor. These individuals come from a wide range of interested parties in American Sāmoa including research, education, business/industry, ASG divisions, fishing, ocean recreation, tourism, and diving, as well as community representatives from five main areas of American Sāmoa: the east and west side of Tutuila, the Manuʻa Islands, Swains Island, and Aunuʻu Island. Thirteen members are non-governmental and the other four members come from related territorial government environmental departments.[22] There are also eight non-voting members that include a student member, the government of Sāmoa, NOAA leadership, the National Park of American Sāmoa, and the U.S. Coast Guard.

Overall, the Sanctuary Advisory Council includes a mix of indigenous and nonnative agents with specialized interests who provide the superintendent with recommendations and advice on policies to manage and protect the sanctuary.

The Sanctuary Advisory Council must meet every six months, but no more than once a month. Meetings are conducted in English. One main goal of this council is to have community representatives bring direct information back to their constituents about the marine sanctuary. Ironically, the first major action of the Sanctuary Advisory Council involved comments on the draft management plan to extend the sanctuary in 2012.

Extension of the Sanctuary

When efforts to expand the sanctuary developed in the 2010s, sentiments towards federally protected waters in American Sāmoa were much different than in 1986. There was more contention and opposition from different members of the community to the augmentation of the national marine sanctuary in the region. As ecology scholar Fikret Berkes has explained, "When fishers are involved in the conservation and management of a fishery, they are more likely to take ownership of it."[23] In contrast, a lack of community involvement could prevent local support for an initiative, as seen in the expansion process in American Sāmoa.

Several environmental factors motivated the expansion of the national marine sanctuary in this region. The increase in commercial longline fishing at the turn of the twenty-first century, major coral bleaching incidents in 1994, 2002, and 2004 (due to ocean changes such as higher temperatures, nutrients, or light), and increased pollution in the local waters encouraged American Sāmoa governors Tau'ese Pita Sunia and Togiola Tulafono to support "setting aside 20% of the coral reef habitat within the territory for long-term protection."[24] The governors were also echoing the 1999 U.S. Coral Reef Task Force's prioritization of protecting 20 percent of all U.S. coral reefs.[25]

In the years since Fagatele's sanctuary designation, at least eighteen scientific studies between 2000 and 2012 also provided greater information on ocean use and the value of the reef surrounding American Sāmoa. For example, a 2007 Fagatele Bay Sanctuary Condition Report described how a crown-of-thorns starfish outbreak, tropical cyclones, elevated ocean temperature, fishing, coral diseases, agriculture, and visitation placed multiple pressures on the resource rich marine environment in American Sāmoa.[26]

The turn of the twenty-first century was also a period in which the United States and nations across the globe started to push for the protection of water regions. According to Callum Roberts, "In 2000, President Bill Clinton issued an executive order, later endorsed by the Bush administration, charging government agencies to create a national network of marine protected areas. . . . At the World Summit on Sustainable Development in 2002, coastal nations of the world pledged to create national networks of marine protected areas by 2012."[27] All of these elements inspired the Office of National Marine Sanctuaries to initiate efforts to expand federally protected waters in American Sāmoa.

The drive to augment the sanctuary was further supported by the first review and evaluation of the Fagatele Bay National Marine Sanctuary management plan that started in 2008. From February to March 2009, NOAA held a fifty-six-day public scoping period "to identify issues and gauge interest within American Samoa for possible sanctuary expansion and designation of additional sanctuary units."[28] Local sanctuary staff and the American Sāmoa Department of Commerce put together a list of discussion topics for three public meetings on February 10, 11, and 12 on the west, east, and center sections of Tutuila. The subjects were (a) Improved Partnerships, (b) Characterization and Monitoring, (c) Spill Prevention, Contingency Planning and Response, (d) Climate Change, (e) Ocean Literacy, (f) Marine Debris, and (g) Site Expansion.[29] According to Lucy Jacob, an American Sāmoa Department of Marine and Wildlife Resources program leader at the time,

> when the public scoping meetings were held in 2009 they were not properly advertised and they were very poorly attended. The staff of Fagatele Bay made the addition of extra sites sound like a vague but unlikely possibility and I am certain that the public felt that they would be fully consulted before any potential site could actually be proposed. However, since those meetings, there have been very few public meetings (evidenced by the public outcry that is occurring) and people are now facing the possibility that their marine areas which are culturally 'owned' by the people could become MPAs [marine protected areas] without them having any say.[30]

Site expansion was only one of seven topics brought up in these sparsely attended meetings. Besides the owners of Swains Island, the local indigenous population did not request an enlargement of the sanctuary. However, after this scoping period, sanctuary management worked diligently on a draft management plan that focused on expanding federally protected waters.

The Sanctuary Advisory Council created a Site Selection Working Group composed of Sanctuary Advisory Council members and community representatives to examine the pros and cons of incorporating additional marine locations into the federally protected and managed area. Sanctuary employees also helped in the assessment process. The Working Group used National Marine Sanctuary

Act guidelines "to evaluate the ecological, cultural, and economic value of the areas proposed" and eventually selected five sites for expansion: Muliāva (Rose Atoll), Larsen Bay, Aunuʻu Island, Taʻu Island, and Swains Island.[31]

Of the thirty-two total community meetings held during this expansion process, twenty-four sessions occurred between July 6, 2009, and April 18, 2011, before the publication of the draft management plan. No meetings were planned after the availability of the document for public review and before the closing of the comment period in January 2012. The overall timing, structure, and content of these sessions demonstrated the more informative nature of these meetings as opposed to the desire to generate specific comments to incorporate feedback and community-based ideas into final expansion plans. Local longline owner Christinna Lutu-Sanchez expressed how, during the meeting held at the American Sāmoa Community College, "there was maybe a 5 minute briefing about this proposal (in summary), and then time was made available for comments. . . . There was NEVER an opportunity for questions and answers for the people to understand more about this proposal. As a matter of fact, we were told that the responses would be forthcoming and that they were just there to collect "comments" . . . how are we to make useful comments if there are numerous questions about this proposal that are unanswered?"[32] Holding a meeting was not the same as fostering community support or engaging in *vā fealoaʻi*. While NOAA listened to and recorded community feedback, a standard mandate of federal government community projects, these gatherings focused on educating the public about the goals set forth by sanctuary management to expand federal protection over local waters. Information and awareness, instead of interaction or appropriate *vā*, guided these activities.

Many in the local community did not feel that the initial comment period provided enough time for villagers to digest and respond to the plan. Selaina Tuimavave stated how "Fagatele is located in the village of Futiga, during the first round of public meetings not one meeting was held in Futiga. With the expansion in review, Larson's Bay is located in the village of Vaitogi. I live in the village of Vaitogi, none of the three public meetings was held in my village. Additionally, the village council of my village was not informed of the plans to expand the sanctuary into our village waters. Aunuʻu is also a proposed site, the village meeting was not held in Aunuʻu but rather in Utumea."[33] Poor advertising and lack of information about the purpose of meetings continued along with inappropriate site selection and low attendance for community meetings, violating Sāmoan concepts of *vā*.

George Tusi also stated how "it was obvious that village communities close to the proposed sites hadn't even heard about the proposals or seen the maps before. But we are told that the Office of Samoan Affairs was told about the plans and that our mayors should have passed on the information."[34] At the beginning of this process, village mayors attended a meeting "to discuss preliminary sanctuary units and solicited help of mayors to engage village stakeholders" on March 30, 2009.[35] Interacting with village mayors, holding twenty-two sessions in villages, and hosting fourteen gatherings for specific families, or *'āiga,* "who could provide village-specific information on fishing activities, coastal management concerns, and other needs of the village" are appropriate steps in a community education process for the region. However, these sessions alone did not result in wide community support for sanctuary expansion.

American Sāmoans likely expected the same level of collaboration that occurred during the establishment of the initial sanctuary: an open and measured communication process where all impacted parties had an opportunity to express their thoughts.[36] In the absence of such *vā fealoa'i,* strong negative community sentiment developed over the expansion that was initiated by sanctuary officials in Washington, D.C., and American Sāmoa, and supported by the American Sāmoa governor's office. In response to vocal concerns over the review process for augmentation, the Sanctuary Advisory Council, American Sāmoa Congressional Delegate Eni Faleomavaega, and members of the public all requested that NOAA extend the comment period, which occurred and ended two months later on March 9, 2012.

Six meetings occurred during this time frame, with the last meeting held on the last day of the extended comment period.[37] During this extra window of opportunity for providing feedback, NOAA worked with the village councils and *mātai* of impacted villages to develop more native knowledge of the plans and purposes for the extension of the sanctuary. Unfortunately, even this flexibility in D.C.-based timelines did not coincide well with the traditional Sāmoan village consensus building process that involves informing different constituents in each village in separate meetings and council advice to the high chief, who makes a decision for the whole community, as discussed in chapter 4. This slow and deliberate process can often take many months. As Jon Barnett and John Campbell have stated about other initiatives in the South Pacific, "community-based approaches can take a long time—for example the three years of the project was considered to be barely adequate."[38] Consequently, NOAA coming to these villages with a two-month period for responses could feel like a lot of pressure and not enough time to make important community decisions.

Save Liuato A. Tuitele and Tofoitaufa Sandra King Young expressed how the "so-called meetings within the villages with the high chiefs were poorly publicized and ineffective in bringing together the right people that make the decisions for the affected villages. The high chiefs and people in the affected villages that were necessary to the deliberations did not attend these sparsely attended meetings. Still the NMS felt they could proceed with the process just because 'they' had the meetings."[39] Since only government employees, stay-at-home moms, youth, retired people, elderly folks, and the unemployed could attend daytime meetings, several felt the appropriate interested parties were not involved in the process. Holding meetings did not equate to extensive community support through traditional methods.

Another anonymous commentator stated:

> The process for public consultations on this proposed set of regulations is deeply flawed. The so-called "public hearings" were stage managed to minimize public input and criticism. . . . The big no-take area is around Aunu'u, but instead of holding the meeting on Aunu'u it was held on Tutuila. That meeting was held as a village council meeting, in which the chiefs on the council are present, and in which traditionally, the villagers do not speak. Speakers had to sign in to be allowed to speak, and were limited to 3 minutes. The Fagatele [sanctuary] people did not answer any questions or respond to any comments. Press was not notified and invited, and one press member seems to have had pressure applied not to report. . . . This whole process is rigged against those who disagree.[40]

In the context of expected extensive, transparent, and deliberate Sāmoan communication and decision-making processes, as well as past cooperation during the establishment of the sanctuary, NOAA's efforts fell short of fully engaging the community, incorporating their needs, addressing their concerns, and following appropriate *vā* and *fa'a Sāmoa*. While a bureaucratically clear comment process was created and expanded by the U.S. federal government, the general sentiment among many in the community remained unsupportive of the quick and cursory demeanor of these meetings. These disconnects between federal versus indigenous priorities and protocols resulted in negative public views of sanctuary expansion at the time and for many years after. In a similar way, at Glacier National Park, "negative opinions of the park service had become a central aspect of tribal policy and a fundamental expression of Blackfeet national identity."[41]

In the end, during the total eight months of the expansion comment period, people provided 188 comments on sixteen different subject areas. Thirteen of the sixteen areas involved negative concerns, with fifty-three specific posts to the online Federal Register opposing some aspect of sanctuary augmentation. Some of those posts also had multiple signatures attached to statements. In general, public remarks expressed concerns over the loss of local indigenous control over ocean resources and the takeover of authority by the federal government.

Several people believed sanctuary expansion was motivated by both the Office of National Marine Sanctuaries' desire to increase their overall power and jurisdiction, as well as local territorial leaders' desire to gain a positive reputation from supporting environmental protections. One anonymous commentator stated that "the main issue here is for the Governor to have a legacy before he goes out of office and for the National Marine Sanctuaries to have a greater area within their network to make more of an impact to their partners in the US and around the world."[42] The Western Pacific Regional Fishery Management Council (Wespac) also claimed that

> the proposed action appears to be another example of the expansionist philosophy of ONMS [Office of National Marine Sanctuaries] . . . to expand its jurisdiction under a veil of protection. . . . the DMP/DEIS [Draft Management Plan/Draft Environmental Impact Statement] fails to provide a clear need for expansion. . . . Examples of ONMS' expansionist regime are common within this program, including Channel Island NMS, Monterey Bay NMS, and Hawaiian Islands Humpback Whale NMS. . . . once the area is designated, ONMS applies the "lock it up and toss the key" approach and then seeks to further expand.[43]

The Council believed that NOAA programs and the augmentation of the sanctuary in American Sāmoa reflected the long-term imperial nature of this federal agency throughout U.S. jurisdiction. Wespac expressed how NOAA always has and always will work towards greater control of ocean use and marine resources throughout the U.S. and its territories. From this perspective, native needs and fishing priorities took backseat positions.

Wespac was also concerned with the lack of scientific rationale for the expansion, the deficient enforcement for violations of sanctuary rules, and the weak federal fiscal situation that could prevent proposed plans from being implemented.[44] On-island scientists also questioned the reasons behind sanctuary expansion. According to Department of Marine and Wildlife Resources biologist Alice Lawrence, "it seems like the most charismatic and nationally important sites have been chosen rather than through any rigorous scientific process. It is evident from public meeting comments and online comments that suggestions were made by one or two members of the public and then discussed with one or two high ranking village representatives."[45] Department biologist Douglas Fenner also stated that "the Fagatele Bay expansion plan shows little if any signs of having used any science to select their expansion sites."[46] Despite these concerns, the final plan moved forward with the originally selected sites. NOAA firmly disputed the claim that science did not prove the need for sanctuary expansion, pointing to a biogeographic assessment and other reports that justified their choices.[47]

At least six people commented on the need to focus on improving the management of Fagatele Bay before expanding to other areas. Lima Tapuaʻi asked NOAA to "concentrate on improving the Fagatele Bay site which hasn't seen many benefits over the last 25 years faʻamolemole [please]."[48] An anonymous commentator also expressed how "very limited success from Fagatele Bay has been demonstrated after 25 years of its establishment. For 25 years the federal government did not provide proper access or signage to the sanctuary, did not effectively enforce the regulations and did not educate people about the regulations."[49] Several people questioned why expansion was necessary when so much more could be done with the existing sanctuary area.

Another topic brought up during both the scoping and comment periods involved the question of whether or not NOAA would incorporate the traditional *mātai* and Community Marine Tenure systems in their leadership.[50] Twenty-three comments to the Federal Register critiqued the process used for sanctuary expansion. Tapuaʻi expressed how "we should all be worried that the Faʻa Samoa wasn't properly followed even though it was boasted about in the plan. . . . There has been no respect for the fishermen that make a small living from our ocean and us people that want to feed our families. Are they really going to include us in future decisions about how to manage these sites?"[51]

To address concerns over the incorporation of indigenous social practices, NOAA explained how they received commendations from the former and current Secretaries of Sāmoan Affairs for their efforts to get community feedback and follow Sāmoan conventions. Paramount Chief Lefiti Falelauliʻi Pese stated that NOAA has "clearly followed our traditional protocols and successfully incorporated Faʻa Samoa into [their] process."[52] NOAA believed such support from local leaders demonstrated their cooperation with customary Sāmoan leadership expectations and *vā*.

But several comments challenged such claims. Department of Marine and Wildlife Resources employee Tepora Lavataʻi said:

let it be known that the Sanctuary officials here have completely disregarded the cultural ways to approach a village community on issues that will affect their people. There is NO documentation that verifies that these communities would like to have the Sanctuary expanding in their communities! Let the unanimous comments from the people of these communities speak for themselves. They were not informed. They weren't involved in the so-called 'conversations' that expressed any interest in the Sanctuary expansion into their village communities. These 'processes' that the Sanctuary officials have continued to work on do not work well in the Sāmoan communities and the Sanctuary officials here should've known better.[53]

To address this concern, NOAA stated that it would create an advisory council working group on Sāmoan cultural heritage to help integrate indigenous management styles into sanctuary administration. While that entity never formed, another committee called the Community Engagement Working Group was created. The only evidence found for this group's activity involved a sanctuary staff member meeting one-on-one with village leadership from a federally protected area to discuss specific issues, as opposed to a consistent effort to engage traditional communication processes in developing sanctuary activities.[54]

At least five letters from villagers proclaimed that NOAA did not go through the appropriate channels for communicating with communities about sanctuary expansion on their ancestral waterfronts. Siaumau Siaumau stated, "I strongly oppose this proposal because your agency did not go through the proper procedures of contacting my family and I about Larsen's Bay in which is part of the land that belongs to our family."[55] Not following traditional Sāmoan contact methods and *fa'a Sāmoa* were seen as deep violations of protocol and trust.

Despite all of these sentiments, NOAA proclaimed that it

has great respect for American Samoa's right to self-governance and for the right of American Samoans to use their family lands in traditional ways without interference from the federal government. For that reason, NOAA has expended a significant amount of effort and resources in consulting with officials of the American Samoa government, the Office of Samoan Affairs, Matai and local representatives, and the public. NOAA's goal throughout the management plan review process has been to create a management structure for the sanctuary that complements and enhances the work of the Territory and local communities in protecting natural resources while also being sensitive to and respectful of American Samoa's unique and rich culture.[56]

NOAA did not want to be accused of cultural insensitivity, ignoring existing forms of ocean management, or violating Sāmoan traditions. However, federal responses to community feedback were often reactionary and defensive, as opposed to being open to major change or vast adjustment of plans.

Several interviewed discussed how the sanctuary expansion process followed Office of National Marine Sanctuaries guidelines and successfully checked off the boxes of federal community engagement requirements. According to Section 922.22 of the National Marine Sanctuary Program Regulations, "if a proposed Sanctuary includes waters within the exclusive economic zone, the Secretary shall notify the appropriate Regional Fishery Management Council(s) which shall have one hundred and twenty (120) days from the date of such notification to make recommendations."[57] As long as these requirements were met, the Office of National Marine Sanctuaries completed their national obligations. But D.C.-based requirements often do not coincide with traditional Sāmoan village consensus building process or *vā fealoaʻi*.

Another set of concerns revolved around the continued belief that marine resources were already being taken care of through existing agencies and historic marine tenure systems. According to Representative Larry Sanitoa, "the American Samoa Government has a process in place with protective policies and the means to enforce federal regulations. The proposed expansion will impose and preempt ASG's right and attempts at self-governance and at best this plan is also a duplication of effort and a waste of money."[58] Worry developed over the infringement of indigenous rights and government waste in the region.

Tuitele and Young also proclaimed that "our local people have been sound stewards of conserving our marine resources off the shores of our villages for thousands of years, because of our respect for the ocean and limited traditional use for subsistence living. This is why we have pristine marine areas that the NMS now want to have jurisdiction over. We have effectively managed and conserved our marine resources close to our shores based on our traditional practices for future sustainability."[59] Based on several similar comments, many in the community believed expansion of the sanctuary would not add any value to existing native protection of local waters and would only complicate existing administrative structures.

In response to claims that protection was not needed in American Sāmoa waters, NOAA stated that the purpose of sanctuaries is not only to protect environments in bad condition, but also to preserve "well-functioning ecosystems of high biological, cultural and historic value."[60] According to the biogeographic assessment of the region, there are seven high-value marine sites in American Sāmoa containing three of four hotspots for coral cover, coral richness, fish biomass or fish richness.[61] NOAA believed that putting regulations in place as preventative measures was better than risking the future loss of such rich, diverse, and unique marine resources in the region. These bioregions became high priority for sanctuary expansion and NOAA worked hard to incorporate these sites into the new management plan through rule making and public education.

NOAA also stated that their regulations would complement territorial government efforts. The final management plan stated how "nothing in the proposal affects American Samoa's right to self-governance, DMWR's authority to manage marine resources in the Territory, or the ownership rights of American Samoans with respect to their lands."[62] Instead, the expanded sanctuary was expected to "provide value-added support and collaboration to existing management efforts. The sanctuary will not take over DMWR's responsibility within the sanctuary units, and the management regime is structured to complement, not replace or be in conflict with, existing authorities."[63] In fact, more programs could be supported with the funding and staff that accompanies a larger sanctuary.

NOAA also explained that they planned to engage in activities that current local agencies were not covering, such as "inventorying, assessing and providing federal protection for maritime heritage resources, and providing state-of-the-art education facilities and technologies."[64] This statement highlighted Western-based approaches to environmental management.

Overall, NOAA clearly addressed comments about sanctuary expansion with steadfast conviction, highlighting the financial, administrative, and long-term benefits that an expanded sanctuary could provide the region and its people. However, such rhetoric did not ease most community concerns over the growth of federal power in American Sāmoa.

There was not total community opposition to sanctuary expansion. According to NOAA, the seven main reasons people supported the management plan included the desire to preserve ocean resources for future generations, the ecological value of Fagalua/Fogamaʻa, the need to protect giant corals near Taʻu, the need to conserve mature fish to keep species numbers high, the ability of sanctuary activities to provide jobs, funding, and tourism to the region, the benefits of educating youth to continue ecologically positive actions in the future, as well as contributions to climate change and ocean conservation research.[65] Eighteen comments, with two posts having multiple signatures, supported the five-site expansion with location-specific regulations.

This pro-growth group of people included some on-island youth who likely participated in educational outreach programs provided by sanctuary staff, demonstrating the effectiveness of environmental education programs on younger generations in American Sāmoa. Jessica Peters stated that "I want to grow up and be able to still go fishing still swimming in the clean waters and be able to continue this long life journey with my kids and grand kids. So therefore, I say yes to Fagatele Bay expansion."[66] Peters agreed with the ecological and scientific reasons to augment federally protected waters in American Sāmoa, while also highlighting the importance of environmental protection for her *'āiga*. Peters also represented one of at least four other youth who expressed their support for this initiative through the Federal Register comment system.

Another community member, Tuai Auva'a, expressed how "if the expansion is for promoting and protection of our coral reefs and wildlife below, let's support it. We were misinformed that this expansion would stop fishermen from fishing in the expanded areas—it's actually not."[67] Supporting environmental reasons for more sanctuary sites, Auva'a explained how a lot of misinformation was circulating in the media and public.

The other major group of supporters involved Governor Togiola Tulafono and several members of his cabinet, including the directors of DMWR, the American Sāmoa Environmental Protection Agency, and the American Sāmoa Department of Commerce, as well as the secretary of Sāmoan Affairs, the manager of the American Sāmoa Coastal Management Program, representatives of the Coral Reef Advisory Group, and the president of the American Sāmoa Community College.[68] However, some doubted the strength of such support since all of these officials were members of the governor's staff who were appointed to their positions. One anonymous commentator questioned, "Why did all the ASG department directors suddenly change their votes one day after the SAC [Sanctuary Advisory Committee] meeting? Was it really that the representatives voted in a way their directors did not want?. . . . for some agencies, it is said that the DOC [Department of Commerce] assistant director was seen entering the agency, and some even say that loud voices were heard. It's not hard to figure out what happened."[69] With a patronage-based government system grounded in high-level political appointments as rewards for loyalty during election campaigns, claiming full government leadership support did not equate to full community support.

While most government-related letters of support expressed basic bureaucratic backing for the expansion of the national marine sanctuary, American Sāmoa Coastal Management Program staff member Sandra Lutu stated,

> I can only express my gratitude to the vision of the current administration of the sanctuary and their respect for our culture, our resources and the ability within the sanctuaries of maximizing our oceans and the support it

has provided our ancestors as well as us today. But even more compelling is the purpose of the plan to protect what we have depended on for so long so it will be there for our children and the future generations. I have read the many comments that are against this expansion and one thing we must remember to grow is that we can agree to disagree. . . . . It is my opinion that the vision of this plan encompasses the benefits for all. Lets expand it together and work together, I am sure in the end it will benefit us all.[70]

Lutu's strong enthusiasm for augmenting the sanctuary focused on protecting the environment for future generations, She praised NOAA for acting in a culturally respectful way. Lutu encouraged opponents to work together and focus on the long-term benefits of protecting larger areas of the ocean. Her sentiments were rare among the comments, but so robust that she provided a second post to say, "I commented earlier but did not clearly indicate my position that we should be open to expansions that not only protect our natural resources but provide the opportunity for further development through research and development for growth and sustenance."[71] Lutu also wanted to emphasize the environmental and research importance of the proposed area for protection. Throughout the expansion process, different members of the indigenous and nonnative community freely expressed a variety of strong opinions about the growth of federally protected zones in American Sāmoan waters.

The Final Plan: 2012

After the publication of the final management plan on July 26, 2012, no comments were received from any member of the U.S. Congress. While the enlargement of this designation involved much controversial debate in American Sāmoa, state politicians showed no visible interest in or concern for this proposal (unlike the minimum wage issue discussed in chapter 2). Consequently, the revised plan for the National Marine Sanctuary of American Sāmoa became official after the close of the sixty-day mandatory Congressional comment period. After three years of community engagement and planning, NOAA expanded its control and protection over vast tracts of the most diverse and vital waters around American Sāmoa on October 15, 2012.

In the final management plan, NOAA addressed the issues that were raised during the comment period. For example, the final plan did allow historical indigenous forms of fishing in specific areas. NOAA adjusted their recommendations for allowable activities within most of the proposed sanctuary areas to avoid significant barriers to native forms of angling or marine sources of financial gain for the indigenous community. NOAA also stated in the final management plan that "the focus of this action must be for the benefit of the American Samoan people, who have managed their ocean resources for 3,000 years. Commenters noted the traditional land management regime, adequate existing management and regulations, village enforcement, a preference to work with local agencies, and a history of failed support from the federal government. These concerns are understandable . . . NOAA has made community engagement the cornerstone of its management plan."[72] On paper, NOAA's reactions to comments seemed sensitive and open to concerns over traditional ocean use and respect for Sāmoan culture.

Overall, NOAA believed allowing subsistence and nonharmful forms of fishing in most sanctuary units, conducting a total of thirty-two community meetings, proposing an advisory council working group on Sāmoan cultural heritage to incorporate indigenous management styles, extending the draft comment period by two months, and getting endorsements from multiple government agencies, including the Office of Sāmoan Affairs, provided enough respectful effort and time with the community to claim a successful management plan review. However, the ways in which NOAA addressed these concerns, in a dense online document written in English, did not coincide well with the needs and circumstances of this indigenous community.

Not everyone in American Sāmoa speaks, let alone reads English. Internet access is hard to come by in the region. One anonymous commentator stated how "not everybody in American Samoa is good at using computers, or writing in English. Submitting on the web may be easy for people in the states, but not for many here."[73] NOAA even acknowledged that not everyone in American Sāmoa has access to the internet. Translation of all documents into the native language, making printed reports more widely available at public places like schools and the library, as well as making efforts to explain the detailed content of these materials through nonwritten forms of communication to impacted villages could have all assisted in getting wider positive support for sanctuary expansion.

In the future, the sanctuary management plan is supposed to be reviewed every five to ten years. Moving forward, an effective way to manage policy discussions with the community would be to meet directly and frequently with all groups living in affected villages to inform them of any proposed changes, provide ample time for them to develop feedback, and work diligently to acknowledge and incorporate their comments into future plans. NOAA could also explain why changes were or were not made through face-to-face follow-up communication. As Barnett and Campbell have stated, projects "need to negotiate local power" and "it takes time to learn, discuss and decide in ways that engage all the constituents within a village . . . the alternative is less widespread commitment."[74] Active responses, continual communication, and *vā fealoaʻi* are highly valued in American Sāmoan culture. These extra steps, as well as full education and awareness, could foster greater understanding, or at least avoid intense animosity, from members of the indigenous community.

Comparative Examples

In comparison, the first efforts to create a national marine sanctuary to protect endangered humpback whales around the Hawaiian Islands occurred in March 1982. With some members of the public "fearing that a marine sanctuary would bring additional restrictions on fishing and vessel traffic. . . . Hawaiʻi's then Governor George Anyoshi suspended further consideration of the site in early 1984."[75] After the closing of Kahoʻolawe weapons range in 1990, Congress once again encouraged the creation of a national marine sanctuary in Hawaiian waters, which became a national marine sanctuary on November 4, 1992, under the condition that the governor of Hawaiʻi could modify the boundaries of the protected area.

Four years later, after "numerous public meetings and hearings were held on each of the main Hawaiian Islands . . . [and] despite divided support from the public," Hawaiʻi governor Benjamin Cayetano approved the sanctuary at the state-level on June 5, 1997. Like comments about the sanctuary in American Sāmoa, ocean users and native peoples had concerns over their ability to continue their water-based activities in the region. Local residents did not want extra federal government control in the area. Some felt enough regulations already existed or were not working in the first place. Just like in American Sāmoa, NOAA steadfastly justified the creation of the sanctuary in Hawaiʻi as necessary and useful to supplement existing regulations and systems to protect nature from human intrusions. Overall, the Office of National Marine Sanctuaries claims they "work cooperatively with the people of Hawaiʻi to protect this important marine ecosystem."[76] In fact, NOAA and the State of Hawaiʻi, through the Department of Land and Natural Resources, jointly manage the sanctuary. In 2012, the sanctuary held a workshop on how to incorporate traditional *aloha ʻāina* (deep love for the land and sea) into sanctuary management.[77]

While American Sāmoans started the original marine sanctuary in Fagatele, neither the expansion nor the sanctuary in Hawaiʻi was initiated by native peoples. The protected area in American Sāmoa involved less community involvement and *vā fealoaʻi* during the expansion process. In the Hawaiʻi case, the public stopped the first attempt to create a sanctuary and was extensively involved in discussions throughout the process. The same year the sanctuary expanded in American Sāmoa, NOAA held a workshop with native experts to incorporate indigenous practices into their management plan in Hawaiʻi. In both cases, NOAA dispossessed native peoples of their water rights for the protection of nature over indigenous groups.

This belief in the authoritative and protective role of the U.S. federal government over the environment has been a cornerstone of U.S. conservation since its founding in the late nineteenth century. As Jacoby has explained, the American conservation movement centered around the "need to use science and the state to protect nature."[78] The goals and actions of new laws reflected "their vision of a just and well-ordered society."[79] Conservation efforts involved setting boundaries, regulations, and enforcement, as well as dictating what you can and cannot do in these federally controlled spaces according to Western scientific and U.S. government standards and rationales. However, "these actions also left behind a troubling legacy of environmental quality at the expense of social justice."[80] The priority of carefully supervised land and waterscapes often erased the historic and current needs and presence of native peoples. As Spence also discussed, U.S. conservation involved a "great deal of management and manipulation to keep original wilderness condition," or at least the idea of a pristine environment, intact.[81] Federal monitoring and control required a lot of staff and hard work to maintain western standards of idealized nature.

Sasha Davis also claimed how the terms "pristine and natural are applied to militarized landscapes to deepen colonial relations, restrict civilian access to contaminated areas, and justify the continued militarization of occupied lands."[82] Whether in Vieques, Puerto Rico, the waters off Kahoʻolawe, or in the remote Pacific Islands region, the shift from intensive and destructive weapons testing to environmental protection of these spaces can enable the U.S. federal government to avoid toxic waste cleanup, land rehabilitation, as well as return of land to native peoples.

The National Park of American Sāmoa provides another interesting point of comparison for federal regulations and control over nature in the U.S. Pacific. Such a protected designation was initiated by the U.S. Congress, like the Hawaiian Islands Humpback Whale National Marine Sanctuary, and became official on October 31, 1988. The goals of this national park are to "preserve and protect the tropical rainforest, coral reefs, archeological and cultural resources of American Samoa, to maintain the habitat of flying foxes, preserve the ecological balance of the Samoan tropical forest, and, consistent with the preservation of these resources, to provide for the enjoyment of the unique resources of the Samoan tropical forest by visitors from around the world."[83] Safeguarding plants, animals, American Sāmoan landmarks and practices, as well as recreation for visitors all mixed together in the justifications for this federal zone.

However, the park's formation presented a challenge to U.S. conservation, because all American Sāmoa lands belong to the native people. According to the National Park System, "early attempts to establish a national park in American Samoa failed when there seemed no way for the government to acquire traditionally owned village lands for a public park. Decades later the High Court of American Samoa and the U.S. Congress developed a compromise allowing lease of the necessary lands for this park. The lease agreement covers many of the visitor and park management practices that can occur within the park."[84] This park could not be established without the direct consent of the Sāmoan people and the specific villages and *ʻāiga* involved. Consequently, the National Parks Service has always had to follow *vā* and *faʻa Sāmoa* to exist, let alone succeed in this region.

In 1993, the National Park Service "signed a 50-year lease with the American Samoa Government. This unique lease initiated a partnership with the villages of Fagasā, Pago Pago, Āfono, Vatia, Taʻū, Fitiʻuta, and Faleāsao. Congress also authorized portions of Ofu and Olosega islands to be included in 2002."[85] The lease provides for fair-market value rent (adjustable every five years), the possibility of renewal, as well as the ability of either side to terminate the contract with one year's notice.[86] Unlike the permanence of national marine sanctuaries, this national park includes flexible, fluid, and changeable parameters.

Today, this location is the only national park south of the equator. This area includes 13,500 total acres with four thousand marine acres that are mostly coral reefs. The park has about five thousand visitors a year and employs an average of twenty-five people (thirty-seven American Conservation Experience members, one volunteer, and twenty-four firefighters). According to the park's website, "all of the park's resources are interwoven within the Samoan culture. In keeping with the meaning of the word Samoa—"sacred earth"—the park helps protect faʻasamoa—the customs, beliefs, and traditions of the 3,000-year-old Samoan culture," providing educational information about aspects of Sāmoan life and legends.[87]

But even as the National Parks System acknowledges the importance of Sāmoan culture and ties to the land, as Spence has stated, federally protected areas are often "pleasureground[s] for the benefit and enjoyment of the people," where

Americans "could go to share their national identity and an appreciation for natural beauty."[88] The National Park of American Sāmoa continues the historic pattern of U.S. nature management in indigenous spaces for Western purposes, which is ultimately a form of native dispossession. However, the terms of the limited leases in American Sāmoa also require the National Parks System to be respectful, accommodating, and sensitive to indigenous peoples and their protocols (aspects of *vā*) throughout all their actions and policies in this region. Ultimately, national park officials understand that the land and the water belong to the native population.

Post-Extension Thoughts

Several government staff who work on marine protection in American Sāmoa expressed how the negatively viewed sanctuary expansion has resulted in overall community hesitance to participate in federal or territorial ocean-zoning programs after 2012. Susan White, superintendent for the Pacific Reefs National Wildlife Refuge Complex, stated that "comments at public meetings and at regulations.gov have been overwhelmingly negative. Ultimately, the negative feelings in the community in regards to the sanctuary's proposed expansion puts all agencies and organizations conducting marine protection work in American Samoa in a bad light."[89] In particular, the National Parks Service and the local Department of Marine and Wildlife Resources have felt the repercussions of the poorly received sanctuary expansion process. To this day, some villagers act hesitantly, if not suspiciously, towards government-related environmental initiatives.

However, National Marine Sanctuary of American Sāmoa deputy superintendent Atuatasi Lelei Peau emphasized the many positive outcomes that developed since sanctuary expansion in 2012. He highlighted work with sanctuary communities to develop and promote ecotourism as a means to "build long lasting protection of sanctuary management areas, and generate job opportunities for village elderly and youth."[90] Peau believed both environmental protection and income opportunities provided by the sanctuary benefited local communities.

In 2012, the Tauese P. F. Sunia Ocean Center was opened. This state-of-the-art gateway for the National Marine Sanctuary of American Sāmoa "is a learning, training and discovery center that celebrates the importance of cultural and natural ocean resources in American Samoa. The exhibits address the value of coral reefs, understanding the ocean ecosystems, how our culture ties into the management of coral reefs, as well as the natural and humanogenic threats to our reefs."[91] There is a small meeting room, small exhibit area/conference room, and a main exhibit area. By 2015, more than twenty-eight thousand people visited this facility from all over American Sāmoa and the world.[92] Twenty-two percent have been local residents and science students. Cruise ships that land in American Sāmoa for the day visit this sanctuary headquarters as part of their land tour. Local schools and other institutions use the meeting facilities on a regular basis. Peau also discussed how the national marine sanctuary highlights Sāmoan folklore, traditional legends, and culture in interpretation about sanctuary management areas. In all these ways, the sanctuary has become a center for education, conference meetings, marine research, and tourism.

However, Peau also acknowledged that there is always room for improvement. "Of course, people always have a negative perspective of federal programs rather than assume these positions, we encourage individuals, communities and organizations to meet with us. By doing so, they gain understanding and awareness of the National Marine Sanctuary of American Sāmoa."[93] The deputy superintendent expressed how misperceptions among the community during expansion efforts were centered on taking rights to land and community use of ocean areas. With the exception of Fagatele Bay, which is the only no-take area in the six sites, all other areas allow some form of fishing. Peau also stated how the primary focus of the sanctuary program involved community livelihoods through stewardship

Today, most people do not talk much about the sanctuary, except in regards to their outreach and education programs. After the expansion, the Sanctuary Advisory Council continued to meet and sanctuary staff worked on several ocean research and awareness efforts. For example, in 2014 the sanctuary participated in the Office of National Marine Sanctuaries' call to action to encourage ocean recreation in marine sanctuaries.[94] This recommendation resulted in the "Get Into Your Sanctuary" project in 2015, where people were encouraged to visit federally protected areas. Students were particularly targeted through a photofishing tournament. To raise awareness on the types of fishing allowed in sanctuary waters, National Marine Sanctuary staff hosted fishing days in different parts of American Sāmoa in April and June 2015. They provided gear for those without rod and reels and taught some how to fish. At the end of the day, photos were taken and posted to Facebook. The kids who submitted the pictures with the most likes received ocean-related prizes such as snorkel gear or rods and reels. This project, which has continued every year through 2018, works to raise awareness of rules and regulations in the sanctuary and combat misconceptions about fishing bans in the region.

At the regional level, post-2012 NOAA programming has become more sensitive to indigenous processes and ways of communicating as a result of the blowback from the enlargement of National Marine Sanctuary of American Sāmoa. Bill Thomas, now the Senior Advisor for Islands, Indigenous and International Issues at NOAA's Office for Coastal Management, explained how anyone working in American Sāmoa needs "to invest in relationships. It's about two people getting to know each other, creating deep relationships."[95] NOAA Pacific Islands regional administrator Michael Tosatto also echoed this sentiment, stating that partnership is key and "a little bit of engagement helps a lot. You need frequent connections. It's really hard to service this territory."[96] Tosatto continued to explain how "it's hard to connect and get things done from Honolulu. It's better to be face-to-face than sending an email. At the very least make a phone call."[97] This regional level of federal administration is more aware than ever about the importance of substantial community contact, as well as continued and open communication.

In conclusion, the National Marine Sanctuary system was initially used by American Sāmoan U.S. colonials as a method to preserve their native marine resources. The successful federal protection of Fagatele Bay provided an example of overlapping local indigenous and federal imperial desires and goals. But once these waters were included in the sanctuary system, activities within this area became subject to specific U.S. government regulations and management long term, dispossessing natives of their ultimate sovereignty in these waters.

Through the years, native American Sāmoans have not hesitated to express either their support for or protest against federal policies. As long as this unincorporated territory remains part of the United States, NOAA should continue to figure out the most effective and ethical way to work with this colonized population. As Mitchell Thomashow urged, bioregional sensibility "requires multiple voices and interpretations," and is "necessarily open-ended and flexible."[98] In addition to involving the community and recording their feedback, a full engagement with issues raised is important. A balance of active education, direct communication, community involvement, *fa'a Sāmoa,* and *vā fealoa'i* are keys to the buy-in and support of indigenous groups for imperial policies. The next chapter discusses local efforts to develop ocean-use policy that acknowledge and integrate traditional native processes and practices with western scientific standards and policies.

CHAPTER 4

The Impact of the U.S. Imperial Grants System
on Indigenous Marine Programs

This chapter explores two American Sāmoa Government (ASG) marine programs centered on territorial waters from the shore to three miles out: the
Community-Based Fisheries Management Program and data collection on fishing
efforts in the region. While local staff members run and maintain these initiatives
on a daily basis, the U.S. federal government funds and regulates most projects.
The expectations attached to grant money has resulted in the incorporation of
western practices and standards into traditional indigenous marine protection
processes. This interweaving of local and U.S. procedures has resulted in greater
ocean health. However, nonnative influences have also shaped the priorities of
the Department of Marine and Wildlife Resources (DMWR), as well as the
methods used to access and monitor fisheries in the region. Traditional fishing
practices, as well as historic forms of indigenous marine knowledge and management, have been regulated and subsumed through this process.

Unlike the minimum wage issue discussed in chapter 2 and the expansion
of the marine sanctuary examined in chapter 3, DMWR has worked diligently
to incorporate cultural traditions like *vā fealoaʻi* (social respect) and *faʻa Sāmoa*
(the Sāmoan way of life) into their processes and polices throughout their programming, enabled by the unique political-legal situation of shared native and
federal governance over waters surrounding American Sāmoa. However, local
territorial staff are still under the overall supervision and management of the
U.S. federal government. Even though these initiatives acknowledge and use
indigenous customs to deeply engage with the community, the types of projects
that get funded by federal agencies encourage western forms of knowledge making, management, and fishing. Required applications, status reports, and strict
deadlines also result in tight U.S. government control over their annual, but
neither guaranteed nor permanent, contributions to approximately 30 percent
of the Gross Domestic Product of this unincorporated territory.[1] Such major

nonnative economic and bureaucratic influences on indigenous marine initiatives are rooted in American Sāmoans' U.S. colonial status as belonging to, but
not part of the United States. This current subjected indigenous situation, or
bioregion, like the other cases analyzed in this book, is generally invisible to the
U.S. public and the wider environmental movement across the globe. Ecology
programs should be conscientious of the impacts Western-based initiatives have
on native lives.

Historical Background

Since the formation of the ASG in 1977, there has always been a local unit dedicated to the growth of fisheries. This bureaucratic entity was first recommended
in 1961 by John C. Marr, director of the Hawaiʻi area Bureau of Commercial
Fisheries, which was the predecessor to the National Marine Fisheries Service.
Marr encouraged "the development of a government agency at the department
level to guide and assist fisheries development, with a priority on the introduction of a suitable small craft for nearshore fisheries."[2] This U.S. government push
to grow fisheries in American Sāmoa through increased fishing effort, as well as
the creation of a standardized bureaucracy occurred at the same time as President John F. Kennedy's initiatives to modernize American Sāmoa through the
creation of more infrastructure and the introduction of modern technologies in
the 1960s discussed in the introduction.

At first, the Office of Marine Resources was a division of the Governor's Office that also conducted ocean assessments.[3] In 1985, Marine Resources director
Ufagafa Ray Tulafono submitted a bill to the American Sāmoa legislature that
successfully changed the status of the office to an independent department. Over
the years, the DMWR has developed multiple projects to conserve and promote
positive ocean use in the region.[4] Overall, this agency aims "to preserve, protect,
perpetuate and manage the marine and wildlife resources within the Territory.
. . . [and] to implement such policy and purpose to the fullest extent."[5] One of
the most successful programs to date has been the Community-Based Fisheries
Management Program. This initiative created customized Village Marine Protected Areas (VMPAs) that effectively incorporated indigenous traditions with
Western ecological priorities. A more challenging but important department
program involved on-the-ground data collection of shore-based and offshore
fishing activities in local waters.

Both of these projects have been largely financed by the U.S. government
grants system. Specifically, the U.S. Federal Sport Fish Restoration Program

(SFR), a division of the U.S. Fish and Wildlife Service under the Department of the Interior, has funded most Department of Marine and Wildlife Resources initiatives. This set of federal monies is earmarked for fishery projects, boating access, and aquatic education run by fish and wildlife agencies in all states of the union, the District of Columbia, and insular areas. The Sport Fish Restoration Act of 1950 created the SFR "to restore and better manage America's declining fishery resources."[6] Capital for this program comes from taxes on fishing equipment, motorboat and small engine fuels, import duties, and interest from the Sport Fish Restoration and Boating Trust Fund. Then "grant funds are disbursed to states for approved grants up to 75% of the project costs and insular areas up to 100% of the project costs."[7] Overall, the Sport Fish Restoration Program promotes the growth and long-term success of fishing and boating through fees of Western-style rod and reel angling, as well as motorized vessels.

The SFR started funding fishery work in American Sāmoa in 1972 with an initial grant of $44,783. Grants have generally increased every year reaching the $100,000 level in 1981, the $500,000 mark in 1988, and the $1 million amount in 2007, staying above that amount through today. In 2018, the program apportioned a total of $351,917,483 throughout U.S. jurisdiction, with American Sāmoa receiving $1,091,964, the average amount that other insular territories received.[8] Every grant lasts one fiscal year. The financial viability of native American Sāmoa ocean programming is highly dependent on continued access to these monies.

Community-Based Fisheries Management Program

In 2000, the Community-Based Fisheries Management Program (CFMP) was created to encourage each village in American Sāmoa to develop their own marine protection policies. Villages volunteered to participate in this initiative and community members decided on ocean use policies through conventional indigenous social and political hierarchies in the region. The overall purpose of the CFMP is "to assist villages in managing and conserving their inshore fishery resources through a voluntary co-management with the government."[9] Allamander Amituana'i and Fatima Sauafea also discussed how the major goals of the project involved the improvement of shore-based fishery resources and the enhancement of village stewardship over marine resources.[10] Other aims of the program include an increase in fish population and general ocean health through community regulation of marine practices. Additionally, this initiative strengthens enforcement capabilities of the village community through territorial government involvement.

In the creation of a VMPA, proper *vā* (social relations) is incorporated. To participate in the program, a village must contact the director of the Department of Marine and Wildlife Resources, who schedules a first meeting. The ASG never initiates contact for the creation of a marine protected area. After an initial face-to-face conversation with a village representative to examine the community's potential to enforce a monitored zone, Community-Based Fisheries Management Program staff members present a program on the possibilities for VMPAs.[11]

Usually three groups are involved in this introductory and educational part of the process. First, the village *mātai,* who compose the village council, are approached. Then a presentation is made to the women's group, as well as the untitled men of the village *(aumaga).* Each of these sections of the community is provided information on the details of how to implement a marine management plan. The village council then picks representatives from the community to form a fishery advisory group. These individuals work together to develop the details of their specific VMPA. Each community creates their own unique regulations from a six-page menu of all potential rules provided by the DMWR. Once a plan is made, the details are presented to the village *mātai* for any feedback or changes. Afterwards, revisions are applied and approved by the village chief. Only after this extended and often slow process is completed will the department start to develop official policies for a specific VMPA.

Possible restrictions for Village Marine Protected Areas include limiting the type of fishing methods, fishing periods, and fishing locations allowed, regulating the amount, type, and/or size of fish that can be taken, as well as banning different types of fishing. According to Community-Based Fisheries Management Program project head Saumaniafaese Uikirifi, "they pick which they want to apply. In some villages spear fishing is illegal. In others it's legal but no flashlight allowed. Some villages only open on weekends or one Saturday throughout the whole year. You pick what you want. Having that menu helps a lot."[12] Ultimately, the high chief of the village makes the final decision to approve the parameters of their specific VMPA and signs an agreement with the Department of Marine and Wildlife Resources. Everyone in the community then usually follows the rules created through this process.

Once the VMPA is in place, "the village provides parallel support, voluntary participation in meetings, and voluntary commitment of labor for enforcement, monitoring, and review of activities. . . . DMWR in turn provides technical

FIGURE 4.01. Village Marine Protected Area sign. (Author photo.)

assistance and advice, workshops and trainings to enhance community understanding of how to manage and protect the marine environment, assistance with
development of the village Fisheries Management Plan and other forms of support to assist with proper implementation of the program."[13] This entire process
shows how the Department of Marine and Wildlife Resources and the community work together closely to develop marine policies that reflect the desires of the
village as a whole through the traditional Sāmoan consensus-building process.

In 2016, VMPAs included "approximately 25 percent of coral reef area in
the territory, with nearly 7 percent of coral reef area within no-take reserves."[14]
Twelve villages participated in this initiative: villages on the eastern side of Tutuila included Aoa, Alofau, Masausi, Amaua and Auto, Sailele, Aua, Vatia. Western villages involved in the Community-Based Fisheries Management Program
included Matuu-Faganeanea, Amanavae, Poloa, and Fagamalo. On the island of
Manuʻa, the villages of Siufaga and Luma also had a Village Marine Protected
Area. Additionally, the village of Alega on the eastern side had a protected area
that was monitored and enforced by the local bar owner. However the region was
not formally part of the Community-Based Fisheries Management Program.

Every month, program staff members try to make face-to-face contact with
people in participating villages on Tutuila. During these community visits, two
program members usually interview either the village mayor or someone else in
the community they see as they drive through the village in their government

vehicle. Staff members often visit on Wednesdays when many are outside for the weekly village cleanup day. These monthly check-ins are an opportunity to review the status of the VMPAs, as well as make inquiries on any violations or challenges to the program.

Initially these protected areas were not official law enforceable by the American Sāmoa Government. After a 2005 court case that questioned the ability of village residents in Fagamalo to enforce Community-Based Fisheries Management Program regulations, the Department of Marine and Wildlife Resources proposed legislation to give the agency the legal authority to police VMPAs.[15] This bill passed in 2008 with the intent "to ensure that the Territory and its surrounding waters are safe habitats for fish, shellfish and other marine life to exist and propagate for the continued use and enjoyment for the people of American Samoa, its future generations and visitors."[16] The priority of this legislation was to protect and hopefully increase sea life populations for future use.

Since the enforcement division of the Department of Marine and Wildlife Resources was short-staffed, as discussed in chapter 3, the agency deputized two representatives from each participating village to keep an eye out for violations of VMPAs in their community. These officials are usually the village mayor and the village policeman. Once appointed by the director of the DMWR, these individuals have the ability to write citations and notify the department of any infractions. Unfortunately, by the time an agency representative can get to the location of a violation, the lawbreaker is frequently gone.[17]

Every year, the program holds a daylong monitoring workshop to train and reward volunteer VMPA officers from each village. Deputies are either initiated or renewed for the year at this session. Deputies can change after every two-year term. According to Uikirifi, this event is a "way to acknowledge village mayors, acknowledge them for their hard work. Those active with us, we give them rod and reels. They are not being paid. They spend a lot of time helping us."[18] While the DMWR does not pay village mayors, the individuals do get a general stipend from the American Sāmoa Government that encourages them to cooperate with government projects like the Community-Based Fisheries Management Program. There are also awards for best VMPA officers. Additionally, this gathering gives the agency an opportunity to share their findings on local fishing statistics, a valued gesture in the community. Past presentations have included topics such as "The Coral Reefs of American Samoa" and the "Creation of a No-Take MPA in Fagamalo's Marine Managed Area."[19]

According to Uikirifi, at the beginning of the program villages wanted to close all access to water resources.[20] At the time, this policy was positively received by communities due to a sense of marine scarcity that was occurring throughout the region. According to a 2000 report by Peter Craig, "Harvested species such as giant clams and parrotfish are overfished, and there is heavy fishing pressure on surgeonfish. Fewer and/or smaller groupers, snappers, and jacks are seen. Most village fishers and elders believe that numbers of fish and shellfish have also declined. Also, in some areas, fish are now toxic with heavy metals."[21] Five years after the start of the Community-Based Fisheries Management Program, a NOAA report stated that "the biomass status of the American Samoa bottomfish complex in 2005 was healthy."[22] Such growth is a major goal of this program.

According to Mark Mitsuyasu, the Fisheries Program Officer for the Western Pacific Regional Fishery Management Council (Wespac), traditional marine management in Sāmoa would conserve during scarcity and use during abundance.[23] More fish in the water led some communities to end angling restrictions. In 2016, the villages of Amaua and Auto decided to change their policies and open up their VMPA to fishing. But any fisher was still expected to get permission from the village mayor to angle in community waters.

That same year, the village of Aoa started discussing the possibility of reclosing their marine protected area after being open for four years. Proponents believed overfishing was having an impact again and wanted to reinstate restrictions so the ocean could continue to grow to feed future generations. Opponents to a closed marine area wanted the opportunity to angle every day to provide for their families. The proposed compromise between these two sides involved a zoning proposal which would allow "one area to fish.... Even if whole area is closed, some methods could be used. No spearfishing, just rod and reel."[24] However, the proposal had to be approved by the village council and was predicted to take a long time to change because of competing views in the community. Due to the historically fluid and changeable nature of indigenous marine policies, the implementation of VMPAs also shifted depending on circumstances.

Tuipagai and Talouavu'u was another area that removed fishing restrictions after a period of ocean recovery time under a Village Protected Area. Sakaio Misifoa, chief of Tuipagai and Talouavu'u, believed this region had other protections to maintain the progress in marine health that occurred through the Community-Based Fisheries Management Program. He claimed that only two people in the village fished. Misifoa further explained how there was "only one way through [to the ocean] and there's a gate."[25] One has to contact the village mayor to enter that area and access the shoreline. Such detailed knowledge of ground-level realities in the community justified opening the waters at that particular point in time.

Uikirifi explained how sometimes "everything going on in village is stopped by one issue. When something like that happens, we leave them alone. They are still part of our program, we'll still work with them. It's not an issue between the program and village" but politics among the village leadership.[26] One time, a group of chiefs told program staff "to be patient and give us time" to sort out other village issues before moving forward.[27] Because *vā fealoaʻi* and the use of a measured and deliberate traditional decision-making process are highly valued in Sāmoan culture, Community-Based Fisheries Management Program staff abide by such requests, in turn gaining trust and respect from village members for following *faʻa Sāmoa*.

When a serious issue develops that impedes the program, Community-Based Fisheries Management Program staff members inform the department's director who talks to the high chiefs. If no agreement can be reached, the agency steps down from working directly with the village. For example, relations with Vatia deteriorated in 2016 and the Department of Marine and Wildlife Resources stopped actively working with the village. According to Uikirifi, "Our program can't provide enforcement right now, but that does not stop us from outreach, conducting awareness through media and youth groups" in that particular community.[28] Community-Based Fisheries Management Program staff members try to maintain some form of contact with any village they have had historic associations with, as long as that communication does not overstep appropriate informal interactions after official relations have stopped. But that outcome is the least desirable and the last resort for the department.

While Village Marine Protected Areas confer territorial government administrative control over local waters in participating villages, communities have the ability to remove restrictions or end the program at any point. As already described, a few villages have already exercised this right. Such fundamental native control of near-shore marine policies significantly differs from the overall federal authority over waters in the national marine sanctuary discussed in chapter 3.

In addition to the ability to end participation in VMPAs, communities can also choose not to participate at all. Of the seventy villages with a coastline in American Sāmoa, only twelve took part in the Community-Based Fisheries Management Program at the time of this study. The majority of villages have chosen not to get involved in the first fifteen years of the project's existence.

Many scholars have discussed the importance of using traditional ecological knowledge (TEK) for successful native conservation programs. Coined by scholars Fikret Berkes, Johan Colding, and Carl Folke, the concept of TEK is known as "a cumulative body of knowledge, practice, and belief, evolving by adaptive processes and handed down through generations by cultural transmission, about the relationship of living beings (including humans) with one another and with their environment."[29] Scholars of traditional ecological knowledge believe indigenous wisdom, particularly in relation to the local environment, can enlarge and enhance Western forms of scientific understanding, research processes, and ecological programs.

Bill Thomas, the Senior Advisor for Islands, Indigenous and International Issues at NOAA's Office for Coastal Management, also discussed how indigenous science involves "inter-generational longitudinal studies at the speed of nature and life. Indigenous management practices have their own checks and balances through village councils that go through a peer-review process. Indigenous science explains how native people came to be here today."[30] The Community-Based Fisheries Management Program in American Sāmoa acknowledges each village's historic right to make decisions on the use of their waters. In this way, traditional ecological knowledge is incorporated into federally funded initiatives to protect local marine resources for future use.

In Sāmoan culture, "ownership of the reefs and their resources was traditionally vested in the chiefs of each village in a like manner to land ownership. Seldom did a member of one village fish on the reefs or within sight of another village."[31] Historically, village boundaries extended into the ocean bordering communal land and out as far as the eye could see. Outsiders needed to ask permission from a leader in the village before fishing in the area.

Ocean-use regulations and conservation policies were also an integral part of ancient Sāmoan fishing and community customs, making contemporary marine protected areas a somewhat familiar concept. According to researcher Richard Wass, "Marine resources were controlled by a council of village chiefs who could institute any management measure they desired or felt necessary. A complex system of taboos reserving certain species and size of fish for the chiefs and restricting effort to certain seasons and locations arose which served to protect the reefs from over-exploitation."[32] American Sāmoans have a long tradition of marine monitoring, connected to their native decision-making structure, which could react to an environmental issue when necessary. Regular customs developed for fishing during specific times and places to avoid overfishing. Michael Tosatto, NOAA Pacific Islands Regional Office director discussed how "*tapu* (or prohibitions) was a sound process. There was a time and place for closed areas. Areas would open and close and there would be a penalty when someone went fishing during the closed period."[33] Through this native system, specific rules could also be implemented quickly and on a temporary basis.

However, traditional ocean-management systems are not the same as western-based marine protected areas. For example, political status and social hierarchies were reinforced by the designation of certain sea life for the exclusive use of village leaders. Peter Eves of the Department of Marine and Wildlife Resources' enforcement division explained how "sea turtles are for the high chief. If one gets caught, it automatically goes to the chief. Now a days, regulations protect them, even their eggs. [However,] Parts of shells are used for ornamental purposes. They [villagers] are still doing it now a days, but we are trying to stop it."[34] Traditional indigenous practices sometimes directly conflict with federal wildlife protection regulations.

Nevertheless, some members of the indigenous community continue to engage in these historical practices of gifting precious sea life to chiefs. According to Tui Atua, some "fish are honorifically referred to as *tamasoaalii* (meaning, the companion of the chief). . . . The use of honorifics denotes status and respect."[35] Offering certain animals to chiefs is part of sacred and central aspects of traditional Sāmoan practices. American Sāmoan U.S. colonials must negotiate between ancient native practices that are still revered today and the possibility of severe punishment based on western ecological standards.

Consequently, Department of Marine and Wildlife Resources enforcement staff members have to balance respect for their indigenous culture and implementing federal laws. Ultimately, Eves stated "no one is above the law" and government regulations work for the greater good.[36] This prioritization of U.S.-based laws shifts the standards of what types of marine practices are acceptable away from traditional indigenous uses towards Western perspectives on sea life preservation. Villagers are also subject to federal endangered species and U.S. wildlife protection laws for marine mammals and coral.[37] Penalties for violations can include fines up to $500 per violation and up to six months in jail.[38] The application of the strictest active law positions nonnative U.S. federal government environmental policies above native practices.

Another difference between indigenous and western marine protection programs involves ultimate authority over marine resources being vested in the territorial government. Instead of rules made and enforced by village chiefs, as well as community self-compliance, the Department of Marine and Wildlife Resources has had the power to enforce regulations in restricted ocean zones since 2008. While the village has to initiate the process to start an official Village Marine Protected Area, overall parameters, management, monitoring are verified and enacted through the American Sāmoan government that is overseen by the U.S. federal government. The DMWR implements a western-style bureaucratic system of rule, logging any activity related to VMPAs in written reports, requiring villages to document restricted zone–related bylaws, approving possible fishing methods from a six-page menu, as well as applying monetary fines and/or prison sentences for violations. This administration creates much written documentation, often in English, as well as Western cash and incarceration methods of punishment.

According to two DMWR staff members, despite the creation of marine protected areas with clear regulations and an enforcement system in place, there was still a lot of illegal fishing. These poachers "park their alia boats, then swim to protected areas" that are two hundred yards off the reef slope. Villagers always confront outsiders to find out what they are doing in their waters, as is tradition. Because each community has their own set of village bylaws, they also have their own justice process. For example, if someone from outside the village fishes at Amanave, it will take about a month to go through the village court."[39] Unsanctioned fishing in village waters has always occurred. However, the methods and authority to deter such activity have shifted with the Community-Based Fisheries Management Program. Some villages joined VMPAs because they did not want outsiders fishing in their waters. When one area closed, people sometimes moved to the next closest unprotected area to fish. This domino effect motivated other villages to join the program to safeguard their oceanfront as well. Village *mātai* set the initial rules and the Department of Marine and Wildlife Resources works in conjunction with village deputies to enforce the written rules of the protected area.

Mātai politics also complicate the creation, implementation, and maintenance of government programs. If one *mātai* does not like another *mātai,* he or she might oppose a project that her or his rival supports, like a Village Marine Protected Area. If the village council does not agree with the protected area, they might not enforce the regulations or punish rule violators. The DMWR has requested the Secretary of Sāmoan Affairs to talk to village mayors, "asking them to look out for us."[40] When an issue surfaces, the department director tries to contact the village's high chief. But if he or she is not responsive, this territorial government official approaches other chiefs. While ultimate legal enforcement lies with the territorial department, the village chiefs oversee both community cooperation and participation. The centrality of proper *vā* in the Sāmoan community adjudication process is why full village support for official marine protected areas is so important.

Another cultural challenge for the Community-Based Fisheries Management Program involves the fact that program staff consists mostly of younger men and women. In Sāmoan culture, it is not appropriate for younger untitled individuals to approach *mātai*. Uikirifi discussed how one key to the CFMP success involved contacting the right person in the correct way for the Sāmoan social-political hierarchy. This native structure led the program to target village mayors to serve as VMPA deputies. Without the buy-in of villagers through proper *vā fealoaʻi* and *faʻa Sāmoa,* the Department of Marine and Wildlife Resources would not have the community support to protect marine areas. DMWR staff members would also barely know about, let alone have a fighting chance to catch quickly mobile lawbreakers.

In 1978, R. E. Johannes, a leading scholar of community-based marine resource management (CBMRM) in the Pacific, believed indigenous-based ocean policies were in decline. The shift to canned and frozen food, as opposed to self-sufficient fishing resulted in less traditional forms of ocean use that he feared would be lost in the future.[41] But in 2012, he admitted that his earlier prediction was incorrect and that CBMRM was rebounding. According to Johannes, "factors contributing to the upsurge include a growing perception of scarcity, the re-strengthening of traditional village-based authority, and marine tenure by means of legal recognition and government support, better conservation education, increasingly effective assistance, and advice from regional and national governments and NGOs. Today's CBMRM is thus a form of cooperative management, but one in which the community still makes and acts upon most of the management decisions."[42] In American Sāmoa, local government support for an indigenous-based community approach to marine protected areas, local fears over fish scarcity, federal funding, as well as extensive education and outreach programs, have resulted in a successful Community-Based Fisheries Management Program in the region. The shared western and native authority created through the 1900 Deeds of Cession was exemplified by this DMWR initiative.

In fact, it seems as if Johannes's 1978 warning stimulated ocean policies administrators to focus on integrating traditional indigenous practices with modern management regulations. In 1982, Wass stated that "historically, the Samoans were very much aware of the need to conserve and protect their marine resources. . . . The acquisition of Western culture and its attendant legal system, however, has caused the disappearance of many of the traditional management methods in the more populated and developed areas. Modern fisheries management requires the resurrection and reinforcement of selected traditional practices and the blending of these with methods and regulations based on comprehensive resource inventories and scientific study."[43] While official village collaboration with government ocean programs did not occur consistently until the creation of the Community-Based Fisheries Management Program in 2000, the current success of the program demonstrates the importance of integrating traditional ecological knowledge-based marine management and appropriate *vā* into government projects in American Sāmoa.

Overall, many scholars have found that "community support for conservation plans consistently emerges as one of the most important factors in maintaining the plans' long-term efficacy, and programs that incorporate customary ecological management practices in their design draw more support from local peoples."[44] Greater native participation and compliance can develop from policies that coincide with established indigenous practices.

Jon Barnett and John Campbell also found that "a careful approach to community engagement is required, and that such approaches cannot be rushed, need to fully respect but not necessarily unquestioningly idealize local knowledges, and are best implemented by people from within the region who understand what it means to live and work in local communities."[45] Patient Community-Based Fisheries Management Program native staff members have been key to bridging indigenous and western approaches to marine management.

In general, the community responded positively to ocean policy management programs when they were actively involved in the process through traditional and familiar indigenous decision-making processes, demonstrating *vā fealoa'i* and *fa'a Sāmoa*. The village deputy for Aoa, La'aloa Taulaga wanted "to thank DMWR and the program for giving him the opportunity to work together."[46] He recalled how after the Village Marine Protected Area started in his community, the area's waters "saw a lot of fish, seasonal fish, mullet not seen before" the creation of a restricted fishing area.[47] Several villages found much value in participating in the Community-Based Fisheries Management Program. Misifoa also recounted how the VMPA was "a good tool to protect our resources, protect for the future. . . . The program was really helpful for the village. . . . more fish, more sharks seen in the area. Turtles are indicators of good and healthy reef, a lot of fish."[48] He also discussed the increase in seasonal fish.

Barnett and Campbell believed "both local and formal technical knowledge is required, as local knowledge may not always be technically correct; technical assessments are greatly enhanced by local input; and decision making based on either, rather than both, is less likely to be effective and locally legitimate."[49] In their research on climate change, a balance of native and Western knowledges and approaches has yielded more success for environmental programs throughout the South Pacific.

When Department of Marine and Wildlife Resources employees conducted biological water sampling and monitoring as part of their grant parameters, staff members gave community members masks and fins to assist in the process. Program members "try to seal a bond with the village. Every time they see us, they already know it's us. . . . when they see that we are trying to take more productive outreach. . . . They really supported us when we're going to the community. They call us because they think they see something."[50] Including villagers in scientific research efforts, as well as enforcement, increases goodwill and support for the Community-Based Fisheries Management Program. Many researchers have corroborated the idea that "because VMPAs are managed by local communities that have a direct interest in their success, compliance with bans on fishing is high within the village."[51] However, Western styles of fishing, data collection, and monitoring were also encouraged through the program's provision of nonnative equipment like rods and reels, as well as masks and fins. Such procedures and materials overshadow traditional native fishing practices and management processes.

The success of the Community-Based Fisheries Management Program can also be hampered by dependence on federal monies. One DMWR employee explained how "all water activities are on hold... Maybe by next month money will come in again. That's the problem. 90% of the department is funded by the federal government. That money goes to the American Sāmoa government, then the government to us. So if folks in government doesn't comply," we lose our funding.[52] That specific grant did not come through until 2017. Incorrectly filling out an application or filing a report late could immediately and indefinitely halt projects in the middle of activity.

Fulfilling all government grant requirements takes a lot of staff time. Each annual application for the Sport Fish Restoration Program requires ten different documents, including a project statement with fifteen subsections. Once monies are awarded, there are six areas of administrative requirements with 520 specific rules. In 2018, there were fourteen terms and conditions that had to be followed to maintain funding. All applications had to be written in English and submitted online.[53] The constant need to reapply for grants on a yearly basis and follow the many complicated, detailed, and frequently changing rules put most DMWR initiatives in a precarious position of never truly knowing how long grants will last, how much money they will receive, or how long a project can be sustained. A lack of U.S. federal funding could also impact the continued participation of local leaders who receive much-appreciated awards and equipment from the program. Such liminal status, which is typical for most U.S. government grant programs, compounded the already variable and unstable U.S.

colonial experiences of American Sāmoans that have been discussed throughout this book.

While the potentially intermittent nature of federal funding could hinder long-term scientific research projects, local management of marine protected areas based on traditional Sāmoan village structures and proper *vā* has continued in this bioregion, or totality of ecological and cultural relationships. The inconsistency of grant money was highly inconvenient but not detrimental to the effectiveness of the program. More funding could result in better program implementation, as shown in the next case study about data collection. However, because the Community-Based Fisheries Management Program is grounded in traditional marine protection and management processes, this initiative has been one of the most successful projects for the DMWR to date.

Data Collection

The topic of data collection and statistics often seems dry and boring. However, the numbers developed from these efforts are extremely critical to successfully accessing U.S. federal grant money. The stronger one's statistics are, the more convincing one's case can be when applying for government funding. American Sāmoa has generally suffered from either a lack of marine data or inconsistencies in the collection of that information. From a western empirical evidence-based perspective, this state of affairs negatively impacts the territorial government's ability to advocate and gain protection for specific access to their ancestral water resources.

After the Office of Marine Resources transitioned into an independent government department in 1985, Director Tulafono made data collection of contemporary local fishing practices in American Sāmoa a major goal.[54] There have been two main types of marine information gathered in the region: shore-based and offshore, or boat-based. The Department of Marine and Wildlife Resources website explained how "the term 'Shore based' covers all fishing activities from shore regardless of where the fishing occurred, inside or outside the reef or lagoon."[55] Any type of angling from a vessel is counted as offshore statistics. The agency's first data collection efforts occurred in 1972.[56] According to Craig Severance, Kitty Simonds, and Robert Franco, "the shoreline subsistence fishery on Tutuila Island was first examined in the late 1970's by Hill (1978) and Wass (1980)."[57] Catch data was first recorded along the south shore of Tutuila, where 35 percent of the people lived. Then, on a per capita basis, data collection was expanded to produce territorial catch statistics. The National Marine Fisheries

Service has monitored the distant-water fleet, or "fishing vessels operating out-side the waters surrounding their own territories," that delivers tuna to canneries in American Sāmoa, either directly or by contract through the Department of Marine and Wildlife Resources since 1963.[58]

By gathering fishery data, Tulafono hoped to provide "baseline data for deci-sion makers to help them with decision-making" on marine policies.[59] This sta-tistical foundation made the region's ocean activity legible to western scientists and grantors, but more detached from indigenous Sāmoan views of water man-agement. Starting off with no federal funding for this project and only eleven staff, most of who were administrative, Tulafono "hired two guys, put them on bus and gave them 50 cents. 25 cents to get in, catch the bus, and walk from village to village. Whatever village they were at by 3pm, they would stop and take the bus back. That's how we did data collection."[60] While staff members traveled by government vehicle in 2016, this catch and grab sampling process remained relatively similar for shore-based fishing data collected in the twenty-first century. However, scholars such as Raymond Buckley, David Itano, and Troy Buckley believed that "the data from 1975 to 1984 can only be used for qualitative comparisons within and between years due to the irregular sampling periods and the lack of standardization in fishing effort and data recording pro-cedures."[61] Data collection and survey information were not consistently done during this period, a problem for Western forms of data analysis.

According to Craig and his co-researchers, "With assistance from WPac-FIN [Western Pacific Fisheries Information Network] in the 1980s, the data collection program was significantly upgraded and expanded to provide bet-ter coverage and statistics for all local boat-based fisheries."[62] Once again, the Western emphasis on the importance of numbers drove the development of the data-collection process in American Sāmoa. WPacFIN is "a partnership be-tween NMFS [National Marine Fisheries Service] and fisheries management agencies in American Samoa, Commonwealth of the Northern Mariana Islands, Guam and Hawaii with the primary objective to monitor U.S. fisheries in the western and central Pacific Ocean. This group collects data on fishing activity and catch in local fisheries and issues reports of fisheries statistics to meet the needs of local and federal fisheries management organizations."[63] This entity supported the collection and dissemination of statistics on marine practices throughout the U.S. Pacific to help government agencies form regional policies. More specifically, WPacFIN provided funding to hire data transcribers, pur-chase data-related equipment like computers, and develop information summa-ries and reports. With such support, the type of marine data obtained for the area became more detailed, specific, and wide-ranging, including vessel-based activities. However, the written documentation of facts was again a foreign process for ocean management in American Sāmoa.

In 1990, the Department of Marine and Wildlife Resources received money from NOAA Fisheries to hire more people for data collection of shore-based fisheries. Researcher Bonnie Ponwith stated that "beginning in 1991, the fishery was again being monitored by a creel and participation survey, conducted 3 days a week, stratified by time of day and type of day (weekday/weekend)."[64] More staff meant more frequent data collection in more areas of the region at different times of day. By the mid-1990s, the DMWR acquired additional funding from NOAA Fisheries, through the Western Pacific Regional Fishery Management Council, for a vehicle and more staff to collect data and interview fishers. No longer relying on the local bus system, staff members could cover more ground in a day's work. In the early 2000s, the department had a "really good data collection system" that surveyed both offshore (boat) and shore-based fishing practices.[65] Through the years, the amount of dedicated employees, type of transportation used, and survey content all increased through growth in federal funding from the United States, solidifying the main purpose of data collection to provide statistics for federal policymaking, including the allotment of grant monies.

In 2015, the DMWR website stated that "collecting fishing method and effort data from roadside observation is an important monitoring system that will help us manage and preserve our marine resources."[66] In 2016, there were three main areas for information gathering on Tutuila. Surveyors visited each section once a day, Monday through Friday. The eastern section spanned from Lauli'i to Tula. The central portion ran from Aua to Nu'uuli. The western section went from Vaiola to Amanave. The survey team randomly picked a side in the morning and drove along the roads, stopping when they saw anyone fishing. Overall, shore-based data collectors tried to interview anglers after they got back from fishing. Surveyors wanted to "estimate catch and effort information and to monitor fishing activity of the shore-based fishery."[67] Staff members interviewed any fisher that was willing to speak with them by the side of road. Questions asked of these individuals included how long they have been fishing, what methods they used, what they caught, and how much of which species and which size they caught. Surveyors also kept count of how many fishers they saw in general. These kinds of data points helped to monitor potential overfishing of U.S.-designated endangered or vulnerable species.

Fishers were familiar with data collectors and could tell when government vehicles were approaching on the road from a distance. Many anglers would informally speak with staff. Priti E. Smith, a surveyor in 2015, stated how "we don't want to interrupt. If they are standing with a rod, we can just talk to them."[68] But some did not want to converse with survey staff. Sometimes fishers did not want to expose their fishing locations. Others wanted to hide illegal catch from surveyors, so left the shore and avoided staff as quickly as possible. Some anglers did not want to talk after returning from the water simply because they were tired.

According to the annual stock assessment of 2017, "the shore-based fishery is mostly gleaning for shellfish and octopus, rod and reel for groupers and jacks and spearfishing for surgeon and parrotfishes."[69] Smith provided more details, estimating that most shore-based fishers were between eighteen and twenty-eight years old, with the oldest fisher being around sixty years old. The majority of anglers were Sāmoan, but some were of other nonnative nationalities, like Korean. These fishers, mostly male, used rods, with a significant number also using spearfishing (mostly at night). Others used netting or sand mining to catch sea life. Women and children engaged in the traditional practice of hand mining, or gleaning of the reef. A few used indigenous woven fish traps called ʻenu.[70] Most of the anglers interviewed were fishing for whatever they could get. Some gave their catch to families in their villages, but most sold their catch on the side of the road. Some fished in their spare time while others fished for entertainment. Most people angled in the central area of the island, like Utulei, Fagaʻalu, and Lions Park, with smaller numbers on the east and west sides of Tutuila.[71] Most fishers also worked by themselves. Surveyors usually saw no more than thirty anglers during the course of one shift.

Due to lack of funding for additional vehicles, auto repairs, and more staff, there were not enough resources on-island to survey all locations at once or on other islands of American Sāmoa. Instead, the shore-based survey team worked under the assumption that if fishing was happening on one side of the island, it was happening at the same frequency in other parts of the island, known as a stratified, randomized data collection program. While data collection has occurred in Manuʻa and random information has been recorded for Ofu-Olosega and Tau, no long-term statistics have been gathered for these and other islands of the territory.

According to Marlowe Sabater, Wespac Fishery Analyst and former DMWR employee, the catch and grab sampling process "is the most fitting for the small island setting. The problem is the actual implementation is not good. There is no overtime pay, compensation time, hazard pay. U.S. Fish and Wildlife Sportfishing doesn't require high quality data."[72] Fishers often go out or return to shore very late at night or very early in the morning. Department of Marine and Wild-life Resources staff members adjust their work schedules according to that of the anglers. Sometimes staff members get calls late at night or early in the morning to survey an incoming boat. In addition to working out in the field in variable weather conditions and different times of day or night, surveyors also spend a lot of time converting the information they collected outside in handwritten notes into computerized data. It is difficult for employees to get additional compensation for working off-hours or providing extended time to complete their work, which could lead to inconsistent or insufficient reporting practices.

Another obstacle to strong data that Sabater identified involved maintaining a sufficient number of interviews on a weekly basis. If a staff member got sick or weather was not favorable, a survey trip could be canceled. If a vehicle got a flat tire, it could be out of commission for several weeks. Sabater also explained how there was "inconsistent implementation of the data standards and lack of follow up on the protocol established to ensure quality data comes out of the [Sport Fish Restoration] program."[73] In contrast to the detailed requirements for grant applications to obtain and maintain federal funding, SFR annual performance reports were only descriptive and did not require any technical information about data collected or the fishery. There was no obligation to record or provide comprehensive information. All of these factors contributed to less reliable data sets for the region, which were priorities for U.S. funding agencies.

NOAA acknowledged that scientific reports on American Sāmoa fisheries were "extremely limited" and reconstructions were "based on a number of un-confirmed critical assumptions and may not accurately reflect changes in fish catch over time."[74] Sabater and Carroll believed "there has been a good estimate of effort since it was easy to detect fishermen from the shore and determine what fishing gear they were using. However, catch data has only been sparse, as very few interviews have been conducted due to low participation in the fishery. Thus, only effort data (expressed in annual fisher hours) were used."[75] While fishing practices could be determined over time from existing data collection, catch information was still problematic. Others involved in American Sāmoa fisheries also acknowledged that many records have been lost or destroyed due to computer failures or storm damage over the years.[76] Despite these drawbacks, this data provided the best available information about shore-based fisheries in American Sāmoa.

Boat-based data collection about local small-scale indigenous commercial alia boats, while not 100 percent complete, did not face as many challenges as shore-based surveys. The Department of Marine and Wildlife Resources staff always knew how many alias were active because they could check the docks on a daily basis to see which boats were missing. These alia owners also had to apply for licenses. In 2015, the department reported twenty local commercial fishers. All boat owners were informed about catch regulations. Through the administration of these Western policies, DMWR staff had close contact with each boat owner.

Both shore-based and offshore methods to collect data use Western-made models and standards. While data collectors were respectful of fishers' time, this program did not include any specific Sāmoan cultural protocols, like *vā fealoa'i* or *fa'a Sāmoa* fostered in the Community-Based Fisheries Management Program. Information was gathered for Western purposes of bureaucratic cash-based grant funding for U.S. government programs. As Barnett and Campbell found in the Climate Witness project in Kabara, Fiji, "extensive use of participatory tools to elicit local knowledge and to engage communities in decision making" was key to this program's success.[77] In a similar way, open communication and integration of the community's conventional practices could enhance or increase the effectiveness of data collection in American Sāmoa.

From 2013 to 2015, alia owners frequently participated in a DMWR subsidy program. Every time an alia boat went out, the captain could voluntarily provide a float plan, which included what time they went out, how long they were out for, what type of fishing they used, specific catch times and locations, as well as the size of their catch and the species caught. In return, alia owners received a large discount on fuel for their next trip. In the summer of 2014, gas was about $4.28 a gallon. Through the Department of Marine and Wildlife Resources subsidy program, fishers only paid $1.75 a gallon for up to fifty gallons.[78] Local fisherman Alvin Mokoma confirmed that the subsidy provided fifty gallons of gas for $87.50.[79] The DMWR also gave alia owners safety equipment such as life jackets and ropes. This initiative offered Western materials and economic incentives for small artisanal fishers to provide fishing data. Mokoma stated that the gas subsidy and free safety gear was "very good. But it did not continue."[80] In 2016, this fisherman hoped the program would restart soon.

Two years after this program started, a DMWR employee questioned the effectiveness of the subsidy project. This individual stated that the discounted fuel "manipulates fishermen to go out more often. If they go more often, it doesn't change fish [data]. There is more fishing now, lesser catch."[81] A high number of boat launchings did not result in greater fish capture. This staff person also expressed how the subsidy program was supposed to be for commercial fishers.

Due to the high benefit of the gas subsidy, some casual boaters claimed to be alias. These vessels would go out for a few days but when they returned, the boat only brought in three fish. Such abuse of this program skewed the data on local commercial fishing.

While increases in grant money helped shore-based information collection by funding more employees and providing better transportation around Tutuila, subsidies for boat-based fishers incentivized the distortion of statistics collected. As evidenced by Mokoma, the financial assistance was a huge help. Monetary compensation could also encourage other alias to fish more frequently. However, to obtain reliable data on local alia commercial fishing efforts, DMWR staff might have benefited from differentiating the mostly subsistence and personal anglers from consistently commercial boat crews. Clear definitions from both territorial officials and federal fishery agencies could improve data collection moving forward. Consideration of ways to incorporate Sāmoan cultural protocols could also result in more ethical use, or at least more general community policing and pressure, for subsidy programs.

Scholar Damon Salesa recounted another failed government subsidy program in Western Sāmoa during New Zealand rule that tried to control a crop-destroying rhinoceros beetle. He explained how "the government put a bounty on the beetles, paying Samoans for each one they brought in. Samoans soon learned that it was more efficient to farm these beetles than to laboriously hunt for them, so began breeding them. New Zealand officials eventually learned what was going on, and so ended the bounty; having lost their value, the beetles were let go, making the problem worse."[82] While the colonial government thought cash incentives would motivate the native population to assist in combatting this pest, Sāmoans creatively figured out how extract the most benefit from the program in the most efficient manner possible. Native peoples completely ignored the underlying governmental reason for this environmental initiative to eliminate a pest. Salesa concluded that "many government efforts are not the best fit for" Sāmoan communities," especially if the goals do not coincide with or resonate with this indigenous group.[83] Cash incentives can encourage targeted groups to figure out how to best take advantage of a particular program, regardless of the government motives, goals, or purposes for a project.

However, such creative native misalignment with Western programs can also have negative impacts on the local community and bioregion. Having reliable data on fishing in American Sāmoa became extremely important in the Large Vessel Prohibited Area (LVPA) reduction discussed in chapter 1, with the ASG lawsuit claiming that the new regulation was based on inaccurate marine use information. Unable to provide solid fishing statistics, alia efforts and their voices were minimized in the discussions and decision-making process to reduce the LVPA.

Now that the consequences of questionable or insufficient data has been demonstrated with the LVPA exemption, fishers might be more motivated work with the Department of Marine and Wildlife Resources to improve this process. Perhaps making data collection a requirement to obtain a commercial fishing license could be a solution to strengthening future data sets. Subsidies could still be provided to encourage the development of local fisheries, but data should not be tied to that program. Providing strong information for policy development should not be seen as something voluntary. To improve statistical information and Western-based policy development in the future, commercial alias need to provide consistent and verifiable data to the DMWR, with or without subsidies.

However, this approach also needs to take into consideration the fact that the desire to quantify commercial fishing involved the initially nonnative desire to bolster Western-based for-profit angling practices that natives have adapted to and incorporated into their contemporary lives, not historic forms of fishing in American Sāmoa. The protection of alia fishing stems from the ultimate goals of U.S. colonization to bolster the tuna industry and make Sāmoans profitable through Western ideals of economic success. As scholar Allen Stayman has claimed, the federal government creates policies for U.S. territories with a focus on "targeted economic supports for the Islands."[84] Financial profitability has guided many programs supported by stateside bureaucrats, including the LVPA and alia program examined in chapter 1 and the labor exemptions discussed in chapter 2.

Ironically, more government money could result in better information gathering on fishing efforts in American Sāmoa. But without a good base of data, it is difficult to convince the government to provide additional funding to a seemingly insignificant or unknown population of fishers. Angling was not a tradition that most families on island engaged in significantly in the twenty-first century, as discussed in the introduction. Recently, local and federal entities have tried to reinvigorate fishing in American Sāmoa. Since 2012, the Western Pacific Regional Fisheries Management Council has funded an annual summer fishery management course for high school students. The National Marine Sanctuary of American Sāmoa has sponsored fishing lessons and angling trips, as well as provided youth with rod and reels. The Department of Marine and Wildlife Resources has also held fishing camps for youth.

Despite the hard work and energy put into each of these programs, fishing statistics have not gone up significantly. Government programs are judged for success on a yearly basis. But sometimes, programs take several years to show positive results. So far, federally funded local ocean-use programs have worked to protect fish species and ocean health, but have not dramatically increased the number of people fishing, especially by traditional methods.

Using information gathered from Department of Marine and Wildlife Resources employees, Wespac staff stated in the 2017 Annual Stock Assessment and Fishery Evaluation Report that "bottomfish fishery performance in American Samoa appeared to show a slight decrease... [while] Coral reef fishery performance appeared to have mixed trends."[85] While past research has shown a decrease in fishing effort in American Sāmoa, recent studies have shown either steady or mixed data on the amount of angling occurring in local waters. Inconsistent results in fishing effort amounts in American Sāmoa do not help the case of local agencies requesting new or continued funding for ocean-use programs.

A 2016 report by Levine and co-researchers found that 47 percent of the 448 people surveyed in fifteen villages on Tutuila, mostly in the central region, never went fishing. Fifty-six percent never gathered marine resources.[86] The rest of those surveyed engaged in these activities in the range of once or less in a month to four or more times a month. While about half of those surveyed engaged in some form of fishing, only 15 percent went out four times or more in a month. Levine and her colleagues found that "most American Samoans purchase seafood from stores or restaurants, with 65% of survey respondents listing this method as their first or second choice for obtaining seafood. Markets and roadside vendors (45%) and fish caught by household members (37%) are also common means for obtaining fish."[87] Fish consumption was generally high, but seafood self-sufficiency was relatively low. All of this data contributes to U.S. federal government decisions on funding for locally initiated marine programs.

Administratively and statistically successful programs regularly receive money, while projects deemed to have a lower impact due to small numbers often get supported in minor or temporary financial ways, if at all. Providing grants based on Western standards and statistics can subsume indigenous practices that cannot be solely justified through numbers. Even if only a handful of people engage in traditional fishing practices, that indigenous group still has a native right to continue their efforts. Such complicated issues of prioritization and support based on local versus federal ideals are the result of the unique shared governance established by the Deeds of Cession.

In conclusion, territorial government staff is constantly applying for federal grants to fund their community marine-related initiatives for this bioregion. However, this money tethers American Sāmoa staff to the guidelines and prerogatives of federal agencies that privilege increased western forms of fishing, boating, and commercialization, as well as overall national environmental priorities. Dependence on U.S. funding shapes the type, knowledge, and management of fishing in American Sāmoa, further distancing the colonized indigenous population from traditional native forms of angling and marine control.

Conclusion

Balancing the Tides highlights the often invisible and unique experiences that typify U.S. colonial status in American Sāmoa. This book shows the influence of U.S. involvement in this Pacific region in the contemporary period and provides a historical understanding of colonial relations between the U.S. federal government and American Sāmoans since the Second World War. While traditional indigenous culture and practices were able to continue after U.S. rule in 1900, as an unincorporated territory of the United States, the region remains under the ultimate control and authority of Washington, D.C. To be viable in the long term and gain community support, local as well as federal policies and regulations must abide by U.S. laws and acknowledge American Sāmoan customs. This work demonstrates both moments of feasible programming and less generative federal and territorial initiatives, as well as the diversity of ideas about marine practices among the indigenous group in the specific bioregion of American Sāmoa.

All four chapters explain how since World War II, the U.S. government has increased involvement and command over economic and environmental policies in American Sāmoa, promoting Western standards, ideals, and processes. The National Oceanic and Atmospheric Administration under the U.S. Department of Commerce, the Department of U.S. Fish and Wildlife as a division of the U.S. Department of Interior, and the U.S. Congress form the basis of the modern administrative colonial state in American Sāmoa. In this setting, state simplification encourages officials to standardize and rationalize "local practices to make them more comprehensible—and ultimately more controllable—by government agencies."[1] Angling practices in American Sāmoa were standardized according to Western forms of fishing technology and a cash-based wage labor commercial fishing industry in chapters 1 and 2. Nonnative scientific principles and bureaucratic government priorities greatly shaped marine practices in chapters 3 and 4. Into the twenty-first century, the U.S. federal government has continued and expanded colonial regulation and authority over the waters of their multiple territories in the U.S. Pacific through the expansion of National Marine Sanctuary of American Sāmoa in 2012 and the development of National Marine Monuments in Hawai'i in 2006. Marine monuments were also created in American Sāmoa and the Marianas Trench, as well as the U.S.-controlled central Pacific islands and atolls of Howland, Baker, Jarvis, Wake, Johnston Atoll, Palmyra Atolls, and Kingman Reef in 2009. The Central Pacific Marine National Monuments were also expanded in 2014.

Another key aspect to the success of marine programs in American Sāmoa revolves around understanding and incorporating aspects of *fa'a Sāmoa* (the Sāmoan way of life). The inclusion of Sāmoan traditions and beliefs, such as *vā* (social relations) and *vā fealoa'i* (social respect), in the process of creating rules and procedures have enabled the successful implementation of American-style industry, government, and environmental expectations and policies in the region. Acknowledging and accommodating *fa'a Sāmoa* practices of attending major *'āiga* events during the workweek, such as funerals, deterred cannery workers from protesting against low wages in chapter 2. Engagement of native groups in the decision-making process increased support for projects such as the establishment of the nation marine sanctuary in chapter 3 and the creation of Village Marine Protected Areas (VMPAs) in chapter 4. In addition to integrating aspects of indigenous customs into initiatives, more effective arrangements incorporated community feedback, like the Community-Based Fisheries Management Program in chapter 4. Sustainable policies also developed when the interests of the federal government and native peoples coincided, such as those of American Sāmoa large-vessel longline owners and the Western Pacific Regional Fishery Management Council (Wespac) in chapter 1. When both sides agreed on a need, like the creation of the Fagatele Bay National Marine Sanctuary in chapter 3, high support was provided. However, this balance was not always easy to achieve due to multiple viewpoints and goals among indigenous groups and government agencies.

As all four chapters reveal, sometimes the priorities and desires of one group of American Sāmoans conflicted with the needs and realities of another. In multiple cases of U.S. conservation projects taking control of native lands, "wage labor pitted residents against not only outside conservationists but also against members of their own communities."[2] Such disagreements over who should benefit from the western cash-based economy and how surfaced in the divide among alia versus large-vessel longliner owners in chapter 1, the debates over minimum wage in chapter 2, and territorial government employees who work closely with

U.S. federal government agencies and their western priorities versus the expectations of village communities in chapters 3 and 4. A multitude of strong and differential positions have developed in the U.S. colonial American Sāmoan community in regards to marine policies.

Into the twenty-first century, the U.S. federal government has been less accommodating of native requests, subsuming indigenous practices and approaches to continental U.S. priorities and agendas, as seen in all four chapters. The reduction of the Large Vessel Prohibited Area (LVPA) in chapter 1, minimum wage increases in chapter 2, the expansion of the marine sanctuary in chapter 3, and the focus on bureaucratic goals for federal funding in chapter 4 demonstrate just a handful of examples where U.S. government motivations overrode native interests in water-related issues.

Many of the regulations over Sāmoan waters were also created to prevent outsiders from spoiling the local environment, particularly through overfishing. However, blanket rules disproportionately impact native peoples, because this group is more likely to be caught in minor, casual, and/or traditional practices that breach federal laws and garner major fines and punishments, such as the LVPA as well as National Marine Sanctuary and VMPA rules. Outside fishers who violate rules often avoid getting caught because this group angles in the region temporarily and can leave quickly with high-speed vessels and technology to spot monitors well ahead of time.

American Sāmoans frequently raise concerns over encroachments on indigenous control over land and water, especially by the U.S. government. Chapters 1, 2, and 3 reveal how ignoring the claims of community members resulted in native protests, justified by the cultural protection guarantees provided in the Deeds of Cession. When American Sāmoans felt the ancestral rights of their *'āiga* were being infringed upon, or they were being forced into certain unacceptable situations, members of the group often took offense to such actions and any related projects. American Sāmoans did not hesitate to speak out against federal agencies like the Western Pacific Regional Fishery Management Council in chapter 1, the U.S. Congress in chapter 2, and the Office of National Marine Sanctuaries in chapter 3. And like with the Cherokee diaspora that historian Gregory Smithers studied, this variety of native American Sāmoan protests and resistances demonstrated an "understanding of how colonialism had affected, and continued to affect" their lives.[3] This Pacific group, like other indigenous peoples, has responded in creative, active, and critical ways to colonial government programs.

In fact, scholar Damon Salesa emphasized the internal and external benefits of Sāmoan creativity in western contexts. He explained how "Pacific people have crafted vibrant and dynamic communities, effectively at lower cost, with less capital, and with limited government assistance.[4] This type of Pacific placemaking identified by Salesa centers around family.[5] As he explained, "Pacific people prioritise investing their social, political and cultural energy, as well as their money and capital, into their families."[6] As a result of such a focus, "fully a quarter of Pacific people rated themselves at the highest level of life satisfaction. . . . Life is tough, but for Pacific people life is also good."[7] Despite occupying the lowest economic and social rungs of colonized societies, Pacific Islanders express high levels of personal comfort and fulfillment. What lessons can we all learn from *fa'a Sāmoa* and *vā* that can lead to more community-oriented fulfillment and move us beyond Western-based standards of achievement through individual materialism? How does one's outlook on life change when a balance in all relationships is the highest priority?

Salesa also discussed how "Pacific people live highly connected and mobile lives, lives that are able to shift people, resources, capital and labour across national boundaries: whether to find capital to build a village church or school, to finance a relative's small business, to participate in the new programmes of seasonal labour migration, or to utilise dual citizenship to realise advantages in the transnational or even global labour markets."[8] While out-migration has its negative consequences on villages in terms of depopulation and absences from important *'āiga* events, continued connectedness across the globe can also augment the social, economic, cultural, and political power of individuals as part of a larger family diaspora. Regardless of where they are physically located across the globe and despite living in lower economic and political scales created and used by Westerners, extended family members can and do rally together and support someone financially and emotionally, almost instantly through internet money-sharing applications and social media.

Another way Sāmoans have melded *fa'a Sāmoa* with contemporary life is to leverage the internet and social media to strengthen their extended family connections across the world. For Salesa, "a key advantage of the internet for Pacific people and communities was that it seemed to obliterate distance, allowing potent Pacific abilities and values of family and relationships to be newly empowered."[9] While some in American Sāmoa have bemoaned the high influence of the internet and social media over the youth population, this technology also has great potential for organizing within the Sāmoan community, as well as building coalitions across similarly subjected groups.

Even without the help of today's communications technology, the formation of the Pacific Panthers in New Zealand in the 1970s showed how strong desires and motivations have existed to connect colonized groups. This organization expanded the definition of Pacific people to include Maori, Sāmoans, Tongans, and South Asians (to name a few) to fight for social justice programs and policies.[10] Despite (or perhaps due to) Americanization and diasporic migration dispersal for economic purposes, different U.S. colonial groups from various locations can draw from their cultural and social values of community to creatively survive, connect, resist, and even thrive in colonial circumstances.

In contrast, American notions of protecting the environment involve Western-based ideas of federal government control, efficiency, appropriate use, and sometimes profitability. Such central elements of the environmental bureaucratic administrations across U.S. jurisdiction can be seen in the reduction of the LVPA in chapter 1, the imposition of minimum wage increases in chapter 2, the expansion of the marine sanctuary in chapter 3, and priorities for federal funding and data collection in chapter 4. In contrast, *fa'a Sāmoa* has always focused on the support and augmentation of the family and the community. Stewardship of the people and the environment, or total bioregion, go hand in hand in American Sāmoan traditional ecological knowledge and indigenous marine management systems, as discussed in chapters 1, 3, and 4.

This contrast in approach has resulted in native peoples being historically frustrated with simplistic government regulatory regimes that do not take their wants and needs into account. Such frustration is shared across communities taken over by federal conservation programs. As an Adirondack resident stated, "The laws were made by men who don't know what we need here. Give us some laws we can take care of and we'll put them through."[11] In a similar way, American Sāmoans have expressed throughout this book their desires to manage and control policies and regulations over the use of their ancestral native waters. The local indigenous population wanted a say in the reduction of the LVPA in chapter 1, minimum wage increases in chapter 2, the expansion of the marine sanctuary in chapter 3, and VMPAs in chapter 4.

The negative reception of indigenous American Sāmoans to Western-based environmental ocean-use and economic policies in the late twentieth century and the early twenty-first century requires an uncomfortable self-confrontation for contemporary Americans. Perhaps the labor and green movement, as well as pro-ecology programs, are not universally helpful, ethical, or just. Maybe a blanket application of scientifically based environmental and labor policies, such as marine protection and minimum wage, are not always appropriate or needed, especially in the context of indigenous rights.

Unfortunately, the voices of American Sāmoans have increasingly not been validated by the policies and actions of U.S. government officials. Twenty-first-century labor and environmental guidelines established in Washington, D.C., often ignore the ground-level reality and daily needs of this indigenous group. This work connects this little known but multidimensional and historic U.S. colonial relationship to familiar continental U.S. issues, like minimum wage and environmental protections, to make visible the significant implications that national ocean-use policies have on both native American Sāmoans and those living in states of the union. To borrow another phrase from Smithers, the story of American Sāmoan experiences is both uniquely American Sāmoan and commonly human.[12]

Balancing the Tides also uses the past to help understand larger contemporary economic and social changes throughout the U.S. Pacific. Other island territories in the region, such as the Commonwealth of the Northern Mariana Islands and Guam, face issues that are similar in American Sāmoa, where U.S. federal funding and presence is also strong and highly influential in their political, financial, environmental, and military structures. Ultimately, the United States wields control over marine practices in all of these areas. American Sāmoans, other Pacific Islanders, and the U.S. federal government need to continue to find more ways to work together in developing collaborative ocean-use programs that also take indigenous rights into serious consideration.

As Jon Barnett and John Campbell found in their research on the South Pacific, ecology programs and policies could benefit from making four specific shifts "in scale—from regional to local; in focus—from impact assessments to adaptation; in nature—from processes driven by experts from outside of the region, to processes driven by people within the region; and in cost—from expensive big projects to relatively cheaper smaller ones."[13] Recentering initiatives around the needs of the ground-level community, figuring out realistic actions for these people to take, empowering native groups to develop their own plans, and focusing on more manageable and attainable projects could all be positive steps moving forward.

Overall, this work places the histories of island territories and possessions at the center of U.S. history narratives. While physically on the periphery of the U.S. empire, the often-invisible experiences of U.S. colonials are critical to understanding U.S. government expansion, development, and policies beyond its official borders over the course of this nation's history. This work contributes to an examination of the in-between, or liminal, encounters of these U.S. colonials, who are neither full-fledged citizens nor foreigners. Subject to U.S. federal laws on a variable basis, U.S. colonials sometimes gain access to unique situations. Other times these imperial wards are disadvantaged by their vague political-legal status, having no independent mechanism to protect their native interests. The combination of U.S. colonial status and indigenous rights complicates marine management throughout the U.S. Pacific.

As Sāmoan scholar Albert Wendt has encouraged, "Our quest should not be for a revival of our past cultures but for the creation of new cultures which are free of the taint of colonialism and based firmly on our own pasts. The quest should be for a new Oceania."[14] Sometimes Western ideas and policies towards marine management coincide with indigenous Sāmoan practices and principles. Other times these two systems conflict. Since "sustainability is a mutual enterprise that pertains as much to human social well-being as to the health of the physical world," figuring out an appropriate balance between the two sides of an indefinite colonial relationship remains the question facing American Sāmoans and the U.S. federal government today.[15] Can new balances in relationships be created?

Such a quandary will continue to be an important issue that the general U.S. public must become aware of and form opinions about for as long as American Sāmoa is an unincorporated territory of the United States. As Byron Caminero-Santangelo discussed, "Any final representation of reality will be impossible, more narrative and dialogue will always be needed" for marine practices and policies in the bioregion of American Sāmoa and beyond.[16] Western-based environmental and labor movements must also acknowledge the impact that their rational and scientific-based initiatives have on indigenous rights and the daily lives of native peoples. Ecological and economic projects should always consider indigenous issues in the development and implementation of both short-term and long-term programs. Native customs, such as *fa'a Sāmoa* and *vā,* can also provide valuable lessons for all inhabitants of the world to learn how to be a more connected and more considerate family of concerned and active global citizens.

Notes

Introduction

1 For a detailed definition and case studies about U.S. colonials, see JoAnna Poblete, *Islanders in the Empire: Filipino and Puerto Rican Laborers in Hawai'i* (Urbana: University of Illinois Press, 2014).

2 See Noenoe Silva, *Aloha Betrayed: Native Hawaiian Resistance to American Colonialism* (Durham, NC: Duke University Press, 2004).

3 See Paul Kramer, *The Blood of Government: Race, Empire, the United States, & the Philippines* (Chapel Hill: University of North Carolina Press, 2006).

4 See Julian Go, *American Empire and the Politics of Meaning: Elite Political Cultures in the Philippines and Puerto Rico during U.S. Colonialism* (Durham, NC: Duke University Press, 2008).

5 See Timothy P. Maga, *Defending Paradise: The United States and Guam, 1898-1950* (New York: Garland Publishing, 1998).

6 "U.S. Department of Commerce, Final Environmental Impact Statement and Management Plan for the Proposed Fagatele Bay National Marine Sanctuary," 26, accessed September 10, 2015, http://americansamoa.noaa.gov/pdfs/fbeis_84ab.pdf.

7 Elizabeth M. DeLoughrey and George B. Handley, *Postcolonial Ecologies: Literatures of the Environment* (New York: Oxford University Press, 2011), 12.

8 Sasha Davis, *The Empires' Edge: Militarization, Resistance, and Transcending Hegemony in the Pacific* (Athens: University of Georgia Press, 2015).

9 Mansel G. Blackford, *Making Seafood Sustainable: American Experiences in Global Perspective* (Philadelphia: University of Pennsylvania Press, 2012), 122, 132.

10 Cluny Macpherson and La'avasa Macpherson, *The Warm Winds of Change: Globalisation in Contemporary Samoa* (Chicago: Auckland University Press, 2010), 9.

11 DeLoughrey and Handley, *Postcolonial Ecologies*, 16.

12 Karl Jacoby, *Crimes Against Nature: Squatters, Poachers, Thieves, and the Hidden History of American Conservation* (Berkley: University of California Press, 2003), 151.

13 Amerika Samoa Humanities Council, *A History of American Samoa* (Honolulu: Bess Press, 2009), 25. See also Geoffrey Irwin, "Voyaging and Settlement," in *Vaka Moana: Voyages of the Ancestors,* ed. K. R. Howe (Auckland: Auckland Museum/David Bateman, 2006), 54-99.

14 *A History of American Samoa*, 26.

15 For an overview of information on the Tongan empire and the origins of the Lapita people from Melanesia, see Glenn Petersen, "Indigenous Island Empires: Yap and Tonga Considered," *The Journal of Pacific History* 35 (2000): 6-27.

16 *A History of American Samoa*, 52.

17 *A History of American Samoa*, 74.

18 *A History of American Samoa*, 74-76. Pages 76 to 84 describe early missionary work in detail.

19 On global empire building in the Pacific and beyond, see Nicholas Thomas, *Islanders: The Pacific in the Age of Empire* (New Haven: Yale University Press, 2012). Matthew Guterl and Christine Skwiot, "Atlantic and Pacific Crossings: Race, Empire, and 'The Labor Problem' in the Late Nineteenth Century," *Radical History Review*, 91 (2005): 40-61; and Marilyn Lake and Henry Reynolds, *Drawing the Global Colour Line: White Men's Countries and the International Challenge of Racial Equality* (Cambridge: Cambridge University Press, 2008).

20 See Kealani R. Cook, "Kahiki: Native Hawaiian Relationships with Other Pacific Islanders 1850-1915" (PhD diss., University of Michigan, 2011), chapter 5.

21 *A History of American Samoa*, 134. For more on Western Sāmoan history, see Frederic M. Miller, Agnes F. Vandome, and John McBrewster, *History of Samoa* (Mauritius: Alphascript Publishers, 2010).

22 Edwin W. Gurr, "Instrument of Cession: Chiefs of Tutuila to United States Government," Navy Department Bureau of Yards and Docks, Navy Department Secretary's Office, Deed of Cession 1, accessed September 7, 2016, http://www.asbar.org/images/unpublished_cases/cession1.pdf.

23 Deed of Cession 1, 2-3.

24 Deed of Cession 2, 2, accessed September 7, 2015, http://www.asbar.org/images/unpublished_cases/cession2.pdf.

25 Deed of Cession 2, 3.

26 Deed of Cession 2, 3.

27 For information on the contradiction of the impersonal and individualistic Western rational-legal system versus Sāmoan communal principles of organization, see Malama Meleisea, *The making of modern Samoa: traditional authority and colonial administration in the history of Western Samoa* (Suva, Fiji: Institute of Pacific Studies of the University of the South Pacific, 1987). For more information on unincorporated territory status, see Kal Raustiala, *Does the Constitution Follow the Flag?: The Evolution of Territoriality in American Law* (Cambridge: Oxford University Press, 2011); Arnold Leibowitz, *Defining Status: A Comprehensive Analysis of U.S. Territorial Policy* (CreateSpace Independent Publishing Platform, 2014); Ediberto Roman, *The Other American Colonies: An International and Constitutional Law Examination of the United States' Nineteenth and Twentieth Century Island Conquests* (Durham: Carolina Academic Press, 2006); Adriel I. Cepeda Derieux, "A Most Insular Minority: Reconsidering Judicial Deference to Unequal Treatment in Light of Puerto Rico's Political Process Failure,"

Columbia Law Review 110, no. 3 (2010): 797-839; and Gerald Neuman and Tomiko Brown-Nagin, *Reconsidering the Insular Cases: The Past and Future of the American Empire* (Cambridge, MA: Human Rights Program, Harvard Law School, 2015).

28 For more information on the coaling station, see Holger Droessler, *"Islands of Labor: Community, Conflict, and Resistance in Colonial Samoa, 1889-1919"* (PhD diss., Harvard University, 2015).

29 Joseph Kennedy, *The Tropical Frontier: America's South Sea Colony* (Mangilao, Guam: Micronesia Area Research Center, 2009), 64-65.

30 For more on the U.S.-Philippine War, see Angel Shaw and Luis Velasco, *Vestiges of War: The Philippine-American War and the Aftermath of An Imperial Dream, 1899-1999* (New York: New York University Press, 2002).

31 Christina Duffy Burnett, "The Edges of Empire and the Limits of Sovereignty: American Guano Islands," *American Quarterly* 57, no. 3 (September 2005): 781, 798.

32 *A History of American Samoa*, 91.

33 Treaties, Cessions, and Federal Laws, American Samoan Bar Association, accessed June 14, 2018, http://www.asbar.org/archive/Newcode/treaties.htm#two.

34 Joseph Kennedy, *The Tropical Frontier: America's South Sea Colony* (Mangilao, Guam: Micronesia Area Research Center, 2009), 97.

35 For an in-depth discussion of the history of legal protests under U.S. rule, see Kirisitina Sailiata, "The Samoan Cause: Colonialism, Culture, and the Rule of Law" (PhD Diss. University of Michigan, 2014).

36 Gordon R. Lewthwaite, Christiane Mainzer, and Patrick J. Holland, "From Polynesia to California: Samoan Migration and Its Sequel," *The Journal of Pacific History* 8 (1973): 133-157.

37 Fa'anofo Lisaclaire Uperesa, "New Fields of Labor: Football and Colonial Political Economies in American Samoa," In *Formations of United States Colonialism,* ed. Alyosha Goldstein, 207-232 (Durham, NC: Duke University Press, 2014), 227.

38 "Table 7.19. Analysis of Arrivals and Departures by Purpose: 2006 to 2016," *Statistical Yearbook 2016*, American Sāmoa Government, Department of Commerce, 109, accessed June 20, 2018, http://doc.as.gov/wp-content/uploads/2011/06/American-Samoa-Statistical-Yearbook-2016.pdf.

39 Most studies of Migration, Remittances, Aid and Bureaucracy (MIRAB) economies do not include American Sāmoa due to its status as a territory of the United States. While remittances are important for the American Sāmoan economy, this economic system plays a more important role in other noncolonized Pacific Island nations. For more information on MIRAB economies in the Pacific, see Jon Fraenkel, "Beyond MIRAB: Do aid and remittances crowd out export growth in Pacific microeconomies?," *Asia Pacific Viewpoint* 47, no. 1 (April 2006): 15-30.

40 Clarence Hall, "Samoa: America's Shame in the South Pacific," *Readers Digest*, July 1961, 111-116.

41 Bureau of Economic Analysis, U.S. Department of Commerce, "Gross Domestic Product for American Samoa Increase for the Second Year in a Row," Table 2.2 Value

Added by Industry as a Percentage of GDP, August 8, 2016, 10, accessed July 31, 2017, https://www.bea.gov/newsreleases/general/terr/2016/asgdp_080816.pdf.

42 Sailiata, "The Samoan Cause," 2.

43 For more information, see Sailiata, "The Samoan Cause," Kennedy, *The Tropical Frontier*, chapter 6; and Holger Droessler, "Whose Pacific? U.S. Security Interests in American Samoa from the Age of Empire to the Pacific Pivot," *Pacific Asia Inquiry*, 4 (Fall 2013): 62.

44 Encyclopedia Britannica, "American Samoa, Constitutional Framework," accessed November 11, 2015, http://www.britannica.com/place/American-Samoa#ref996263. See also *A History of American Samoa*, 261; and Fofō I. F. Sunia, *The Story of the Legislature of American Samoa: In Commemoration of the Golden Jubilee 1948—1998* (Auckland: GP Print of New Zealand, 1998).

45 *A History of American Samoa*, 303-304.

46 "Economic Development," *American Samoa Annual Report to the Secretary of the Interior for Fiscal Year 1975*, The Office of Samoan Information, Pago Pago, 1975, 26.

47 Economic Development," *American Samoa Annual Report to the Secretary of the Interior for Fiscal Year 1976*, The Office of Samoan Information, Pago Pago, 1976, 34.

48 For more on American Sāmoa's role in World War II, see Kennedy, *The Tropical Frontier*, chapter 7.

49 *A History of American Samoa*, 245.

50 Va'amua Henry Sesepasara, interview by author, June 4, 2015, Utueli, American Sāmoa.

51 Nate Ilaoa, interview by author, June 3, 2015, Fagatogo, American Sāmoa.

52 Alfred Judd, "1926 Expanded Notes on the Ethnology of American Samoa," Bishop Museum Archives, Honolulu, Hawai'i.

53 Frank J. Drees, "Samoa and Her People: A group of anecdotes about my travels by longboat and trail over a large part of the Islands of Samoa."

54 "Population and Housing Profile: 2000 Geography: American Samoa," United States Census Bureau, 3-4, accessed July 19, 2016, https://www.census.gov/census2000/pdf/amsamstatelevel.pdf.

55 A. Levine, M. Dillard, J. Loerzel, and P. Edwards, *National Coral Reef Monitoring Program Socioeconomic Monitoring Component: Summary Findings for American Samoa, 2014*, NOAA Technical Memorandum CRCP 24, NOAA Coral Reef Conservation Program, Silver Springs, MD, March 2016, 13 and 14, accessed July 27, 2017, https://docs.lib.noaa.gov/noaa_documents/NOS/CRCP/TM_CRCP/TM_CRCP_24.pdf.

56 For a discussion of the impact of globalization on Sāmoan society in independent Sāmoa, see Macpherson and Macpherson, *The Warm Winds of Change*.

57 For examples of the allure of U.S. consumer culture, see Lizabeth Cohen, *A Consumers' Republic: The Politics of Mass Consumption in Postwar America* (New York: Vintage Books, 2004); Gary S. Cross, *An All-Consuming Century: Why Commercialism Won in Modern America* (New York: Columbia University Press, 2000); and Victoria De Grazia, *Irresistible Empire: America's Advance Through Twentieth-Century Europe* (Cambridge: Belknap Press, 2006).

58 Marlowe Sabater, interview by author, August 10, 2016, Honolulu, Hawaiʻi.

59 Alvin "Eo" Mokoma, interview by author, June 21, 2016, Pago Pago, American Sāmoa; Mika Letuane, interview by author, June 24, 2016, Fagatogo, American Sāmoa; Mathaew Atafua, interview by author, June 22, 2016, Nuʻuuli, American Sāmoa; Chief Faimealelei/Tauese Apelu Soʻoaʻmalelagi, interview by author, June 22, 2016, Nuʻuuli, American Sāmoa; and Tasele Masunu, interview by author, June 22, 2016, Nuʻuuli, American Sāmoa.

60 On importance of water over land, see Epeli Hauʻofa, *We Are the Ocean: Selected Works* (Honolulu: University of Hawaiʻi Press, 2008); and Alice Te Punga Somerville, *Once Were Pacific: Maori Connections to Oceania* (Minneapolis: University of Minnesota Press, 2012).

61 "About Your Sanctuary," National Oceanic & Atmospheric Administration, accessed September 23, 2015, http://americansamoa.noaa.gov/about/welcome.html.

62 Sailiata, "A Samoan Cause." The other works in order mentioned are J. A. C. Gray, *Amerika Samoa: A History of American Samoa and Its United States Naval Administration* (Annapolis: United States Naval Institute, 1960); J. Robert Shaffer, *American Sāmoa: 100 Years Under the United States Flag* (Honolulu: Island Heritage Publishing, 2000); Kennedy, *The Tropical Frontier*, and *A History of American Samoa.*

63 Robert W. Franco, *Samoan Perceptions of Work: Moving Up and Moving Around* (New York: AMS Press, 1991).

64 Saʻiliemanu Lilomaiava-Doktor, "Faʻa-Samoa and population movement from the inside out: the case of Salelologa, Savaiʻi" (PhD dissertation, University of Hawaiʻi, 2004); Saʻiliemanu Lilomaiava-Doktor, "Samoan Transnationalism: Cultivating "Home" and "Reach," in *Migration and Transnationalism: Pacific Perspectives*, ed. by Helen Lee and Tupai Steve Francis (Acton, A.C.T.: Australian National University, 2009); and Saʻiliemanu Lilomaiava-Doktor, "Beyond 'Migration': Samoan Population Movement *(Malaga)* and the Geography of Social Space *(Vā),*" *The Contemporary Pacific* 21, no. 1 (2009): 1-32.

65 Faʻanofo Lisaclaire Uperesa, "Fabled Futures: Migration and Mobility for Samoans in American Football," *Contemporary Pacific* 26, no. 2 (2014): 281-301. Also see Uperesa, "Fabled Futures: Development, Gridiron Football, and Transnational Movements in American Samoa." (PhD diss., Columbia University, 2010); and Uperesa, "New Fields of Labor." Uperesa also wrote an article about consumption and identity in American Sāmoa. Uperesa, "Tales of the Tala (Dollar): Notes on Cars, Consumption, and Class in American Samoa," in *At Home And In The Field: Ethnographic Encounters In Asia And The Pacific Islands,* ed. Suzanne S. Finney, Mary Mostafanezhad, Guido Carlo Pigliasco, and Forrest Wade Young (Honolulu: University of Hawaiʻi Press, 2015), 175-183.

66 Kathleen M. McGeehan, "Cultural and Religious Belief Systems, Tsunami Recovery and Disaster Risk Reduction in American Samoa in the Aftermath of the September 29, 2009 Tsunami" (Master's thesis, University of Hawaiʻi, 2012); and Sherri Brokopp Binder, "Resilience and Disaster Recovery in American Samoa: A Case Study of the 2009 Pacific Tsunami" (Master's thesis, University of Hawaiʻi, 2012). See references for

fishery-based research in chapters 1 and 4. There are also some books about Sāmoan culture and events prior to U.S. rule.

67 Fofō Sunia, Email to author, November 2, 2018.

68 Albert Wendt, "Tatauing the Postcolonial Body," in Inside Out: Literature, Cultural Politics, and Identity in the New Pacific, ed. Vilsoni Hereniko and Rob Wilson, 399-412 (Lanham, MD: Rowman and Littlefield, 1999), 402.

69 Lilomaiava-Doktor, "Beyond "Migration," 12.

70 Lilomaiava-Doktor, "Beyond "Migration," 14 and 16.

71 Lilomaiava-Doktor, "Beyond "Migration," 13.

72 For examples, see Fofō I. F. Sunia, Lupe o le Foaga (Apia: Department of Education, American Sāmoa, 1997) and 'Aumua Mata'itusi Simanu in SLD, 13). Also note, indigenous ideology is not static. The divisions in society such fluidity creates is discussed in chapter 1.

73 Lilomaiava-Doktor, "Beyond "Migration," 18.

74 Lilomaiava-Doktor, "Beyond "Migration," 15.

75 Sunia, Email to author.

76 Tamasailau M. Suaalii-Sauni, I'uogafa Tuagalu, Tofilau Nina Krifi-Alai, and Namoi Fuamatu, Su'esu'e Manogi: In Search of fragrance: Tui Atua Tupua Tamasese Ta'isi and the Samoan Indigenous Reference (Apia, Sāmoa: The Centre for Samoan Studies, National University of Samoa, 2009), 109.

77 Damon Ieremia Salesa, Island Time: New Zealand's Pacific Futures (Wellington, New Zealand: Bridget Williams Books, 2017), Kindle Locations, 1142-1143.

78 Salesa, Island Time, Kindle Locations, 1136-1137.

79 Miranda Cahn, "Indigenous Entrepreneurship, Culture and Micro-enterprise in the Pacific Islands: Case Studies from Samoa," Entrepreneurship and Regional Development, no. 20 (2008): 3.

80 Susan Maiava, A Clash of Paradigms: Intervention, Response and Development in the South Pacific (Abingdon, Oxon: Routledge, 2018), 79.

81 Lilomaiava-Doktor, "Fa'a-Samoa," 172.

82 Lilomaiava-Doktor, "Fa'a-Samoa," 9.

83 Byron Caminero-Santangelo, "In Place," in Postcolonial Ecologies, ed. DeLoughrey and Handley, 292.

84 Caminero-Santangelo, "In Place," 292.

85 DeLoughrey and Handley, Postcolonial Ecologies, 24.

86 Jacoby, Crimes, 203.

87 Macpherson and Macpherson, The Warm Winds of Change, 83.

88 See Fikret Berkes, Sacred Ecology (New York: Routledge, 2012).

89 DeLoughrey and Handley, Postcolonial Ecologies, 17.

90 According to DeLoughrey and Handley, "Although postcolonial nations are the lowest in terms of carbon emissions, they are the most vulnerable to climate change." DeLoughrey and Handley, Postcolonial Ecologies, 26. See also Jon Barnett and John R.

Campbell, *Climate Change and Small Island States: Power, Knowledge, and the South Pacific* (London: Earthscan, 2010).

91 Blackford, *Making Seafood Sustainable,* 214.

92 For example, U.S. Fisheries allows the landing of sharks as long as the fin is attached. American Sāmoa DWMR does not allow any shark fishing. While legal under U.S. regulations, shark fishing is prohibited three miles from shore and on American Sāmoan land. According to Peter Eves, DMWR enforcement supervisor, "the strictest law applies." Peter Eves, interview by author, June 20, 2016, Fagatogo, American Sāmoa.

93 DeLoughrey and Handley, *Postcolonial Ecologies,* 28.

Chapter 1: Native Commercial Fishing and Indigenous Debates over Regulations in the U.S. Pacific

1 NOAA Fisheries, NOAA, "Our Mission," accessed October 9, 2015, http://www.nmfs.noaa.gov /aboutus/our_mission.html.

2 NOAA Fisheries, "Our Mission."

3 "An Act to place certain submerged lands within the jurisdiction of the governance of Guam, the Virgin Islands, and American Samoa, and for other purposes," Public Law 93-435, October 5, 1974, 88 Stat., 1210, accessed July 17, 2017, http://uscode.house.gov /statutes/pl/93/435.pdf.

4 Another approximately twenty-two million tons of seafood was caught for fishmeal. "Positive outlook for global seafood as demand surges for multiple species in markets across the world," GLOBEFISH—Analysis and information on world fish trade, Food and Agriculture Organization of the United Nations, March 19, 2018, accessed June 26, 2018, http://www.fao.org/in-action/globefish/market-reports/resource-detail/en /c/1109513/.

5 Augustin Krämer, *The Samoa Islands: An Outline of a Monograph with Particular Consideration of German Samoa* (Honolulu: University of Hawai'i Press, 1994); Peter Henry Buck (Te Rangi Hiroa), *Samoan Material Culture* (New York: Kraus, 1971); Lowell Don Holmes, Samoan Village (Toronto, ON: Thomson Learning, 1974); Karen Armstrong, David Herdrich, and Arielle Levine, "Historic Fishing Methods in American Samoa," National Oceanic and Atmosphere Administration, June 2011, accessed October 9, 2015, http://docs.lib.noaa.gov/noaa_documents/NMFS/PIFSC/TM _NMFS_PIFSC/NOAA_Tech_Memo_PIFSC_24.pdf.

6 Armstrong, Herdrich and Levine, "Historic Fishing Methods," 3.

7 Brian Fagan, *Fishing: How the Sea Fed Civilization* (New Haven: Yale University Press, 2018), Kindle Locations 430-433.

8 Afoa Lutu, Interview by author, June 24, 2015, Fagatogo, American Sāmoa.

9 Ma'a Maea, Interview by author, August 4, 2014, American Sāmoa and James Gurr, Interview by author, June 17, 2015, Mapusaga, American Sāmoa.

10 Craig J. Severance, Kitty Simonds, and Robert W. Franco, *Justification and Design of Limited Entry Alternatives for the Offshore Fisheries of American Samoa, and an Examination of Preferential Fishing Rights for Native People of American Samoa within a Limited Entry Context: Final Report: Submitted to Kitty Simonds* (Hilo: Anthropology, University of Hawai'i at Hilo, 1989), December 1, 1989, 54. Bonito boat fishing is also described in detail in Armstrong, Herdrich and Levine, "Historic Fishing Methods in American Samoa," 19-20.

11 Sesepasara, Interview by author.

12 Armstrong, Herdrich and Levine, "Historic Fishing Methods," 4 and 7.

13 P. Craig, A. Green, and F. Tuilagi, "Subsistence Harvest of Coral Reef Resources in the Outer Islands of American Samoa: Modern, Historic and Prehistoric Catches," *Fisheries Research* 89, no. 3 (March 2008): 1.

14 Fagan, *Fishing*, Kindle Locations 380-381.

15 Arielle Levine and Stewart Allen, "American Samoa as a Fishing Community," NOAA Technical Memorandum NMFS-PIFSC-19," NOAA, July 2009, accessed October 9, 2015, http://docs.lib.noaa.gov/noaa_documents/NMFS/PIFSC./TM_NMFS_PIFSC/NOAA_Tech_Memo_PIFSC_19.pdf, 37.

16 Theodore Koboski, "Socio-Cultural and Economic Barriers to Small Vessel/Indigenous Participation in the American Samoan Longline Fishery." (B.S. Thesis in Marine Sciences, Honors College, University of Maine, 2014), 8.

17 David G. Itano, "The Development of Small-Scale Fisheries for Bottomfish in American Samoa (1961-1987)," *SPC Fisheries Newsletter* (1996), 28-29.

18 See chapter 2.

19 Alvin Eo Mokoma, Interview by author, June 21, 2016, Pago Pago, American Sāmoa and Tony Langkilde, Interview by author, June 20, 2016, Fagatago, American Sāmoa.

20 Armstrong, Herdrich and Levine, "Historic Fishing Methods," 39.

21 Armstrong, Herdrich and Levine, "Historic Fishing Methods," 37.

22 Itano, "Development of Small-Scale Fisheries," 1.

23 Levine and Allen, "American Samoa as a Fishing Community," 42.

24 Levine and Allen, "American Samoa as a Fishing Community," 35.

25 Levine and Allen, "American Samoa as a Fishing Community," 43.

26 NOAA Fisheries, *American Samoa Pelagic Longline Fishing*, accessed November 13, 2015, http://www.fpir.noaa.gov/SFD/pdfs/american-samoa-longline-reg-summary.pdf.

27 Paul Dalzell and Eric Kingma, "Potential Modifications to the American Samoa Pelagic Longline Limited Entry Permit Program," Western Pacific Regional Fishery Management Council, accessed November 13, 2015, http://www.wpcouncil.org/wp-content/uploads/2011/03/150CM_Action-Item_ASLLMod.pdf.

28 Levine and Allen, "American Samoa as a Fishing Community," 45.

29 NOAA Fisheries, *Pacific Islands Fisheries Science Center*, accessed November 13, 2015, http://www.pifsc.noaa.gov/wpacfin/as/Data/ECL_Charts/ae3bmain.htm.

30 NOAA Fisheries, *Pacific Islands Fisheries Science Center*.

31 Fagan, *Fishing,* Kindle Locations 282 and 3972.

32 Fagan, *Fishing,* Kindle Locations 3983-3991.

33 Fagan, *Fishing,* Kindle Locations 3994.

34 Blackford, *Making Seafood Sustainable,* 14.

35 Blackford, *Making Seafood Sustainable,* 15.

36 "A gross registered ton is a measure of storage space equal to one hundred cubic feet." Blackford, *Making Seafood Sustainable,* 14.

37 "Welcome," National Environmental Policy Act, accessed July 12, 2018, https://ceq.doe.gov/.

38 "EPR History," United Sates Environmental Protection Agency, accessed July 12, 2018, https://www.epa.gov/history.

39 Blackford, *Making Seafood Sustainable,* 20.

40 Blackford, *Making Seafood Sustainable,* 24.

41 "Fishery Conservation and Management Act of 1976," Digest of Federal Resource Laws of Interest to the U.S. Fish and Wildlife Service, accessed July 12, 2018, https://www.fws.gov/laws/lawsdigest/fishcon.html.

42 See Andrew F. Smith, *American Tuna: The Rise and Fall of an Improbable Food* (Berkeley: University of California Press, 2012), chapter 7.

43 Blackford, *Making Seafood Sustainable,* 123.

44 Levine and Allen, "American Samoa as a Fishing Community," 35.

45 Itano, "A Review of the Development of Bottomfish Fisheries in American Samoa," *Department of Marine and Wildlife Resources Biological Report Series,* no. 26 (October 1991): 4.

46 William Sword, Interview by author, June 23, 2016, Utulei, American Sāmoa.

47 Itano, "A Review of the Development," 5.

48 Levine and Allen, "American Samoa as a Fishing Community," 35.

49 J J. John Kaneko and Paul K. Bartram, "Operational Profile of a Highliner in the American Samoa Small-scale (Alia) Longline Albacore Fishery," SOEST 05-03, JIMAR Contribution, School of Ocean and Earth Science and Technology, 7. http://imina.soest.hawaii.edu/PFRP/soest_jimar_rpts/kaneko_bartram_alia_fishery.pdf. Accessed November 13, 2015.

50 Fagan, *Fishing,* Kindle Location 68.

51 Koboski, "Socio-Cultural and Economic Barriers," 2. Also see John Kurien and Rolf Willmann, "Special Considerations for Small-Scale Fisheries Management in Developing Countries" in *A Fishery Manager's Guidebook,* ed. Kevern L. Cochrane and Serge M. Garcia (Oxford: Wiley-Blackwell, 2009), 404-424.

52 Levine and Allen, "American Samoa as a Fishing Community," 35.

53 Dalzell and Kingma, "Potential Modifications," 11.

54 Levine and Allen, "American Samoa as a Fishing Community," 36.

55 Koboski, "Socio-Cultural and Economic Barriers," 10.

56 Mokoma, Interview by author.

57 Mokoma, Interview by author. Others who love fishing or feel that fishing is in

their blood include Tony Langkilde, Interview by author; Mathaew Atafua, Interview by author, with translator Saumaniafaese Uikirifi, June 22, 2016, Nuʻuuli, American Sāmoa; Mika Letuane, Interview by author, June 24, 2016, Fagatogo, American Sāmoa; Tasele Masunu, Interview by author, with translator Uikirifi, June 22, 2016, Nuʻuuli, American Sāmoa; and Sword, Interview by author.

58 Maea, Interview by author, August 4, 2014.

59 Maea, Interview by author, August 4, 2014.

60 Christinna Lutu-Sanchez, Interview by author, June 21, 2016, Utulei, American Sāmoa.

61 Levine and Allen, "American Samoa as a Fishing Community,"45.

62 Levine and Allen, "American Samoa as a Fishing Community," 45.

63 Levine and Allen, "American Samoa as a Fishing Community," 44.

64 Levine and Allen, "American Samoa as a Fishing Community," 44.

65 Levine and Allen, "American Samoa as a Fishing Community," 45.

66 Joseph M. O'Malley, and Samuel G. Pooley, "A Description and Economic Analysis of Large American Samoa Longline Vessels," Working Paper no. SCTB15 GEN 2, July 27, 2002, 45-46, accessed November 13, 2015, http://imina.soest.hawaii.edu/PFRP /sctb15/papers/GEN-2.pdf, and Levine and Allen, "American Samoa as a Fishing Community."

67 Blackford, *Making Seafood Sustainable,* 1.

68 "American Samoa: 1982-2014 Annual Total Estimated Commercial Landings," NOAA, National Marine Fisheries Service, August 6, 2015, accessed November 13, 2015, https://www.pifsc.noaa.gov/wpacfin/as/Data/ECL_Charts/ ae3bmain.htm.

69 Krista Corry, Interview by author, June 24, 2015, Pago Pago, American Sāmoa.

70 Lutu-Sanchez, Interview by author.

71 Lutu-Sanchez, Interview by author.

72 Corry, Interview by author.

73 Lutu-Sanchez, Interview by author.

74 Fili Sagapolutele, "Governor Lolo looks to AG for Next step in Longliner Battle," *Samoa News,* March 31, 2015, accessed March 31, 2015, http://samoanews.com/content/en /gov-lolo-looks-ag-next-step-longliner-battle#sthash.4OMAl2DE.dpuf.

75 Western Pacific Regional Fishery Management Council, "Navigating the Western Pacific Council Process: A Guide to the Western Pacific Regional Fishery Management Council," Fifth Edition, 2013, 4, accessed June 25, 2018, http://www.wpcouncil.org/wp -content/uploads/2013/04/COUNCIL_PROCESS_GUIDEv5_FINAL.pdf.

76 Blackford, *Making Seafood Sustainable,* 213.

77 Thomas A. Okey, "Membership of the eight regional Fishery Management Councils in the United States: Are special interests over-represented?" *Marine Policy,* 27 (2003): 193; and Blackford, *Making Seafood Sustainable,* 40.

78 H.R.5946—Magnuson-Stevens Fishery Conservation and Management Reauthorization Act of 2006, 109th Congress (2005-2006), accessed July 12, 2018, https://www .congress.gov/bill/109th-congress/house-bill/5946.

79 "Western Pacific Regional Fishery Management Council home page," accessed June 25, 2018, http://www.wpcouncil.org/.

80 Western Pacific Regional Fishery Management Council, "Navigating the Western Pacific Council Process," 8.

81 Blackford, *Making Seafood Sustainable,* 50.

82 "Pelagics Fishery Ecosystem Plan," Western Pacific Regional Fishery Management Council, accessed July 17, 2018, http://www.wpcouncil.org/fishery-plans-policies-reports /pelagics_fe/.

83 Okey, "Membership," 194.

84 Okey, "Membership," 194.

85 Blackford, *Making Seafood Sustainable,* 37.

86 Levine and Allen, "American Samoa as a Fishing Community," 37.

87 Dalzell and Kingma, "Potential Modifications," Abstract.

88 *American Samoa Longline Fishery,* Report, December 1, 2005, accessed July 19, 2016, http://www.nmfs.noaa.gov/pr/pdfs/fisheries/american_samoa_longline.pdf.

89 "Fisheries Off West Coast States and in the Western Pacific; Western Pacific Pelagic Fisheries; American Samoa Longline Limited Entry Program," *Federal Register— Rules and Regulations,* 99th ser., no. 70 (March 24, 2005): 29646, accessed July 19, 2016, http://www.federalregister.com/Browse/AuxData/161AA659-4AF8-4EB8-B93D -58A793E6B3BB.

90 NOAA, "American Samoa Longline Limited Entry Program," accessed November 11, 2015, http://www.fpir. noaa.gov/SFD/SFD_aslle.html.

91 NOAA Fisheries, Sustainable Fisheries Division, "Fishing Permits," accessed August 20, 2018, http://www.fpir.noaa. gov/SFD/SFD_permits_index.html.

92 Lutu-Sanchez, Interview by author.

93 Levine and Allen, "American Samoa as a Fishing Community," 46.

94 Ilaoa, Interview by author.

95 Levine and Allen, "American Samoa as a Fishing Community," 36 and 48.

96 Koboski, "Socio-Cultural and Economic Barriers," 22.

97 "Summary of Action Items, 1," Western Pacific Regional Fishery Management Council, accessed July 20, 2016, www.wpcouncil.org/wp-content/uploads/2011/03 /Summary-of-Action-Items.docx. See also Walter Ikehara, "Report on Implementation of the American Samoa Pelagic Longline Limited Access Program" NOAA Fisheries Service, Pacific Islands Region, 2006.

98 "Purse Seine Fishing," International Seafood Sustainability Foundation, January 19, 2016, accessed November 11, 2015, http://iss-foundation.org/about-tuna/fishing -methods/ purse-seine/.

99 For more detail, see NOAA Fisheries "Purse Seine: Fishing Gear and Risks to Protected Species," accessed November 11, 2015, http://www.nmfs.noaa.gov/pr/interactions /gear/purseseine.htm.

100 "Fishing Techniques: Tuna Purse Seining." Food and Agriculture Organization

of the United Nations, Fisheries and Aquaculture Department of the United Nations, accessed November 11, 2015, http://www.fao.org/fishery/fishtech/40/en.

101 Levine and Allen, "American Samoa as a Fishing Community," 37.

102 "Western Pacific Pelagic Fisheries; Purse Seine Prohibited Areas Around American Samoa," Federal Register, April 6, 2011, accessed July 21, 2016, https://www.federal register.gov/documents/2011/04/ 06/2011-8212/western-pacific-pelagic-fisheries-purse -seine-prohibited-areas-around-american-samoa.

103 U.S. Department of Commerce, NOAA, "Fisheries in the Western Pacific; Pelagic Fisheries; Purse Seine Prohibited Areas Around American Samoa," 50 CFR Part 665, *Federal Register,* Proposed Rules, Volume 76, July 11, 2011, 40674, accessed July 19, 2017, https://www.gpo.gov/fdsys/pkg/FR-2011-07-11/pdf/2011-17357.pdf.

104 Barnett and Campbell, *Climate Change.*

105 "Annual Catch Limits," Wespac website, accessed August 9, 2017, http://www .wpcouncil.org/managed-fishery-ecosystems/annual-catch-limits/.

106 Callum Roberts, *The Unnatural History of the Sea* (Washington D.C.: Island Press/Shearwater Books, 2007), 322.

107 Roberts, *The Unnatural History,* 338.

108 "The State of the World Fisheries and Aquaculture: Meeting the Sustainable Development Goals," and Agriculture Organization of the United Nations, accessed July 17, 2018, http://www.fao.org/3/i9540en/I9540EN.pdf.

109 Roberts, *The Unnatural History,* 338.

110 Okey, "Membership," 195.

111 Suaalii-Sauni, Tuagalu, Krifi-Alai, and Fuamatu, *Su'esu'e Manogi,* 175-176.

112 Suaalii-Sauni, Tuagalu, Krifi-Alai, and Fuamatu, *Su'esu'e Manogi,* 107.

113 Roberts, *The Unnatural History,* 350. Also see Arielle Levine and Fatima Sauafea-Le'au, "Traditional Knowledge, use, and Management of Living Marine Resources in American Samoa: Documenting Changes Over Time through Interviews with Elder Fishers," *Pacific Science* 67 (2013): 395-407; and Fikret Berkes, *Sacred Ecology* (New York: Routledge, 2012).

114 Barnett and Campbell, *Climate Change.*

115 Blackford, *Making Seafood Sustainable,* 140.

116 Fagan, *Fishing,* Kindle Locations 4850-4852.

117 Fagan, *Fishing,* Kindle Locations 4966-4967.

118 NOAA Fisheries, "PIFSC Report on the American Samoa Longline Fishery Year 2013," March 14, 2014, accessed November 13, 2015, https://www. pifsc.noaa.gov /library/pubs/DR-14-006.pdf.

119 See "Potential Collapse Of Am. Samoa Longline Fishery Discussed: Fisheries Council Meeting Blames Low Prices, Chinese Competition," *Samoa News,* June 19, 2014, accessed June 19, 2014, http://pidp.eastwestcenter.org/pireport/2014/June/06 -19-05.htm; and Itano, "The Development of Small-Scale Fisheries."

120 Westpac Council, "Federal Fishery Managers Amend American Samoa Large

Vessel Prohibited Area to Promote Optimal Yield, Efficiency and Non-Discrimination in the Local Albacore Fishery," Western Pacific Regional Fishery Management Council, March 20, 2015, accessed July 19, 2016, http://www.wpcouncil.org/2015/03/20 /press-release-federal-fishery-managers-amend-american-samoa-large-vessel-prohibited -area-to-promote-optimal-yield-efficiency-and-non-discrimination-in-the-local-albacore -fishery/.

121 Westpac Council, "Federal Fishery Managers."

122 Michael Tosatto, Interview by author, August 8, 2016, Ford Island, O'ahu, Hawai'i.

123 Lutu-Sanchez, Interview by author.

124 Corry, Interview by author.

125 "121st Meeting of the Scientific and Statistical Committee," Western Pacific Regional Fishery Management Council, Report, October 13-14, 2015, 1-10, accessed July 26, 2016, http://www.wpcouncil. org/wp-content/uploads/2015/10/cm34-Report-of -the-121st-SSC-Meeting.pdf, 2.

126 "Bottomfish Catch Limits Could Increase for American Samoa, Decrease for Guam," *Marianas Variety*, October 16, 2015, accessed July 26, 2016, http://www.mvariety .com/cnmi/cnmi-news/local/80811-bottomfish-catch-limits-could-increase-for american-samoa-decrease-for-guam.

127 Westpac Council, "Federal Fishery Managers."

128 "Pacific Island Pelagic Fisheries; Exemption for Large U.S. Longline Vessels To Fish in Portions of the American Samoa Large Vessel Prohibited Area," Federal Register, February 03, 2016, accessed July 26, 2016, https://www.federalregister.gov/documents /2016/02 /03/2016-01891/pacific-island-pelagic-fisheries-exemption-for-large-us-longline -vessels-to-fish-in-portions-of-the.

129 Julie St. Louis, "American Samoa Fights Feds for Fishing Zone," *Courthouse News Service,* March 9, 2016, accessed July 27, 2016, http://www.courthouse news.com /american-samoa-fights-feds-for-fishing-zone/.

130 "Decision Making Getting on the Nerves of Alia Association," Talanei.com, October 23, 2015, accessed November 3, 2015, http://www.talanei.com/news/Decision -making-getting-on-the-nerves-of-alia-asso/22107882.

131 "Fish sold by canneries?" comment on "Decision making getting on the nerves of alia association," Talanei.com, October 23, 2015, accessed November 3, 2015, http:// www.talanei.com/news/Decision-making-getting-on-the-nerves-of-alia-asso/22107882.

132 Koboski, "Socio-Cultural and Economic Barriers," 22.

133 "Recommendation," comment on "Decision making getting on the nerves."

134 Koboski, "Socio-Cultural and Economic Barriers," 27.

135 Draft Regulatory Amendment Fishery Ecosystem Plan for Pelagic Fisheries of the Western Pacific Region Approval of an exemption for large (>50ft LOA) longline vessels to fish in the Large Vessel Prohibited Areas (LVPA) in American Samoa Including a Draft Environmental Assessment, March 5, 2015, 18.

136 Sagapolutele, "Am. Samoa Looks At Options To Maintain Large Vessel Protected

Area Opening Area to Longliners Proposed by Fishery Management Council," *Pacific Islands Report,* April 1, 2015, accessed July 27, 2016, http://pidp.org/pireport/2015/April /04-01-14.htm.

137 Joyetter Feagaimaalii-Luamanu, "Fono Calls for Wespac to Leave 50nm Zone in Place," *Samoa News,* November 3, 2015, accessed July 17, 2016, http://www.samoanews .com/content/en/ fono-calls-Wespac-leave-50nm-zone-place.

138 Lolo Moliga to Penny Pritzker, "Re: Official Comment on the proposed changes to the Large Vessel Prohibited Area in the U.S. EEZ waters around the islands of the territory of American Samoa," September 16, 2015, 3. Exhibit D, *Territory of American Samoa versus National Marine Fisheries Service et al,* Civil No. 16-00095.

139 Corry, Interview by author.

140 Lutu-Sanchez, Interview by author.

141 Maea, Interview by author, June 19, 2015, Fagatogo, America Sāmoa.

142 Sagapolutele, "LVPA Not Being Utilized to its Full Potential Says Local Long-line Owner," SamoaNews.com, September 2, 2015, accessed November 3, 2015, https:// www.samoanews.com/content/en/lvpa-not-being-utilized-its-full-potential-says-local -longline-owner?quicktabs_3=0&quicktabs_1=1.

143 Corry, Interview by author.

144 Corry, Interview by author.

145 Sagapolutele, "Gov. Lolo Looks to AG for Next Step in Longliner Battle."

146 Macpherson and La'avasa Macpherson, *Warm Winds,* 9.

147 Caminero-Santangelo, "In Place," 296.

148 "Pacific Island Pelagic Fisheries; Exemption for Large U.S. Longline Vessels to Fish in Portions of the American Samoa Large Vessel Prohibited Area" *Federal Register* 81, no. 22 (February 3, 2016): 5619, accessed July 12, 2018, https://www.gpo.gov/fdsys /pkg/FR-2016-02-03/html/2016-01891.htm.

149 "Pacific Island Pelagic Fisheries; Exemption," 5622.

150 "Pacific Island Pelagic Fisheries; Exemption," 5619. Discussion of comments did not specific how many specific people made the same comments. Descriptors were limited to the distinction of one or several comments.

151 "Pacific Island Pelagic Fisheries."

152 *Territory of American Samoa v. National Marine Fisheries Service,* 15.

153 *Territory of American Samoa v. National Marine Fisheries Service,* 13.

154 "Order granting in part and denying in part plaintiff's motion for summary judgment and denying defendants' counter-motion for summary judgment," *Territory of American Samoa versus National Marine Fisheries Service, et al,* Civil 16-00095 LEK-KJM, 28, accessed July 18, 2017, https://www.gpo.gov/fdsys/pkg/USCOURTS -hid-1_16-cv-00095/pdf/USCOURTS-hid-1_16-cv-00095-0.pdf.

155 "Order granting," 39.

156 Sagapolutele, "Lolo Administration responds with praise of court's LVPA ruling," *Samoa News,* March 22, 2017, accessed July 18, 2017, http://www.samoanews.com /local-news/lolo-administration-responds-praise-court%E2%80%99s-lvpa-ruling.

157 Sagapolutele, "Lolo Administration responds."

158 Sagapolutele, "NOAA cautious in motion for reconsideration of LVPA lawsuit," *Samoa News,* June 24, 2017, accessed July 17, 2017, http://www.samoanews.com/local -news/noaa-cautious-motion-reconsideration-lvpa-lawsuit/.

159 Sagapolutele, "NOAA cautious."

160 Sagapolutele, "No adverse impacts."

161 Sagapolutele, "'No adverse impacts on catch rates' since LVPA reduced," *Samoa News,* May 15, 2017, accessed July 17, 2017, http://www.samoanews.com/local-news /%E2%80%9Cno-adverse-impacts-catch-rates%E2%80%9D-lvpa-reduced.

162 Sagapolutele, "NOAA cautious."

163 Sagapolutele, "No adverse impacts."

164 Sagapolutele, "Tautai o Samoa Association pleads for help in LVPA battle," *Samoa News,* June 19, 2017, accessed July 17, 2017, http://www.samoanews.com/local -news/tautai-o-samoa-association-pleads-help-lvpa-battle.

165 Sagapolutele, "Tautai o Samoa Association pleads." *Samoa News,* June 16, 2018.

166 "Federal Managers recommend 4-yr LVPA exemption for American Samoa longliners," accessed August 22, 2018, http://www.samoanews.com/federal-managers -recommend-4-yr-lvpa-exemption-american-samoa-longliners.

167 Fagan, *Fishing,* Kindle Location 5006.

168 Koboski, "Socio-Cultural and Economic Barriers," 35.

169 See C. Béné, G. Macfadyen, E. H. Allison, "Increasing the Contribution of SmallScale Fisheries to Poverty Alleviation and Food Security," FAO Fisheries Technical Paper No. 481, Food and Agriculture Organization of the United Nations, Rome: 2007; and Koboski, "Socio-Cultural and Economic Barriers," 4.

170 Kurien and Willmann, "Special Considerations for Small-Scale Fisheries Management in Developing Countries," 404; and "Small-scale fishers and communities," People and Communities, Fisheries and Aquaculture Department, Food and Agriculture Organization of the United Nations, accessed July 11, 2018, http://www.fao.org /fishery/ssf/people/en.

Chapter 2: Minimal Returns

1 Levine and Allen, "American Samoa as a Fishing Community," 17-18.

2 Andrew F. Smith, *American Tuna: The Rise and Fall of an Improbable Food* (Berkeley: University of California Press, 2012), x.

3 Smith, *American Tuna,* xi.

4 Smith, *American Tuna,* 171.

5 For a similar example, see Sam Erman, "Meanings of Citizenship in the U.S. Empire: Puerto Rico, Isabel Gonzalez, and the Supreme Court, 1898 to 1905," *Journal of American Ethnic History* 27 (2008): 5-33.

6 For more on this topic, see Thomas Alexander Aleinikoff, *Semblances of Sovereignty* (Cambridge: Harvard University Press, 2002).

7 For more information, see "Citizens Class: Abramoff, Inc.," *Moyers on America,* November 3, 2015, accessed October 1, 2015, http://www.pbs.org/moyers/moyersonamerica /print/marianasclass_print.html.

8 Stephen Dinan, "Territories snared in wage debate: Hill backpedals on minimum pay rate for Samoa, Marianas," *Washington Times,* October 18, 2010.

9 Dinan, "Territories snared."

10 Dinan, "Territories snared."

11 Aumua Amata, "Aumua Makes Impassioned Plea on House Floor for American Samoa's Economic Well-Being," United States Congresswoman Aumua Amata, accessed October 2, 2015, https://radewagen.house.gov/media-center/press-releases /aumua-makes-impassioned-plea-house-floor-american-samoas-economic-well.

12 Blackford, *Making Seafood Sustainable,* ix.

13 Roberts, *The Unnatural History,* 280.

14 Blackford, *Making Seafood Sustainable,* 17.

15 Blackford, *Making Seafood Sustainable,* 169.

16 Blackford, *Making Seafood Sustainable,* 156.

17 Blackford, *Making Seafood Sustainable,* 156.

18 Blackford, *Making Seafood Sustainable,* 156.

19 Richard J. Barnet and John Cavanagh, *Global Dreams: Imperial Corporations and the New World Order* (New York: Simon & Schuster, 1994), 271.

20 Barnet and Cavanagh, *Global Dreams,* 275.

21 Allen Stayman, "U.S. Territorial Policy: Trends and Current Challenges," Pacific Islands Policy 5, 2009, 1.

22 Barry Leonard, "Minimum Wage in American Samoa 2007: Economic Report," U.S. Department of Labor, Employment Standards Administration, Wage and Hour Division, May 2007.

23 Leonard, "Minimum Wage in American Samoa 2007," 62.

24 "American Samoa Investment Guide—Department of Commerce," American Sāmoa Government Department of Commerce, accessed November 10, 2015, http:// doc.as.gov/invest-in-american-samoa/investment-guide-2014/.24.

25 H. Rex Lee, September 27, 1962, Box D-15, Folder Star-Kist Foods Incorporated, 15B-SK, American Sāmoa Archives, Tafuna.

26 John R. Luckey, "Buy American Act, Buy America Act, Little Buy American Act, The Berry Amendment: Which is What and Who's on First?" Report no. NB-2012-07119, Congressional Research Library, Washington, D.C.: American Law Division: 2012, 1.

27 Luckey, *Buy American Act,* 2.

28 Mark Mitsuyasu, interview by author, August 10, 2016, Honolulu, Hawai'i.

29 Barnet and Cavanagh, *Global Dreams,* 275.

30 Brett Butler, interview by author, August 3, 2014, Utueli, American Sāmoa.

31 For example, Sonny Thompson, interview by author, August 2, 2014, Utueli, American Sāmoa and Carlos Sanchez, interview by author, August 8, 2014, Utueli, American Sāmoa.

32 Carlos Gonzales, interview by author, July 31, 2014, Atu'u, American Sāmoa.

33 Dan Sullivan, interview by author, June 26, 2015, Pago Pago, American Sāmoa.

34 "Closure of Fishing Grounds Helping Foreign Competitors," *talanei.com,* October 23, 2015, accessed October 30, 2015, http://www.talanei.com/news/Closure-of -fishing-grounds-helping-foreign-competi/22107267.

35 Barnet and Cavanagh, *Global Dreams,* 281.

36 Barnet and Cavanagh, *Global Dreams,* 282.

37 For more information on oil refining in the U.S. Virgin Islands, see David Bond, "Oil in the Caribbean: Refineries, Mangroves, and the Negative Ecologies of Crude Oil," *Comparative Studies in Society and History* 59, no. 3 (2017): 600-628; and Matthew Johnson, "Black Gold of Paradise: Negotiating Oil Pollution in the US Virgin Islands, 1966-2012," *Environmental History* 24, no. 4 (2019): 1-27.

38 "Don't Industrialize Samoa, Native Son Pleads at Hearing," *Honolulu Star-Bulletin,* March 10, 1956.

39 U.S. Congress. House, Committee on Education and Labor, Minimum Wages in Certain Territories, Possessions, and Oversea Areas of the United States, 84th Congress, 2nd Session, February 15, 1956, 21-22.

40 For reference to the Department of Defense sentiments, see *Congressional Record,* July 11, 1956, 12303.

41 U.S. Congress, House of Representatives, Committee on Education and Labor, Amendment to Increase the Minimum Wage. Hearings, 84th Congress, 1st Session, June 1, 1955, and forward Washington, U.S. Govt. Print. Off., 1955, 1180-1181.

42 U.S. Congress, House of Representatives, Subcommittee on Insular Affairs of the Committee on Natural Resources, *The Economic Effects of the Recently Increased Minimum Wage,* 110th Congress, Second Session, February 22, 2008, 3.

43 House Hearings, 1956, 13-14.

44 U.S. Congress, *Recently Increased Minimum Wage,* 3

45 *Congressional Record,* July 11, 1956, 12303.

46 William G. Whittaker, "Minimum Wage in the Territories and Possessions of the United States: Application of the Fair Labor Standards Act," 2008, accessed May 3, 2017 http://congressionalresearch. com/RL30235/document.php.

47 See chapter 1, footnote 83.

48 "American Samoa: Alternative for Raising Minimum Wages to Keep Pace with the Cost of Living and Reach the Federal Level," Report to Congressional Committees, U.S. GAO, December 2016, 19, accessed August 10, 2017, http://www.gao.gov /assets/690/681370.pdf.

49 "American Samoa Statistical Yearbook," Department of Commerce, 2009, 155, ac-

cessed August 10, 2017, http://www.doc.as/wp-content/uploads/2011/06/2009-Statistical
-Yearbook.pdf.

50 U.S. Congress, *Recently Increased Minimum Wage*, 6.

51 George Miller, "Proceedings and Debates of the U.S. Congress," *Congressional
Record,* July 17, 2012, 112th Congress, 2nd Session Issue: Vol. 158, No. 107."

52 For more history on the Special Industry Committee of American Sāmoa, see
Whittaker, "The Federal Minimum Wage and American Samoa," April 8, 2008,
accessed August 10, 2017, http://congressionalresearch.com/RL34013/document.
php?study=The+Federal+Minimum+Wage+and+American+Samoa.

53 See JoAnna Poblete, *Islanders in the Empire* (Urbana: University of Illinois Press,
2014), chapters 3 and 4.

54 Togiola Tulafono, interview by author, June 17, 2015, Utueli, American Sāmoa.

55 Tulafono, interview by author.

56 Thompson, interview by author.

57 Patricia Letuli, interview by author, August 8, 2014, Pago Pago, American Sāmoa.

58 "H.R. 3021-American Samoa Job Protection & Expansion Act of 2017," 115th Congress (2017-2018), accessed July 6, 2017, https://www.congress.gov/bill/115th-congress
/house-bill/3021/cosponsors?pageSort=lastToFirst&loclr=cga-member.

59 Fili Sagapolutele, "Minimum wage continued as issues of economy vs. cost of living," *Samoa News,* June 27, 2017, accessed July 6, 2017, http://www.samoanews.com
/local-news/minimum-wage-continues-issue-economy-vs-cost-living.

60 Sagapolutele, "Businesses Line Up Firmly Against Min. Wage Increase," *Samoa
News,* May 5, 2015, accessed October 1, 2015, http://www.samoanews.com/content/en
/businesses-line-firmly-against-min-wage-increase?quicktabs_1=0&quicktabs_3=1.

61 U.S. Department of Labor, Office of the Assistant Secretary for Policy, "Impact of
Increased Minimum Wages on the Economies of American Samoa and the Commonwealth of the Northern Mariana Islands," accessed November 3, 2015, https://www.doi
.gov/sites/doi.gov/files/uploads/ascnmi.pdf.

62 "Tofaeono Hollywood," comment on "Businesses Line Up Firmly."

63 "Troyboy," comment on "Businesses Line Up Firmly."

64 Amata, "Aumua Makes Impassioned Plea."

65 Amata, "Aumua Makes Impassioned Plea."

66 "Guest," comment on "Businesses Line Up Firmly."

67 "Steve," comment on "Businesses Line Up Firmly."

68 "Niuveve," comment on "Businesses Line Up Firmly." There were eight additional
emotional responses to posts for this particular article.

69 James C. Scott, *Seeing like a State: How Certain Schemes to Improve the Human
Condition Have Failed* (New Haven: Yale University Press, 1998).

70 Armstrong, Herdrich and Levine, "Historic Fishing Methods," 6.

71 Felix Keesing, *Modern Samoa: Its Government and Change Life* (Stanford: Stanford University Press, 1934), 30-31.

72 Other proposals for economic development, like call centers and tourism, have

been proposed over the years, but none of these projects have been successful so far. Obstacles to these endeavors include lack of infrastructure and limited number of flights to the region per week.

73 Amata, "Aumua Makes Impassioned Plea."

74 Sagapolutele, "Study says $5.67 min wage needed for local family of six," *Samoa News,* December 12, 2016, accessed July 6, 2017, http://www.samoanews.com/local -news/study-says-567-min-wage-needed-local-family-six.

75 Letuli, interview by author.

76 Taeaoafua Dr. Meki Solomona, interview by August 6, 2014, Utueli, American Sāmoa.

77 Joe Taeao, comment on "Except for Canneries, Min Wage Hike Has Min Impact," *Samoa News,* October 21, 2015, accessed October 26, 2015, http://www.samoanews.com /content/ en/except-canneries-min-wage-hike-has-min-impact#sthash.xkaptLrD.dpuf.

78 "Pomasame," comment on "Except for Canneries."

79 John Wasko, interview by author, June 31, 2014, Fagatogo, American Sāmoa.

80 United States Department of Commerce, Economic and Statistics Administration, Foreign Trade Division, "U.S. Trade with Puerto Rico and U.S. Possessions, 2005," FT895/05, Table 4, F-1 , accessed November 10, 2015, https://www.census.gov/prod /2006pubs/ft895a05.pdf.

81 For most recent statistics, see U.S. Department of Commerce, Economic and Statistics Administration, Foreign Trade Division, "U.S. Trade with Puerto Rico and U.S. Possessions annual reports," Table 4, F-1 .

82 Blackford, *Making Seafood Sustainable,* 174.

83 See Moon-kie Jung, *Reworking Race: The Making of Hawaii's Interracial Labor Movement* (New York: Columbia University Press, 2006), Edward Beechert, *Working in Hawaii: A Labor History* (Honolulu: University of Hawai'i Press, 1985), and Poblete, *Islanders.*

84 April Merleaux, *Sugar and Civilization: American Empire and the Cultural Politics of Sweetness* (Chapel Hill: University of North Carolina Press, 2015).

85 Butler, interview by author.

86 Lave Tuiletufuga, "Starkist Attacks," *Samoa News,* March 28, 1994.

87 Tuiletufuga, "Union Challenge," *Samoa News,* May 11, 1994.

88 Tuiletufuga, "Teamsters," *Samoa News,* March 3, 1994.

89 See Rick Halpern, "The Iron Fist and the Velvet Glove: Welfare Capitalism in Chicago's Packinghouses, 1921-1933," *Journal of American Studies* 26, no. 2 (August 1992): 159-183; and Nikki Mandell, *The Corporation as Family: The Gendering of Corporate Welfare, 1890-1930* (Chapel Hill: University of North Carolina Press, 2002).

90 U.S. Department of Labor, "Impact of Increased Minimum Wages on the Economies of American Samoa and the Commonwealth of the Northern Mariana Islands," *8.*

91 "Cannery Workers Happy But Also Concerned," Talanei.com, October 1, 2015,

accessed October 15, 2015, http://www.talanei.com/news/Cannery-workers-happy-but
-also-concerned/ 22028736.

92 See "American Samoa Statistical Yearbook 2016," American Samoa Department of
Commerce, Research and Statistics Division, 124 and "Commonwealth of the Northern
Mariana Islands: Preliminary Observations on the Implementation of Federal Immigra-
tion Laws," United States Government Accountability Office, April 27, 2017, 6.

93 Dinan, "Territories Snared in Wage Debate."

94 U.S. Congress, House—Foreign Affairs; Judiciary; Education and the Workforce;
Insular Areas Act of 2011, 112th Congress, 1st session, 2011, House of Representatives,
112-149, accessed November 3, 2015, https://www.congress.gov/bill/112th-congress
/senate-bill/2009?q=%7B%22search%22%3A%5B%22samoa+wage+delay+2011%22%5
D%7D&resultIndex=35.

95 George Miller, *Congressional Record,* July 17, 2012.

96 Bureau of East Asian and Pacific Affairs, "U.S. Relations With Marshall Islands,"
Fact Sheet, U.S. Department of State, December 27, 2016, accessed July 25, 2018, https://
www.state.gov/r/pa/ei/bgn/26551.htm.

97 Stayman, "U.S. Territorial Policy," 17.

98 Nick Wing, "American Samoa Minimum Wage Freeze Approved By Congress,"
The Huffington Post, September 18, 2012, accessed October 1, 2015, http://www
.huffingtonpost.com/2012 /07/19/american-samoa-minimum-wage_n_1687975.html.

99 See JoAnna Poblete-Cross, "Bridging Indigenous and Immigrant Struggles: A
Case Study of American Sāmoa," *American Quarterly* 62 (2010): 501-522.

100 Sagapolutele, "Amended Minimum Wage Hike Bill Passes Senate: Contains
Retroactive Clause for 40 Cent Raise," *Samoa News,* October 1, 2015, accessed October
1, 2015, http://www.samoanews.com/content/en/amended-minimum-wage-hike-bill-
passes-senate#sthash.MiEefHO5.dpuf.

101 "Senator Makes Fight Tougher for Am Samoa's Min Wage," *Samoa News,* October 13, 2015, accessed October 13, 2013, http://www.samoanews.com/content/en
/senator-makes-fight-tougher-am-samoa%E2%80%99s-min-wage.

102 Amata, "Aumua Makes Impassioned Plea."

103 See more at Sagapolutele, "Except for Canneries, Min Wage Hike Has Min
Impact," *Samoa News,* October 21, 2015, accessed October 26, 2015, http://www
.samoanews.com/content /en/except-canneries-min-wage-hike-has-min-impact#sthash
.xkaptLrD.dpuf.

104 For more information, see Suzanne Heller Clain, "Explaining the Passage of
Living Wage Legislation in the U.S," *Atlantic Economic Journal* 40 (2012): 315-327.

105 Stephen Dinan, "Territories Snared in Wage Debate."

106 Amata, "Aumua Makes Impassioned Plea."

107 See "Amata introduces bill to keep businesses in American Samoa," *Samoa News,*
June 21, 2017, accessed July 6, 2017, http://www.samoanews.com/local-news/amata
-introduces-bill-keep-businesses-american-samoa; Fili Sagapolutele, "Min wage hike
will be final nail in coffin for local economy, says DOC," *Samoa News,* June 22, 2017,
accessed July 6, 2017, http://www.samoanews.com/local-news/min-wage-hike-will-be

-final-nail-coffin-local-economy-says-doc; and Sagapolutele, "Minumum wage continued as issue."

108 Sagapolutele, "Minumum wage continues as issue."

109 Sagapolutele, "StarKist Moves Should Not Be A Surprise, Says TriMarine," *Samoa News,* November 4, 2015, accessed November 4, 2015, http://www.samoanews.com/content /en/ starkist-moves-should-not-be-surprise-says-tri-marine?quicktabs_1=0.

110 Sagapolutele, "StarKist Moves Should Not Be A Surprise."

Chapter 3: The Devolution of Marine Sanctuary Development in American Sāmoa

1 Mark David Spence, *Dispossessing the Wilderness: Indian Removal and the Making of the National Parks* (New York: Oxford University Press, 1999), 3.

2 U.S. Department of Commerce, "Final Environmental Impact Statement and Management Plan for the Proposed Fagatele Bay National Marine Sanctuary," Executive Summary, accessed October 23, 2015, http://americansamoa.noaa.gov/pdfs/fbeis _84ab.pdf.

3 Spence, *Dispossessing,* 71 and 4.

4 U.S. Department of Commerce, NOAA, Fagatele Bay National Marine Sanctuary Science Series "Changes in the Coral Reef Communities of Fagatele Bay National Marine Sanctuary and Tutuila Island (American Samoa), 1982-1995," accessed October 23, 2015, http://americansamoa.noaa.gov/pdfs/changes_coral.pdf.

5 "NOAA Helps American Samoa Tackle a Thorny Issue," National Ocean Service, accessed June 14, 2018, https://oceanservice.noaa.gov/news/may15/crown-of-thorns .html.

6 U.S. Department of Commerce, "Changes in the Coral Reef Communities," 6-7.

7 Bill Thomas, interview by author, August 8, 2016, Ford Island, Oʻahu, Hawaiʻi.

8 U.S. Department of Commerce, "Final Environmental Impact Statement and Management Plan," C-16-18.

9 U.S. Department of Commerce, "Final Environmental Impact Statement and Management Plan," C-3.

10 U.S. Department of Commerce, "Final Environmental Impact Statement and Management Plan," C-3.

11 U.S. Department of Commerce, "Final Environmental Impact Statement and Management Plan," Executive Summary, C-16-18.

12 Jacoby, *Crimes,* 119.

13 U.S. Department of Commerce, "Final Environmental Impact Statement and Management Plan," C-4.

14 National Marine Sanctuary of American Samoa, "Faʻa-Samoa and the National Marine Sanctuary of American Samoa," accessed July 17, 2017, http://americansamoa .noaa.gov/about/faasamoa.html.

15 Bill Thomas, interview by author.

16 Tuifagalua Fuimaono, interview by author, June 23, 2016, Futiga, American Sāmoa; and Chirstina Muaimalae Fuimaono, interview by author, June 23, 2016, Futiga, American Sāmoa.

17 "American Samoa Coast Management Program," American Samoa Department of Commerce, accessed August 23, 2018, http://doc.as.gov/resource-management/ascmp/.

18 Jacoby, *Crimes,* 35.

19 Peter Eves, interview by author, June 8, 2015, Fagatogo, American Sāmoa.

20 U.S. Department of Commerce and NOAA, "Expansion of Fagatele Bay National Marine Sanctuary, Regulatory Changes, and Sanctuary Name Change; Final Rule," *Federal Register* 77, no. 144 (July 26, 2012): 43947, accessed October 23, 2015, http://americansamoa.noaa.gov/pdfs/77_fr_43942_final.pdf.

21 Jacoby, *Crimes,* 184 and 35-36.

22 U.S. Department of Commerce, NOAA, *National Marine Sanctuary of American Samoa Advisory Council Charter,* 2014, 1-18, accessed October 23, 2015, http://americansamoa.noaa.gov/pdfs/charter-2014.pdf.

23 Fikret Berkes, *Sacred Ecology* (New York: Routledge: 2012), 168.

24 Tauʻese Pita Sunia was governor from 1998 to 2003. Togiola Tulafono was governor from 2003 to 2012. U.S. Department of Commerce, "Expansion of Fagatele Bay National Marine Sanctuary; Final Rule," 43942. Also see Fofō Sunia, interview by author, Togiola Tulafono, interview by author, and "Expansion of Fagatele Bay National Marine Sanctuary Name Change," Regulations.gov, accessed October 23, 2015, http://www.regulations.gov/#!documentDetail;D=NOAA-NOS-2011-0243-0192.

25 "Building a National Network of Marine Protected Areas for Coral Reefs," U.S. Coral Reef Task Force, July 1, 2008, accessed October 23, 2015, http://www.coralreef.gov/ecosystem/ marinepro.html.

26 U.S. Department of Commerce, NOAA, "Fagatele Bay National Marine Sanctuary: Condition Report 2007," report, August 2007, ii-40, accessed October 23, 2015, http://americansamoa.noaa.gov/html/docs/fb_condition.pdf.

27 Roberts, *The Unnatural History,* 373.

28 U.S. Department of Commerce, "Expansion of Fagatele Bay National Marine Sanctuary; Final Rule," 43942. See also U.S. Department of Commerce, "Expansion of Fagatele Name Change."

29 U.S. Department of Commerce, "Expansion of Fagatele Bay; Final Rule," R10-D.

30 Lucy Jacob, "Comment from Lucy Jacob," Regulations.gov, January 6, 2012, 1, accessed August 26, 2016, https://www.regulations.gov/document?D=NOAA-NOS-2011-0243-0089.

31 U.S. Department of Commerce, "Expansion of Fagatele Bay National Marine Sanctuary; Final Rule," 43943. Also see U.S. Department of Commerce, "Expansion of Fagatele By National Marine Sanctuary, Name Change."

32 "Comment from Christinna Lutu-Sanchez," Regulations.gov, January 6, 2012, 1,

accessed August 26, 2016, https://www.regulations.gov/document? D=NOAA-NOS
-2011-0243-0109.

33 "Comment from Selaina Tuimavave," Regulations.gov, January 6, 2012, 1, accessed August 26, 2016, https://www.regulations.gov/document?D=NOAA-NOS-2011-0243-0086.

34 "Comment from George Tusi," Regulations.gov, January 6, 2012, accessed August 26, 2016, https://www.regulations.gov/document?D=NOAA-NOS-2011-0243-0020.

35 U.S. Department of Commerce, NOAA "Fagatele Bay National Marine Sanctuary Management Plan and Environmental Impact Statement," June 2012, 51, accessed October 27, 2015, http://americansamoa.noaa.gov/management/pdfs/fbnms_mp_eis.pdf.

36 U.S. Department of Commerce, "Fagatele Bay Management Plan and Environmental Impact Statement," 51-52.

37 For a chart on the dates and target groups for each community meeting, see U.S. Department of Commerce, "Management Plan and Environmental Impact Statement," 49-51.

38 Barnett and Campbell, *Climate Change,* 129.

39 "Comment from Save Tuitele," Regulations.gov, March 9, 2012, accessed August 26, 2016, https://www.regulations.gov/document?D=NOAA-NOS-2011-0243-0180.

40 "Comment from Anonymous Anonymous," Regulations.gov, January 6, 2012, accessed August 26, 2016, https://www.regulations.gov/document?D= NOAA-NOS-2011 -0243-0028.

41 Spence, *Dispossessing,* 98.

42 "Comment from Anonymous Anonymous," Regulations.gov, January 6, 2012, accessed August 26, 2016, https://www.regulations.gov/document?D=NOAA-NOS -2011-0243-0010. Also see "Comment from Controversial Lelei," Regulations.gov, January 6, 2012, accessed August 26, 2016, https://www.regulations.gov/document?D = NOAA-NOS-2011-0243-0138.

43 Kitty M. Simonds to Gene Brighouse, December 29, 2011, 3, accessed August 26, 2016, http://www.wpcouncil.org/news/docs/2011/WPRFMC%20Comments%20on%20 FBNMC%20DMP&DEIS_FINAL.pdf.

44 Kitty M. Simonds to Gene Brighouse, 13.

45 "Letter from Alice Lawrence," Regulations.gov, January 6, 2012, 7, accessed May 25, 2016, https://www.regulations.gov/document?D=NOAA-NOS-2011-0243-0161.

46 "Comment from Douglas Fenner," Regulations.gov, March 9, 2012, 1, accessed August 26, 2016, https://www.regulations.gov/document?D=NOAA-NOS-2011-0243-0179.

47 Kendall Matthew and Matthew Poti, *A Biogeographic Assessment of the Samoan Archipelago,* Technical Memorandum NOS NCCOS 132, NOAA, Silver Spring, MD: Biogeography Branch Center for Coastal Monitoring and Assessment, July 2011, Executive Summary, accessed October 28, 2015, http://sanctuaries.noaa.gov/about/pdfs /samoa_report.pdf.

48 "Comment from Lima Tapuaʻi," Regulations.gov, March 9, 2012, accessed August 25, 2016, https://www.regulations.gov/document?D=NOAA-NOS-2011-0243-0190.

49 "Comment from Anonymous Anonymous," https://www.regulations.gov /document?D=NOAA-NOS-2011-0243-0010.

50 U.S. Department of Commerce, "Expansion of Fagatele Bay National Marine Sanctuary; Final Rule," 43955.

51 "Comment from Lima Tapuaʻi."

52 U.S. Department of Commerce, "Expansion of Fagatele Bay National Marine Sanctuary; Final Rule," 43957.

53 "Comment from Tepora Lavataʻi," Regulations.gov, January 6, 2012, 1, accessed August 26, 2016, https://www.regulations.gov/document?D=NOAA-NOS-2011-0243-0134.

54 See "Superintendent's Update Report," November 2012 to March 2013," 2, accessed July 14, 2017, http://americansamoa.noaa.gov/pdfs/sac-update-0413.pdf.

55 "Comment from Siaumau Siaumau," Regulations.gov, January 6, 2012, h accessed August 26, 2016, ttps://www.regulations.gov/document?D=NOAA-NOS-2011-0243-0082.

56 U.S. Department of Commerce, "Expansion of Fagatele Bay National Marine Sanctuary; Final Rule," 43957.

57 U.S. Government Printing Office, "National Marine Sanctuary Program Regulations, Subpart C—Designation of National Marine Sanctuaries," Electronic Code of Federal Regulations, accessed August 24, 2016, http://www.ecfr.gov/cgibin/retrieve ECFR?gp=&SID=c5dc3424ae799143c42a14559dafc551&mc=true&r=PART&n=pt1 5.3.922#sp15.3.922.c.

58 "Comment from Larry Sanitoa," Regulations.gov, January 9, 2012, accessed August 25, 1016, https://www.regulations.gov/document?D=NOAA-NOS-2011-0243-0119.

59 "Comment from Save Tuitele."

60 Matthew and Poti, *A Biogeographic Assessment,* 175-176.

61 Matthew and Poti, *A Biogeographic Assessment,* iv.

62 U.S. Department of Commerce, "Expansion of Fagatele Bay National Marine Sanctuary; Final Rule," Use Existing Management (R2), 15 CFR Part 922.

63 U.S. Department of Commerce, "Expansion of Fagatele Bay National Marine Sanctuary; Final Rule," Use Existing Management (R2).

64 U.S. Department of Commerce, "Expansion of Fagatele Bay National Marine Sanctuary; Final Rule," Use Existing Management (R2).

65 U.S. Department of Commerce, "Expansion of Fagatele Bay National Marine Sanctuary Name Change," Response to Public Comment, Support for Preferred Alternative.

66 "Comment from Jessica Peters," Regulations.gov, December 1, 2011, accessed August 25, 2016, https://www.regulations.gov/document?D=NOAA-NOS-2011-0243-0047.

67 "Comment from Tuai Auvaʻa," Regulations.gov, November 30, 2011, accessed August 25, 2016, https://www.regulations.gov/document?D=NOAA-NOS-2011-0243-0034.

68 U.S. Department of Commerce, "Expansion of Fagatele Bay National Marine Sanctuary Name Change," Response to Public Comment, Support for Preferred Alternative.

69 "Comment from Anonymous Anonymous." Regulations.gov, March 12, 2012,

accessed August 26, 2016, https://www.regulations.gov/document?D=NOAA-NOS-2011
-0243-0182.

70 "Comment from Sandra Lutu," Regulations.gov, January 5, 2012, accessed July 11,
2017, https://www.regulations.gov/document?D=NOAA-NOS-2011-0243-0074.

71 "Comment from Sandra Lutu."

72 U.S. Department of Commerce, "Expansion of Fagatele Bay National Marine
Sanctuary; Final Rule," Use Existing Management (R2).

73 "Comment from Anonymous Anonymous," Regulations.gov, November 28, 2011,
accessed August 26, 2016, https://www.regulations.gov/document?D=NOAA-NOS-2011
-0243-0029.

74 Barnett and Campbell, *Climate Change,* 131, 134.

75 "Sanctuary Designation," Hawaiian Islands Humpback Whale National Marine
Sanctuary, https://hawaiihumpbackwhale.noaa.gov/management/designation.html. Accessed August 12, 2018.

76 "Sanctuary Designation."

77 "Aloha ʻĀina Guidance Document," Hawaiian Islands Humpback Whale National Marine Sanctuary, accessed August 12, 2018, https://hawaiihumpbackwhale
.noaa.gov/council/council_aloha_aina_guidance.html.

78 Jacoby, *Crimes,* 198.

79 Jacoby, *Crimes,* 1.

80 Jacoby, *Crimes,* 198.

81 Spence, *Dispossessing,* 88.

82 Sasha Davis, *Empires' Edge: Militarization, Resistance, and Transcending Hegemony in the Pacific* (Athens: University of Georgia Press, 2015), 26.

83 "Fact Sheet," National Park of American Sāmoa, accessed August 12, 2018, https://
www.nps.gov/npsa/learn/news/fact-sheet.htm.

84 "Laws and Policies," National Park of American Sāmoa, accessed August 12, 2018,
https://www.nps.gov/npsa/learn/management/lawsandpolicies.htm.

85 "National Park of American Samoa Celebrates 25th Anniversary," National Park
of American Sāmoa, accessed August 12, 2018, https://www.nps.gov/npsa/learn/news
/25th-anniversary.htm.

86 "Original ASG/National Park of American Samoa lease," National Park of American
Sāmoa, accessed August 12, 2018, https://home.nps.gov/npsa/learn/management/upload
/asmleaseop2.pdf.

87 "Fact Sheet."

88 Spence, *Dispossessing,* 4.

89 Susan White, "Comment: Letter from Department of Interior, Fish and Wildlife Service," Regulations.gov, January 9, 2012, accessed August 26, 2016, https://www
.regulations.gov/document?D=NOAA-NOS-2011-0243-0155.

90 Atautasi Lelei Peau, interview by author, June 22, 2015, Utueli, American Sāmoa.

91 "Tauese P.F. Suina Ocean Center," NOAA, National Marine Sanctuary of

American Samoa, accessed October 28, 2015, http://american samoa.noaa.gov/about/ocean
-center.html.

92 Joseph Paulin, interview by author, June 15, 2015, Utueli, American Sāmoa.

93 Peau, interview by author.

94 U.S. Department of Commerce, NOAA, National Marine Sanctuary, "A Call
to Action from the Marine Protected Areas Federal Advisory Committee and the National Marine Sanctuary Advisory Councils, Destination Marine Protected Areas:
Sustaining America's Most Treasured Ocean Places for Recreation and Stewardship,"
June 2014, accessed October 28, 2015, http://americansamoa. noaa.gov/council/pdfs
/action-0614.pdf.

95 Thomas, interview by author.

96 Tosatto, interview by author, August 8, 2016, Ford Island, O'ahu, Hawai'i.

97 Tosatto, interview by author.

98 Mitchell Thomashow, "Toward a cosmopolitan bioregionalism," in *Bioregionalism,* ed. Michael Vincent McGinnis (New York: Routledge, 2005), 130.

Chapter 4: The Impact of the U.S. Imperial Grants System on Indigenous Marine Programs

1 Bureau of Economic Analysis, "Gross Domestic Product," Table 2.2, 10.

2 David Itano, "A Review of the Development of Bottomfish Fisheries in American
Samoa," *Department of Marine and Wildlife Resources Biological Report Series,* no. 26
(October 1991): 2.

3 Peter Craig, Bonnie Ponwith, Fini Aitaoto, and David Hamn, "The Commercial,
Subsistence, and Recreational Fisheries of American Samoa," *Marine Fisheries Review*
55 (1993): 109-116.

4 David G. Itano, "The Development of Small-Scale Fisheries for Bottomfish in
American Samoa (1961-1987)," *SPC Fisheries Newsletter,* 1.

5 "Chapter 3 — Office of Marine and Wildlife Resources: A.S.C.A. Code 24, §§.0301,"
American Samoa Bar Association, accessed November 4, 2015, http://www.asbar.org
/index.php?option= com_content&view=category&id=603&Itemid=172.

6 "Sport Fish Restoration Program — Overview," U.S. Fish and Wildlife Service:
Wildlife and Sport Fish Restoration Program, May 1, 2015, accessed October 23, 2015,
http://wsfrprograms.fws.gov/Subpages/GrantPrograms/SFR/SFR.htm.

7 "Sport Fish Restoration Program — Overview."

8 Deputy Director of Fish and Wildlife Service, "Certificate of Apportionment of
$351,917,483 of the Appropriation for Dingell-Johnson Sport Fist Restoration," March 20,
2018, Sport Fish Restoration Program — Funding, U.S. Fish and Wildlife Service website, accessed August 24, 2018, https://wsfrprograms.fws.gov/Subpages/GrantPrograms
/SFR/SFRFinalApportionment2018.pdf.

9 Laurie Richmond and Arielle Levine, "Institutional Analysis of Community-based Marine Resource Management Initiatives in Hawai'i and American Samoa," NOAA Technical Memorandum NMFS-PIFSC-35, November 2012, accessed October 22, 2015, http://www.academia.edu/15396383/NOAA_ Technical_Memorandum_NMFS-PIFSC-35 _Institutional_Analysis_of_Community-based_Marine_Resource_Management _Initiatives_in_Hawaii_and_American_Samoa.

10 Allamander Amituana'i and Fatima Sauafea, "Improving Community Skills and Knowledge to Build, Enhance and Promote Environmental Stewardship," in *Samoa Ministry of Natural Resources and Environment,* Proceedings of 2004 National Environment Forum, 4.

11 See personal communication (Sauafea-Le'au, 2008) in Arielle S. Levine and Laurie S. Richmond, "Examining Enabling Conditions for Community-Based Fisheries Co-management: Comparing Efforts in Hawai'i and American Samoa," *Ecology and Society* 19 (2014): 5.

12 Saumaniafaese Uikirifi, interview by author, June 11, 2015, Fagatogo, American Sāmoa.

13 Levine and Allen, "American Samoa as a Fishing Community," 53.

14 Jeremy M. Raynal, Arielle S. Levine and Mia T. Comeros-Raynal, "American Samoa's Marine Protected Area System: Institutions, Governance, and Scale," *Journal of International Wildlife Law and Policy* 19, no. 4 (December 2016): 310.

15 Raynal et al., "American Samoa's Marine Protected Area System," 312.

16 "Chapter 10 — Community-Based Fisheries Management Program, 24.1002 Purpose," American Samoa Bar Association, accessed July 24, 2017, http://www.asbar.org /index.php?option=com_content&view=category&id=887&Itemid=294.

17 Uikirifi, interview by author, June 22, 2016, Fagatogo, American Sāmoa.

18 Uikirifi, interview by author, June 11, 2015.

19 "No Take MPA documents," The Department of Marine and Wildlife Resources blog, accessed July 24, 2017, https://www.scribd.com/document/115527329 /Government-Leaders-and-Village-Mayors-Workshop-on-Oct-15-2010.

20 Uikirifi, interview by author, June 11, 2015.

21 Peter Craig, "The Status of the Coral Reefs in American Samoa," in *American Samoa's state of the reefs,* American Sāmoa Government, 183-184, accessed July 24, 2017, https://www.coris.noaa.gov/portals/pdfs/status_coralreef_samoa.pdf.

22 Robert B. Moffitt, Jon Brodziak, and Thomas Flores, "Status of the bottomfish resources of American Samoa, Guam, and Commonwealth of the Northern Mariana Islands, 2005," Pacific Islands Fisheries Science Center, Administrative Report H-07-04, October 2007, 16, accessed July 27, 2017, https://repository.library.noaa.gov/view /noaa/3543.

23 Mitsuyasu, interview by author.

24 Uikirifi, interview by author, June 11, 2015.

25 Sakaio Misifoa, interview by author, with translator Uikirifi, June 22, 2016, Afo-fau, American Sāmoa.

26 Uikirifi, interview by author, June 22, 2016.

27 Uikirifi, interview by author, June 22, 2016.

28 Uikirifi, interview by author, June 22, 2016.

29 Fikret Berkes, Johan Colding, and Carl Folke, "Rediscovery of Traditional Ecological Knowledge as Adaptive Management," *Ecological Applications* 10 (2000): 1251.

30 Bill Thomas, interview by author.

31 Richard C. Wass, "The Shoreline Fishery of American Samoa—Past and Present," in *Unesco Seminar on Marine and Coastal Processes in the Pacific,* Proceedings of Marine and Coastal Processes in the Pacific: Ecological Aspects of Coastal Zone Management, Motupore Island, Papua New Guinea, Jakarta, Indonesia: UNESCO, 14-17 June 1980, 57. See also Levine and Allen, "American Samoa as a Fishing Community," Armstrong, Herdrich, and Levine, "Historic Fishing Methods," 21, and R. E. Johannes, "Traditional Marine Conservation Methods in Oceania and Their Demise," *Annual Review of Ecology and Systematics* 9 (1978): 350.

32 Wass, "The Shoreline Fishery," 58.

33 Tosatto, interview by author.

34 Eves, interview by author, June 8, 2015, Fagatogo, American Sāmoa.

35 Suaalii-Sauni et al., *Su'esu'e Manogi,* 108.

36 Eves, interview by author.

37 For more details, see "24.1026 Protection of other Marine Life in a Village Marine Protected Area" and "24.1027 Endangered Species," in Chapter 10—Community-Based Fisheries Management Program."

38 "Endangered Species Act, Section 11, Penalties and Enforcement," U.S. Fish and Wildlife Service, accessed November 14, 2018, https://www.fws.gov/endangered/laws-policies/section-11.html.

39 DMWR Staff Member 1 and 2, interview by author, June 16, 2015, Fagatogo, American Sāmoa.

40 Uikirifi, interview by author, June 11, 2015.

41 R. E. Johannes, "Traditional Marine Conservation Methods in Oceania and their Demise," Annual Review of Ecology and Systematics, 9, 1978, 349-364.

42 Johannes, "The Renaissance of Community-Based Marine Resource Management in Oceania," *Annual Review of Ecology and Systematics* 33, no. 1 (2002): 317.

43 Richard C. Wass, "Characterization of Inshore Samoan Fish Communities," *DMWR Biological Report Series* 6 (1982): 1.

44 J. A. Drew, "Use of Traditional Ecological Knowledge," 1287. See also M. King and U. Faasili, "Community-based Management of Subsistence Fisheries in Samoa," *Fisheries Management and Ecology* 6 (1999): 133-144, S. M. Evans and A. C. Birchenough, "Community-based Management of the Environment;" R. E. Johannes, "The Renaissance," S. Aswani, and R. J. Hamilton, "Integrating Indigenous Ecological Knowledge and Customary Sea Tenure with Marine and Social Science for Conservation of

Bumphead Parrotfish (Bolbometopon muricatum) in the Roviana Lagoon, Solomon Islands," *Environmental Conservation* 31 (2004): 69-83.

45 Barnett and Campbell, *Climate Change,* 132.

46 Laʻaloa Taulaga, interview by author, with translator Uikirifi, June 22, 2016, Faga-togo, American Sāmoa.

47 Taulaga, interview by author.

48 Misifoa, interview by author.

49 Barnett and Campbell, *Climate Change,* 131.

50 Department of Marine and Wildlife Resources Staff Member 1, interview by author, June 16, 2015, Fagatogo, American Sāmoa.

51 DMWR Staff Member 1, interview by author. See also S. M. Evans, and A. C. Birchenough, "Community-based Management of the Environment: Lessons from the Past and Options for the Future," *Aquatic Conservation: Marine and Freshwater Ecosystems* 11 (2001): 137-147; S. A. Clarke, A. L. Wai-yin, Y. M. Mak, R. Kennish, and N. Haggan, "Consultation with Local Fishers on the Hong Kong Artificial Reefs Initiative," *ICES Journal of Marine Science* 59 (2002): S171-177; D. O. Obura, S. Wells, J. Church, and C. Horrill, "Monitoring of Fish and Fish Catches by Local Fishermen in Kenya and Tanzania," *Marine and Freshwater Research* 53 (2002): 215-222; Alan T. White, Catherine A. Courtney, and Albert Salamanca, "Experience with Marine Protected Area Planning and Management in the Philippines," *Coastal Management* 30 (2002): 1-26.

52 DMWR Staff Member 1, interview by author.

53 See "Title 2: Grants and Agreements, Part 200—Uniform Administrative Requirements, Cost Principles, And Audit Requirements For Federal Awards" of the Electronic Code Of Federal Regulations, Effective January 6, 2017, accessed July 31, 2017, https://www.fws.gov/grants/atc.html; and U.S. Fish and Wildlife Service, Wildlife and Sport Fish Restoration Program Application Guidelines, OMB Control No. 1018-0109, accessed July 31, 2017, https://wsfrprograms.fws.gov/home.html.

54 Ufagafa Ray Tulafono, interview with author.

55 "Creel Survey Program," Department of Marine and Wildlife Resources, accessed October 22, 2015, http://asdmwr.org/srgp/creel-survey.

56 Richard C. Wass, "The Shoreline Fishery."

57 Severance, Simonds, and Franco, "Justification and Design."

58 Craig, Ponwith, Aitaoto, and Hamn, "Commercial, Subsistence, and Recreational Fisheries," 110. See also Harry Burnette Hill, *The Use of Nearshore Marine Life as a Food Resource by American Samoans* (Master's thesis, University of Hawaiʻi, 1978), Honolulu: Pacific Islands Studies Program, Miscellaneous Work Papers, University of Hawaiʻi, 1978. For more info on distant-water fleets, see Ramon Bonfil et al., "Distant Water Fleets: An Ecological, Economic and Social Assessment," Fisheries Centre Research Reports 6, no. 6, 1998.

59 Ufagafa Ray Tulafono, interview by author.

60 Ufagafa Ray Tulafono, interview by author.

61 Raymond M. Buckley, David G. Itano, and Troy W. Buckley, "Fish Aggregation

Device (FAD) Enhancement of Offshore Fisheries in American Samoa," *Bulletin of Marine Science* 44 (March 1989): 4.

62 Craig, Ponwith, Aitaoto, and Hamn, "The Commercial, Subsistence, and Recreational Fisheries," 109.

63 "WPacFIN Program," NOAA Fisheries: Pacific Islands Fisheries Science Center, accessed July 28, 2016, https://pifsc-www.irc.noaa.gov/frmd/wpacfin.php.

64 Bonnie Ponwith, "The Pala Lagoon Subsistence Fishery," *Department of Marine and Wildlife Resources Biological Report Series*, 27th ser. (1992), 28.

65 Ufagafa Ray Tulafono, interview by author. Also see Levine and Allen, "American Samoa as a Fishing Community," 25.

66 "Creel Survey Program."

67 "Creel Survey Program."

68 Priti E. Smith, interview by author, June 22, 2015, Utueli, American Sāmoa.

69 Marlowe Sabater, Asuka Ishizaki, Thomas Remington, and Sylvia Spalding, *Annual Stock Assessment and Fishery Evaluation Report: Fishery Ecosystem Plan for the American Samoa Archipelago 2017*, Western Pacific Regional Fishery Management Council, 3, accessed August 24, 2018, http://www.wpcouncil.org/wp-content/uploads/2018/07/American-Samoa-FEP-SAFE-Report-2017-Final-Optimized.pdf.

70 Information on fishing styles and gender breakdown from Ilaoa, Email with author, August 7, 2017.

71 Smith, interview by author.

72 Sabater, interview by author.

73 Sabater, Email with author, August 8, 2017.

74 Levine and Allen, "NOAA Technical Memorandum NMFS-PIFSC-19," 26.

75 Sabater and Carroll, "Trends in Reef Fish Population and Associated Fishery," 322.

76 Nate Iloa, interview by author, Kristine Bucchianeri, interview by author, June 3, 2015, Fagatogo, American Sāmoa. Michael Crook, interview by author.

77 Barnett and Campbell, *Climate Change*, 134.

78 DMWR staff member 3, interview by author, June 8, 2015, Fagatogo, American Sāmoa.

79 Mokoma, interview by author.

80 Mokoma, interview by author.

81 DMWR Staff Member 3, interview by author.

82 Salesa, *Island Time*, Kindle Locations 2208-2211.

83 Salesa, *Island Time*, Kindle Locations 2212-2213.

84 Allen P. Stayman, *U.S. Territorial Policy: Trends and Current Challenges* (Honolulu, East-West Center, 2009), 1.

85 Sabater et al., *Annual Stock Assessment*, v.

86 A. Levine, M. Dillard, J. Loerzel and P. Edwards, "National Coral Reef Monitoring Program Socioeconomic Monitoring Component: Summary Findings for American Samoa, 2014," NOAA Technical Memorandum CRCP 24, NOAA Coral

Reef Conservation Program, Silver Spring, MD, March 2016, 13, accessed July 27, 2017, https://docs.lib.noaa.gov/noaa_documents/NOS/CRCP/TM_CRCP/TM_CRCP_24.pdf.

87 Levine et al, *National Coral Reef Monitoring,* 14.

Conclusion

1 Jacoby, *Crimes,* 29.

2 Jacoby, *Crimes,* 64.

3 Smithers, *The Cherokee Diaspora,* 3.

4 Salesa, *Island Time,* Kindle Locations 2213-2214.

5 Salesa, *Island Time,* Kindle Location 2216.

6 Salesa, *Island Time,* Kindle Locations 2225-2226.

7 Salesa, *Island Time,* Kindle Locations 2237-2239.

8 Salesa, *Island Time,* Kindle Locations 1129-1133.

9 Salesa, *Island Time,* Kindle Locations 1354-1357.

10 *Polynesian Panthers: A Documentary,* directed by Salmon Dan, Kay Ellmers, Nevak 'Ilolahia, and Tūmanako Productions. Tūmanako Productions, 2010.

11 Jacoby, *Crimes,* 66.

12 Smithers, *The Cherokee Diaspora,* 24.

13 Barnett and Campbell, *Climate Change,* 136.

14 Albert Wendt, "Towards a New Oceania," *Mana Reivew* 1 (1976): 53.

15 DeLoughrey and Handley, *Postcolonial Ecologies,* 25.

16 Caminero-Santangelo, "In Place," 296.

Selected Bibliography

Primary Sources

Archives

American Sāmoa Historical Preservation Office, Nuʻuuli
American Sāmoa Archives, Tafuna
National Archives at San Francisco
Sāmoa News
Special Collections, Feleti Barstow Public Library, Utulei

Government Documents and Reports

American Sāmoa Government
    Department of Commerce
    Department of Marine and Wildlife Resources
Central Intelligence Agency
Code of Federal Regulations
Congressional Record
Congressional Reports
Congressional Research Service
Executive Office of the President
Federal Register
National Park Service
Pacific Islands Regional Office
Regulations.gov
U.S. Census Bureau
U.S. Congress
    Committee Hearings
U.S. Coral Reef Task Force
U.S. Department of Agriculture
U.S. Department of Commerce
    National Oceanic & Atmospheric Administration Fisheries
        National Marine Fisheries Services

National Marine Sanctuary of American Samoa
National Ocean Service
Office of National Marine Sanctuary
Pacific Islands Fisheries Science Center
U.S. Department of Labor
U.S. Fish and Wildlife Service
U.S. Government Accountability Office
U.S. Government Printing Office
U.S. Representative Aumua Amata Coleman Radewagen
Western Pacific Regional Fishery Management Council

Non-Governmental Documents and Reports

American Samoa Bar Association
Food and Agriculture Organization of the United Nations
Pacific Island Forum Fisheries Agency
StarKist
United Nations
Fisheries and Aquaculture Department

Media Sources

Cascadia Times
Courthouse News Service
Honolulu Star-Bulletin
The Huffington Post
Marianas Variety
Pacific Islands Report
Sāmoa News
Talanei
Undercurrent News
Washington Examiner
The Washington Times

Partial List of Individual Interviews

American Sāmoa Advisory Council Member, interview by author, August 7, 2014.
    Nuʻuuli, American Sāmoa.
Anonymous, interview by author, August 4, 2014. Pago Pago, American Sāmoa.
Atafua, Mathaew, interview by author, June 22, 2016. Nuʻuuli, American Sāmoa.
Brooke, Samantha, interview by author, August 8, 2016. Ford Island, Oʻahu, Hawaiʻi.
Bucchianeri, Kristine, interview by author, June 3, 2015. Fagatogo, American Sāmoa.

Butler, Brett, interview by author, August 3, 2014. Utueli, American Sāmoa.

Soʻoaʻmalelagi, Tauese Apelu/Chief Faimealelei, interview by author, June 22, 2016. Nuʻuuli, American Sāmoa.

Clark, Tim, interview by author, June 5, 2015. Pago Pago, American Sāmoa.

Corry, Krista, interview by author, June 24, 2015. Pago Pago, American Sāmoa.

Crook, Michael, interview by author, June 10, 2015. Utueli, American Sāmoa.

Department of Marine and Wildlife Resources (American Samoa) Staff Member 1, interview by author, June 16, 2015. Fagatogo, American Sāmoa.

Department of Marine and Wildlife Resources (American Samoa) Staff Member 2, interview by author, June 16, 2015. Fagatogo, American Sāmoa.

Department of Marine and Wildlife Resources (American Samoa) Staff Member 3, interview by author, June 8, 2015. Fagatogo, American Sāmoa.

Matagi-Tofiga, Ruth, interview by author, July 29, 2014. Fagatogo, American Sāmoa.

Solomona, Meki Taeaoafua, interview by author, August 6, 2014. Utueli, American Sāmoa.

Eves, Peter, interview by author, June 8, 2015. Fagatogo, American Sāmoa.

Eves, Peter, interview by author, June 20, 2016. Fagatogo, American Sāmoa.

Fenner, Doug, interview by author, June 15, 2016. Utueli, American Sāmoa.

Fuimaono, Christina Muaimalae, interview by author, June 23, 2016. Futiga, American Sāmoa.

Fuimaono, Tuifagalua, interview by author, June 23, 2016. Futiga, American Sāmoa.

Gonzales, Carlos, interview with author, July 31, 2014. Atuʻu, American Sāmoa.

Gurr, James, interview by author, June 17, 2015. Mapusaga, American Sāmoa.

Hall, Richard, interview by author, August 9, 2016. Ford Island, Oʻahu, Hawaiʻi.

Ilaoa, Nate, interview by author, July 30, 2014. Fagatogo, American Sāmoa.

Langkilde, Tony, interview by author, June 17, 2016. Fagatogo, American Sāmoa.

Langkilde, Tony, interview by author, June 20, 2016. Fagatogo, American Sāmoa.

Letuane, Mika, interview by author, June 24, 2016. Fagatogo, American Sāmoa.

Letuli, Patricia, interview by author, August 8, 2014. Pago Pago, American Sāmoa.

Levine, Arielle, interview by author, March 24, 2016. San Diego, California.

Lutu, Afoa, interview by author, June 24, 2015. Fagatogo, American Sāmoa.

Lutu-Sanchez, Christinna, interview by author, June 21, 2016. Utulei, American Sāmoa.

Luva, Rafa, interview by author, August 4, 2014. Utueli, American Sāmoa.

Maea, Maʻa, interview by author, August 4, 2014. Fagatogo, American Sāmoa.

Masunu, Tasele, interview by author, June 22, 2016. Nuʻuuli, American Sāmoa.

Misifoa, Sakaio, interview by author, with translator Uikirifi, June 22, 2016. Afofau, American Sāmoa.

Mitsuyasu, Mark, interview by author, August 10, 2016. Honolulu, Hawaiʻi.

Mokoma, Alvin Eo, interview by author, June 21, 2016. Pago Pago.

Paulin, Joseph, interview by author, June 15, 2015. Utueli, American Sāmoa.

Peau, Atautasi Lelei, interview by author, June 22, 2015. Utueli, American Sāmoa.

Rogers-Kaʻaekuahiwi, Leila Hokulani, interview by author, August 9, 2016. Ford Island, Oʻahu, Hawaiʻi.

Sabater, Marlowe, interview by author, August 10, 2016. Honolulu, Hawaiʻi.

Sanchez, Carlos, interview by author, August 8, 2014. Utueli, American Sāmoa.

Sesepasara, Vaʻamua Henry, interview by author, June 4, 2015. Utueli, American Sāmoa.

Smith, Priti E, interview by author, June 22, 2015. Utueli, American Sāmoa.

Sullivan, Dan, interview by author, June 26, 2015. Pago Pago, American Sāmoa.

Sunia, Fofō, interview by author, June 24, 2015. Tafuna, American Sāmoa.

Sword, William, interview by author, June 23, 2016. Utulei.

Taulaga, Laʻaloa, interview by author, with translator Uikirifi, June 22, 2016. Fagatogo, American Sāmoa.

Thomas, Bill, interview by author, August 8, 2016. Ford Island, Oʻahu, Hawaiʻi.

Thompson, Sonny, interview by author, August 2, 2014. Utueli, American Sāmoa.

Tosatto, Michael, interview by author, August 8, 2016. Ford Island, Oʻahu, Hawaiʻi.

Tucher, Frederick, interview by author, August 9, 2016. Ford Island, Oʻahu, Hawaiʻi.

Tulafono, Togiola, interview by author, June 17, 2015. Utueli, American Sāmoa.

Tulafono, Ufagafa Ray, interview by author, June 23, 2015. Pago Pago, American Sāmoa.

Uikirifi, Saumaniafaese, interview by author, June 11, 2015. Fagatogo, American Sāmoa.

Uikirifi, Saumaniafaese, interview by author, June 22, 2016. Fagatogo, American Sāmoa.

Wasko, John, interview by author, June 31, 2014. Fagatogo, American Sāmoa.

"WestPac Fisheries Council Meeting." Interview by author, August 7, 2014. Nuʻuuli, American Sāmoa.

Secondary Sources

Aleinikoff, Thomas Alexander. *Semblances of Sovereignty the Constitution, the State, and American Citizenship.* Cambridge, MA: Harvard University Press, 2002.

Amerika Samoa Humanities Council. *A History of American Samoa.* Honolulu: Bess Press, 2009.

Amituanaʻi, Allamander, and Fatima Sauafea. "Improving Community Skills and Knowledge to Build, Enhance and Promote Environmental Stewardship." Proceedings of 2004 National Environment Forum. Samoa Ministry of Natural Resources and Environment, no. 4. Apia, Samoa (2005).

Aswani, S., and R. J. Hamilton. "Integrating Indigenous Ecological Knowledge and Customary Sea Tenure with Marine and Social Science for Conservation of Bumphead Parrotfish (Bolbometopon muricatum) in the Roviana Lagoon, Solomon Islands." *Environmental Conservation* 31, no. 1 (2004): 69-83.

Barnet, Richard J., and John Cavanagh. *Global Dreams: Imperial Corporations and the New World Order.* New York: Simon & Schuster, 1994.

Barnett, Jon, and John R. Campbell. *Climate Change and Small Island States: Power, Knowledge, and the South Pacific.* London: Earthscan, 2010.

Berkes, Fikret. *Sacred Ecology.* New York: Routledge, 2012.

Binder, Sherri Brokopp. "Resilience and Disaster Recovery in American Samoa: A Case Study of the 2009 Pacific Tsunami." Master's thesis, University of Hawai'i, 2012.

Blackford, Mansel G. *Making Seafood Sustainable: American Experiences in Global Perspective.* Philadelphia: University of Pennsylvania Press, 2012.

Blackford, Mansel G. *Pathways to the Present U.S. Development and Its Consequences in the Pacific.* Honolulu: University of Hawai'i Press, 2007.

Bond, David. "Oil in the Caribbean: Refineries, Mangroves, and the Negative Ecologies of Crude Oil." *Comparative Studies in Society and History* 59, no. 3 (2017): 600-628.

Brock, Richard E. "Preliminary Study of the Feeding Habits of Pelagic Fish Around Hawaiian Fish Aggregation Devices or Can Fish Aggregation Devices Enhance Local Fisheries Productivity?" *Bulletin of Marine Science* 37, no. 1 (July 1985): 40-49.

Buck, Peter Henry (Te Rangi Hiroa) *Samoan Material Culture.* New York: Kraus, 1971.

Buckley, Raymond M., David G. Itano, and Troy W. Buckley. "Fish Aggregation Device (FAD) Enhancement of Offshore Fisheries in American Samoa." *Bulletin of Marine Science* 44, no. 2 (March 1989): 942-949.

Cahn, Miranda. "Indigenous Entrepreneurship, Culture and Micro-enterprise in the Pacific Islands: Case Studies from Samoa," *Entrepreneurship and Regional Development,* no. 20 (2008): 1-18.

Caminero-Santangelo, Byron. "In Place." In *Postcolonial Ecologies: Literatures of the Environment,* edited by Elizabeth M. DeLoughrey and George B. Handley, 291-306. New York: Oxford University Press, 2011.

Cepeda Derieux, Adriel I. "A Most Insular Minority: Reconsidering Judicial Deference to Unequal Treatment in Light of Puerto Rico's Political Process Failure." *Columbia Law Review* 110, no. 3 (2010): 797-839.

"Citizens Class: Abramoff, Inc." *Moyers on America.* Public Broadcasting Service. 2006, accessed November 3, 2015, http://www.pbs.org/moyers/moyersonamerica /print/marianasclass_print.html.

Clain, Suzanne Heller. "Explaining the Passage of Living Wage Legislation in the U.S." *Atlantic Economic Journal* 40, no. 3 (2012): 315-327.

Clarke, S. A., A. L. Wai-yin, Y. M. Mak, R. Kennish, and N. Haggan. "Consultation with Local Fishers on the Hong Kong Artificial Reefs Initiative." *ICES Journal of Marine Science* 59, supplement (2002): S171-177.

Coburn, Senator Tom, M. D. *Tax Decoder.* December 2014, accessed February 11, 2016, https://web.archive.org/web/20141210013518/http://www.coburn.

senate.gov/public/index.cfm?a=Files.Serve&File_id=e1f80788-49ce-4bef-b30d-2c2d074a4f7e. 31.

Cohen, Lizabeth. *A Consumers' Republic: The Politics of Mass Consumption in Postwar America*. New York: Vintage Books, 2004.

Cook, Kealani R. "Kahiki: Native Hawaiian Relationships with Other Pacific Islanders 1850-1915." PhD diss., University of Michigan, 2011.

Craig, P., A. Green, and F. Tuilagi. "Subsistence Harvest of Coral Reef Resources in the Outer Islands of American Samoa: Modern, Historic and Prehistoric Catches." *Fisheries Research* 89, no. 3 (March 2008): 230-240.

Craig, Peter, Bonnie Ponwith, Fini Aitaoto, and David Hamn. "The Commercial, Subsistence, and Recreational Fisheries of American Samoa." *Marine Fisheries Review* 55, no. 2 (1993): 109-116.

Crocombe, Marjorie Tuainekore, R. G. Crocombe, eds. *Polynesian Missions in Melanesia: From Samoa, Cook Islands and Tonga to Papua New Guinea and New Caledonia*. Suva, Fiji: Institute of Pacific Studies, University of the South Pacific, 1982.

Cross, Gary S. *An All-Consuming Century: Why Commercialism Won in Modern America*. New York: Columbia University Press, 2000.

Davis, Sasha. *The Empires' Edge: Militarization, Resistance, and Transcending Hegemony in the Pacific*. Athens: University of Georgia Press, 2015.

DeLoughrey, Elizabeth M., and George B. Handley. *Postcolonial Ecologies: Literatures of the Environment*. New York: Oxford University Press, 2011.

Diaz, Vicente M. *Repositioning the Missionary: Rewriting the Histories of Colonialism, Native Catholicism, and Indigeneity in Guam*. Honolulu: University of Hawai'i Press, 2010.

Drew, Joshua A. "Use of Traditional Ecological Knowledge in Marine Conservation." *Conservation Biology* 19, no. 4 (June 30, 2005): 1286-1293.

Droessler, Holger. "Islands of Labor: Community, Conflict, and Resistance in Colonial Samoa, 1889-1919." PhD diss., American Studies, Graduate School of Arts & Sciences, Harvard University, 2015.

Droessler, Holger. "Whose Pacific? U.S. Security Interests in American Samoa from the Age of Empire to the Pacific Pivot." *Pacific Asia Inquiry* 4, no. 1 (Fall 2013): 58-65.

Duffy Burnett, Christina, and Burke Marshall. *Between Foreign and Domestic: The Doctrine of Territorial Incorporation, Invented and Reinvented*. Durham: Duke University Press, 2001.

Erman, Sam. "Meanings of Citizenship in the U.S. Empire: Puerto Rico, Isabel Gonzalez, and the Supreme Court, 1898 to 1905." *Journal of American Ethnic History* 27, no. 4 (2008): 5-33.

Evans, S. M., and A. C. Birchenough. "Community-based Management of the Environment: Lessons From the Past and Options for the Future." *Aquatic Conservation: Marine and Freshwater Ecosystems* 11, no. 2 (2001): 137-147.

Fa'asili, Ueta, and Fatima Sauafea. *Technical Input into the Community Fisheries Management Program of American Samoa.* Report no. 6, Field Report. Secretariat of the Pacific Community. Noumea, New Caledonia: Secretariat of the Pacific Community, 2001.

Fagan, Brian. *Fishing: How the Sea Fed Civilization.* New Haven, Yale University Press, 2018.

Fairbairn-Dunlop, Peggy. "'E au le inailau a tamaitai': Women, Education and Development, Western Samoa." PhD diss., Macquarie University, Sydney, 1991.

Finney, Suzanne S., Mary Mostafanezhad, Guido Carlo Pigliasco, and Forrest Wade Young, eds. *At Home And In The Field: Ethnographic Encounters In Asia And The Pacific Islands.* Honolulu: University of Hawai'i Press, 2015.

Franco, Robert W. *Samoan Perceptions of Work: Moving Up and Moving Around.* New York: AMS Press, 1991.

Frusher, S. D. "Utilization of Small Scale Fish Aggregation Devices by Papua New Guineas Artisanal Fishermen." *Department of Primary Industry.* Wewak, Papua New Guinea.

Goggans, Jan, and Aaron DiFranco. *The Pacific Region.* Westport, CT: Greenwood Press, 2004.

Goldstein, Alyosha, ed. *Formations of U.S. Colonialism.* Durham: Duke University Press, 2014.

Gray, J. A. C. *Amerika Samoa; A History of American Samoa and Its United States Naval Administration.* Annapolis: United States Naval Institute, 1960.

Guha, Ramachandra. *The Unquiet Woods: Ecological Change and Peasant Resistance in the Himalaya.* Berkeley: University of California Press, 2000.

Guterl, Matthew, and Christine Skwiot. "Atlantic and Pacific Crossings: Race, Empire, and 'The Labor Problem' in the Late Nineteenth Century." *Radical History Review,* no. 91 (2005): 40-61.

Halpern, Rick. "The Iron Fist and the Velvet Glove: Welfare Capitalism in Chicago's Packinghouses, 1921-1933." *Journal of American Studies* 26, no. 2 (August 1992): 159-183.

Hau'ofa, Epeli. *We Are the Ocean: Selected Works.* Honolulu: University of Hawai'i Press, 2008.

Herrold-Menzies, Melinda. "Peasant Resistance Against Nature Reserves." In *Reclaiming Chinese Society: The New Social Activism.* Edited by You-tien Hsing and Ching Kwan. Lee, 85-86. London: Routledge, 2010.

Hill, Harry Burnette. "The Use of Nearshore Marine Life as a Food Resource by American Samoans." Master's thesis, University of Hawai'i, 1978.

Holmes, Lowell Don. *Samoan Village.* Toronto, ON: Thomson Learning, 1974.

Irwin, Geoffrey. "Voyaging and Settlement." In *Vaka Moana: Voyages of the Ancestors,* edited by K. R. Howe, 54-99. Auckland: Auckland Museum/David Bateman, 2006.

Itano, David G. "The Development of Small-Scale Fisheries for Bottomfish in American Samoa (1961-1987)." *SPC Fisheries Newsletter,* 1996.

Jacoby, Karl. *Crimes Against Nature: Squatters, Poachers, Thieves, and the Hidden History of American Conservation.* Berkley: University of California Press, 2003.

Johannes, R. E. "Traditional Marine Conservation Methods in Oceania and Their Demise." *Annual Review of Ecology and Systematics* 9, no. 1 (1978): 349-364.

Johannes, R. E. "The Renaissance of Community-Based Marine Resource Management in Oceania." *Annual Review of Ecology and Systematics* 33, no. 1 (2002): 317-340.

Johnson, Matthew. "Black Gold of Paradise: Negotiating Oil Pollution in the US Virgin Islands, 1966-2012." *Environmental History* 24, no. 4 (2019): 1-27.

Kaneko, J., Bartram, P. "Operational profile of a highliner in the American Samoa small-scale (alia) albacore fishery." SOEST 05-04, JIMAR Contribution 05-357, 2004.

Kaplan, Amy, and Donald E Pease. *Cultures of United States Imperialism (New Americanists).* Durham: Duke University Press, 1993.

Keesing, Felix. *Modern Samoa: Its Government and Change Life.* Stanford: Stanford University Press, 1933.

Kennedy, Joseph. *The Tropical Frontier: America's South Sea Colony.* University Station, Mangilao, Guam: Micronesian Area Research Center, University of Guam, 2009.

Kilarski, Stacey, Daniel Klaus, Jennifer Lipscomb, Kimbrely Matsoukas, Robert Newton, and Abigail Nugent. "Decision Support for Coral Reef Fisheries Management: Community Input as a Means of Informing Policy in American Samoa." Master's thesis, University of California at Santa Barbara, 2006.

King, Michael, and Ueta Fa'asili. "Community-based Management of Subsistence Fisheries in Samoa." *Fisheries Management and Ecology* 6, no. 2 (1999): 133-144.

King, Michael, and Ueta Fa'asili. "A Network of Small, Community-owned Village Fish Reserves in Samoa." *Secretariat of the Pacific Community: Traditional Marine Resource Management and Knowledge.* Information Bulletin 11 (September 1999): 2-6.

Koboski, Theodore. "Socio-Cultural and Economic Barriers to Small Vessel/Indigenous Participation in the American Samoan Longline Fishery," B.S. Thesis, University of Maine, 2014.

Koya, C. N. Haneefa, and A. K. V. Naseer. "Community Participation in Reef Management: An Example of Benign "Dredging" from India." *Coral Reefs* 18, no. 4 (1999): 320.

Krämer, Augustin. *The Samoa Islands: An Outline of a Monograph with Particular Consideration of German Samoa.* Honolulu: University of Hawai'i Press, 1994.

Kuramitsu, Minako. "What is 'The Local' in Women's Participation? The Contexts of Two Development Programs in Samoa." *Geographical Review of Japan, Series B* 74, no. 1 (2001): 15-32.

Kurien, John, and Rolf Willmann. "Special Considerations for Small-Scale Fisheries Management in Developing Countries." In *A Fishery Manager's Guidebook,* edited by Kevern L. Cochrane and Serge M. Garcia, 404-424. Oxford: Wiley-Blackwell, 2009.

Lake, Marilyn, and Henry Reynolds. *Drawing the Global Colour Line: White Men's Countries and the International Challenge of Racial Equality.* Cambridge: Cambridge University Press, 2008.

Lee, Helen, and Steve Tupai. Francis. *Migration and Transnationalism: Pacific Perspectives.* Acton, A.C.T.: Australian National University Press, 2009.

Leibowitz, Arnold H. *Defining Status: A Comprehensive Analysis of U.S. Territorial Policy.* CreateSpace Independent Publishing Platform, 2016.

Levine, Arielle, and Fatima Sauafea-Le'au. "Traditional Knowledge, Use, and Management of Living Marine Resources in American Samoa: Documenting Changes Over Time Through Interviews with Elder Fishers." *Pacific Science* 67, no. 3 (2013): 395-407.

Levine, Arielle, and Laurie Richmond. "Using Common-pool Resource Design Principles to Assess the Viability of Community-based Fisheries Co-management Systems in American Samoa and Hawai'i." *Marine Policy* 62 (December 2015): 9-17.

Levine, Arielle S., and Laurie S. Richmond. "Examining Enabling Conditions for Community-Based Fisheries Comanagement: Comparing Efforts in Hawai'i and American Samoa." *Ecology and Society* 19, no. 1 (2014): Article 24.

Lilomaiava-Doktor, Sa'iliemanu. "Beyond 'Migration': Samoan Population Movement *(Malaga)* and the Geography of Social Space *(Vā)*." *The Contemporary Pacific* 21, no. 1 (2009): 1-32.

Lilomaiava-Doktor, Sa'iliemanu. "Fa'a-Samoa and population movement from the inside out: the case of Salelologa, Savai'i." PhD dissertation, University of Hawai'i, 2004.

Lilomaiava-Doktor, Sa'iliemanu. "Samoan Transnationalism: Cultivating "Home" and "Reach." In *Migration and Transnationalism: Pacific Perspectives.* Edited by Lee Helen and Tupai Francis Steve. Acton, A.C.T.: Australian National University, 2009.

Luckey, John R. *Buy American Act, Buy America Act, Little Buy American Act, The Berry Amendment: Which is What and Who's on First?* Report no. Open-file report NB-2012-07119. Congressional Research Library. Washington, D.C.: American Law Division, 2012.

Macpherson, Cluny, and La'avasa Macpherson. *The Warm Winds of Change:Globalisation in Contemporary Samoa.* Chicago: Auckland University Press, 2010.

Maiava, Susan. *A Clash of Paradigms: Intervention, Response and Development in the South Pacific.* Abingdon, Oxon: Routledge, 2018.

Mandell, Nikki. *The Corporation as Family: The Gendering of Corporate Welfare, 1890-1930.* Chapel Hill: University of North Carolina Press, 2002.

Matsumoto, Walter M., Thomas K. Kazama, and Donald C. Aasted. "Anchored Fish Aggregating Devices in Hawaiian Waters." *Marine Fisheries Review* 43, no. 9 (September 1981): 1-13.

McGeehan, Kathleen M. "Cultural and Religious Belief Systems, Tsunami Recovery and Disaster Risk Reduction in American Samoa in the Aftermath of the September 29, 2009 Tsunami." Master's thesis, University of Hawaiʻi, 2012.

McGregor, Davianna Pomaikaʻi. Nā Kuaʻāina: Living Hawaiian Culture. Honolulu: University of Hawaiʻi Press, 2007.

Meleisea, Malama. The Making of Modern Samoa: Traditional Authority and Colonial Administration in the History of Western Samoa. Suva, Fiji: Institute of Pacific Studies, University of the South Pacific, 1987.

Miller, Frederic M., Agnes F. Vandome, and John McBrewster. History of Samoa. Mauritius: Alphascript Publishers, 2010.

Moore, Donald S. "Contesting Terrain in Zimbabwe's Eastern Highlands: Political Ecology, Ethnography, and Peasant Resource Struggles." Economic Geography 29, no. 3 (1993): 380-401.

Munro, Doug, and Andrew Thornley. The Covenant Makers: Islander Missionaries in the Pacific. Suva, Fiji: Pacific Theological College, The Institute of Pacific Studies at the University of the South Pacific, 1996.

Neuman, Gerald L., and Tomiko Brown-Nagin. "Reconsidering the Insular Cases: The Past and Future of the American Empire." Master's thesis, Harvard Law School, 2015.

Neumann, Roderick P. Imposing Wilderness: Struggles Over Livelihood and Nature Preservation in Africa. Berkeley: University of California Press, 1998.

Neumann, Roderick P. "Political Ecology of Wildlife Conservation in the Mt. Meru Area of Northeast Tanzania." Land Degradation and Development 3, no. 2 (1992): 85-98.

Obura, D. O., S. Wells, J. Church, and C. Horrill. "Monitoring of Fish and Fish Catches by Local Fishermen in Kenya and Tanzania." Marine and Freshwater Research 53, no. 2 (2002): 215-222.

Okey, Thomas A. "Membership of the eight Regional Fishery Management Councils in the United States: are special interests over-represented?" Marine Policy 27, no. 3 (2003): 193-206.

Peet, Richard, and Michael Watts. Liberation Ecologies: Environment, Development, Social Movements. London: Routledge, 1996.

Peluso, Nancy Lee. Rich Forests, Poor People: Resource Control and Resistance in Java. Berkeley: University of California Press, 1992.

Petersen, Glenn. "Indigenous Island Empires: Yap and Tonga Considered." Journal of Pacific History 35, no. 1 (2000): 5-27.

Poblete, JoAnna. Islanders in the Empire: Filipino and Puerto Rican Laborers in Hawaiʻi. Urbana: University of Illinois Press, 2014.

Poblete-Cross, JoAnna. "Bridging Indigenous and Immigrant Struggles: A Case Study of American Sāmoa." American Quarterly 62, no. 3 (2010): 501-522.

Raustiala, Kal. Does the Constitution Follow the Flag?: The Evolution of Territoriality in American Law. Cambridge: Oxford University Press, 2009.

Raynal, Jeremy M., Arielle S. Levine, and Mia T. Comeros-Raynal. "American Samoa's Marine Protected Area System: Institutions, Governance, and Scale." *Journal of International Wildlife Law and Policy* 19, no. 4 (2016): 301-316.

Roberts, Callum. *The Unnatural History of the Sea.* Washington, D.C.: Island Press/ Shearwater Books, 2007.

Roman, Ediberto. *The Other American Colonies: An International and Constitutional Law Examination of the United States' Nineteenth and Twentieth Century Island Conquests.* Durham: Carolina Academic Press, 2006.

Sabater, Marlowe G., and Benjamin P. Carroll. "Trends in Reef Fish Population and Associated Fishery after Three Millennia of Resource Utilization and a Century of Socio-Economic Changes in American Samoa." *Reviews in Fisheries Science* 17, no. 3 (2009): 318-335.

Sailiata, Kirisitina. "The Samoan Cause: Colonialism, Culture, and the Rule of Law." PhD diss., University of Michigan, 2014.

Salesa, Damon Ieremia. *Island Time: New Zealand's Pacific Futures.* Wellington, New Zealand: Bridget Williams Books, 2017.

Shaffer, J. Robert. *American Sāmoa: 100 Years Under the United States Flag.* Honolulu, HI: Island Heritage Publishing, 2000.

Smith, Allan H., and Fikret Berkes. "Solutions to the 'Tragedy of the Commons': Sea-urchin Management in St Lucia, West Indies." *Environmental Conservation* 18, no. 2 (1991): 131-136.

Smith, Andrew F. *American Tuna: The Rise and Fall of an Improbable Food.* Berkeley: University of California Press, 2012.

Somerville, Alice Te Punga. *Once Were Pacific: Māori Connections to Oceania.* Minneapolis: University of Minnesota Press, 2012.

Sparrow, Bartholomew H. *The Insular Cases and the Emergence of American Empire.* Lawrence: Kansas University Press, 2006.

Spence, Mark David. *Dispossessing the Wilderness: Indian Removal and the Making of the National Parks.* New York: Oxford University Press, 1999.

Suaalii-Sauni, Tamasailau M, I'uogafa Tuagalu, Tofilau Nina Krifi-Alai, and Namoi Fuamatu. *Su'esu'e Manogi: In Search of fragrance: Tui Atua Tupua Tamasese Ta'isi and the Samoan Indigenous Reference.* Apia, Samoa: The Centre for Samoan Studies, National University of Samoa, 2009.

Sunia, Fofō I. F. *The Story of the Legislature of American Samoa: In Commemoration of the Golden Jubilee 1948—1998.* Auckland: GP Print of New Zealand, 1998.

Thomas, Nicholas. *Islanders: The Pacific in the Age of Empire.* New Haven: Yale University Press, 2010.

Turner, Rachel. "An Assessment of Public Perceptions for the Planning of Environmental Education." *Ocean and Coastal Management* (2005), 1-13.

Uperesa, Fa'anofo Lisaclaire. *Fabled Futures: Development, Gridiron Football, and Transnational Movements in American Samoa.* PhD diss., Anthropology, Columbia University, 2010.

Uperesa, Faʻanofo Lisaclaire. "Fabled Futures: Migration and Mobility for Samoans in American Football." *The Contemporary Pacific* 26, no. 2 (2014): 281-301.

Uperesa, Faʻanofo Lisaclaire. "New Fields of Labor: Football and Colonial Political Economies in American Samoa." In *Formations of US Colonialism,* edited by Alyosha Goldstein, 207-232. Durham: Duke University Press, 2014.

Uperesa, Faʻanofo Lisaclaire. "Tales of the Tala (Dollar): Notes on Cars, Consumption, and Class in American Samoa." In *At Home And In The Field: Ethnographic Encounters In Asia And The Pacific Islands,* edited by Suzanne S. Finney, Mary Mostafanezhad, Guido Carlo Pigliasco, and Forrest Wade Young, 175-183. Honolulu: University of Hawaiʻi Press, 2015.

Vieitas, Claudia F., Gustave G. Lopez, and Maria A. Marcovaldi. "Local Community Involvement in Conservation—The Use of Mini-guides in a Programme for Sea Turtles in Brazil." *Oryx* 33, no. 2 (1999): 127-131.

Wass, Richard C. "*The Shoreline Fishery of American Samoa—Past and Present.*" In UNESCO Seminar on Marine and Coastal Processes in the Pacific, 51-83. Proceedings of Marine and Coastal Processes in the Pacific: Ecological Aspects of Coastal Zone Management, Motupore Island, Papua New Guinea. Jakarta, Indonesia: UNESCO, June 14-17, 1980.

Wendt, Albert. "Towards a New Oceania." *Mana Review* 1 (1976): 49-61.

Wendt, Albert. "Tatauing the Postcolonial Body." In *Inside Out: Literature, Cultural Politics, and Identity in the New Pacific,* edited by Vilsoni Hereniko and Rob Wilson, 399-412. Lanham, MD: Rowman & Littlefield, 1999.

White, Alan T., Catherine A. Courtney, and Albert Salamanca. "Experience with Marine Protected Area Planning and Management in the Philippines." *Coastal Management* 30, no. 1 (2002): 1-26.

Worster, Donald. *Nature's Economy: A History of Ecological Ideas.* Cambridge: Cambridge University Press, 1994.

98–100, 104; in DMWR programs,
111, 118, 121–122, 123–124, 125; fishing
and, 26; fishing regulation process and,
24, 46, 48, 49, 51; importance, 15; in
tuna canning industry, 58; violations,
15–16, 24, 46, 48, 49, 94–96,
98–100, 104
Van Camp Seafood Company, 61, 66, 67
Vatia, 107, 115, 118
village chiefs. *See* chiefs
village councils, 52, 89, 94, 95, 96, 114,
117, 119, 121
Village Marine Protected Areas
(VMPAs): effects, 123; establishment,
112, 114; goals, 116–117, 121;
implementation roles, 114–116,
117–118, 120–122, 123–124; legal basis,
116; number of, 115, 118; regulations,
114, 117, 118; sign, **115**; violations, 121.
See also Community-Based Fisheries
Management Program
village mayors, 95, 115, 116, 121, 122
VMPAs. *See* Village Marine
Protected Areas

wages: in American Sāmoa, 58–60,
65–67, 68–70, 72, 77–82; in Hawaiʻi,
67–68; local control, 10; local
perspectives, 69–73, 81; in mainland
United States, 79, 80; minimum, 57,
58–60, 65–67, 69, 72, 73, 77–82; in
other Pacific island nations, 72
wages, in tuna canning industry:
competing interests and, 58–59;
increases, 61, 68–69, 73, 79–80, 81;
industry views, 68–69, 73, 81–82;
local perspectives, 71, 73, 81; set by
industry committee, 67, 68, 80; U.S.
laws on, 59–60, 65–67, 77–79; worker
perspectives, 75, 77
Washington Times, 59, 60
Wass, Richard C., 119, 122

Wendt, Albert, 15, 18, 141
Wespac. *See* Western Pacific Regional
Fishery Management Council
Western Pacific Fisheries Information
Network (WPacFIN), 126–127
Western Pacific Regional Fishery
Management Council (Wespac):
coordinator, 12; establishment, 14;
funding for data collection, 127;
jurisdiction, 23; on marine sanctuary
expansion, 97; meetings, 39, 48, 51;
members, 39, 46–47; policies and
programs, 39–40, 42–44, 46–55, 132;
reports, 133; scope and structure, 38–39
Western Sāmoa, 6, 37, 131
White, Susan, 108
wilderness preservation, 86, 91
workers, in tuna canning industry:
company benefits, 76; experiences,
73–77; from Independent Sāmoa,
75; productivity, 66; treatment by
companies, 71; unionization efforts,
75–76. *See also* wages
World War II, 9, 11
WPacFIN (Western Pacific Fisheries
Information Network), 126–127

Young, Tofoitaufa Sandra King, 95–96,
100

JoAnna Poblete is an associate professor of history at Claremont Graduate University. Her research and teaching involve studies of colonialism and empire; migration and labor; comparative ethnic studies; Asian American and Pacific Islander studies; indigenous and environmental history; identity; oral history, and twentieth-century U.S. history. Having received her MA and PhD in History from UCLA and a BA in History from UC Davis, Poblete has taught at several academic institutions, including UNC Chapel Hill, University of Wyoming, and UCLA. At CGU, she has taught courses in oral history methodology, Pacific worlds, twentieth-century U.S. identities, nineteenth-century expansionism, comparative histories, U.S. immigration, as well as environment and indigeneity.

Her first book, *Islanders in the Empire: Filipino and Puerto Rican Laborers in Hawai'i,* received the Best Book Award in History from the Filipino Section of the Association for Asian American Studies in 2018. Poblete has also published articles in *American Quarterly* and the *Pacific Historical Review.* She has a forthcoming chapter in the *Cambridge History of America in the World* on the American Island Empire in the nineteenth century, an essay on liminal status and comparative history in *Critical Filipinx Studies Keywords Project,* and has started her third book project on the impact of the oil industry on the unincorporated territory of the U.S. Virgin Islands. In 2018, Poblete received the Faculty Diversity Award for Outstanding Teaching among the seven Claremont Colleges.